Mielai Irenai

Su šilčiausiais

Prisiminimais —

Laimonas
Briedis

2012. 01. 09

Laimonas Briedis

VILNIUS
City of Strangers

Laimonas Briedis

VILNIUS
City of Strangers

baltos lankos

CEU PRESS

UDK 711(474.5)
        Br-197

The publication of this book was supported by the Ministry of
Culture of the Republic of Lithuania (Culture Support Foundation)

Author
Laimonas Briedis

Editor
Elizabeth Novickas

Designer
Dalia Šimavičiūtė

On the cover:
Saint Casimir Catholic Church in Vilna.
Photo by S. F. Fleury, circa 1896. (Lithuanian National Museum)

ISBN 978-9955-23-196-7

Distributed by

Central European University Press
Budapest – New York
Nádor utca 11, H-1051 Budapest, Hungary
Tel: (+36-1) 327-3138
Fax: (+36-1) 327-3183
E-mail: ceupress@ceu.hu
Website: http://www.ceupress.com

400 West 59th Street, New York NY 10019, USA
Telephone (+1-212) 547-6932, Fax: (+1-646) 557-2416
E-mail: mgreenwald@sorosny.org

ISBN 978-963-9776-44-9

Library of Congress Cataloging-in-Publication Data

Briedis, Laimonas.
  Vilnius: city of strangers / Laimonas Briedis.
     p. cm.
  Includes bibliographical references and index.
  ISBN 978-9639776449 (pbk. : alk. paper)
  1. Vilnius (Lithuania)--History. 2. Vilnius (Lithuania)--Description and travel. 3. Travelers--
Lithuania--Vilnius--History. I. Title.

  DK505.935B75 2009
  947.93--dc22

                        2008049724

Printed in Lithuania

For David

ACKNOWLEDGEMENTS

The cityscape of Vilnius directed my work, but I take full responsibility for any inaccuracies in my map of its history. I am grateful to those who read and commented on various drafts of the manuscript: Derek Gregory, Modris Eksteins, Thomas Salumets, Gerry Pratt and Robert North. For assistance offered in their particular areas of expertise I would like to thank Elizabeth Novickas, Aida Novickas, Dalia Šimavičiūtė, Ernesta Bražėnaitė, Austėja Pečiūra, Fayette Hickox, Cecile Kuznitz, Antanas Sileika, Violeta Kelertas, Antanas Kubilas, Juozas Statkevičius, Inga Vidugirytė-Pakerienė, Jurgis Pakerys, Judita and Eugenijus Čuplinskas, Kristina Sabaliauskaitė, Mindaugas Kvietkauskas, Alma Lapinskienė, Péter Inkei, Irena Veisaitė, Leonidas Donskis, Laima Vincė, Darius Ross, Dovilė Kėdikaitė, Jadvyga Dragūnas, and Aida, Kęstutis, Jonas and Mona Ivinskis. The support of my family was instrumental in helping me to complete the manuscript, and I also profited from the knowledgeable assistance of the staff at the Vilnius University Library, the Lithuanian Art Museum, the National Museum of Lithuania, the Library of the Lithuanian Academy of Sciences and the Institute of Lithuanian Literature and Folklore. The research for this book was in part funded by the doctoral and postdoctoral grants from the Social Science and Humanities Research Council of Canada.

CONTENTS

PROLOGUE:	Departures	11
CHAPTER ONE:	The Brink of Europe	19
CHAPTER TWO:	Mapping Sarmatia	41
CHAPTER THREE:	Enlightenment Shadows	63
CHAPTER FOUR:	Napoleon's Curse	81
CHAPTER FIVE:	Russian Intrigue	125
CHAPTER SIX:	German Intrusion	163
CHAPTER SEVEN:	The Absent Nation	193
CHAPTER EIGHT:	Maelstrom Europe	221
	Notes	253
	Illustrations	270
	Cited works	275
	Index	282

1. Frontispiece from *La cosmographie universelle*, 1556.

PROLOGUE:

Departures

The map
pinned on the wall,
a name underlined,
the undiscovered city,
the roads to it
charted.

"Precaution," Johannes Bobrowski

One could say that all of Europe must converge in the Lithuanian capital, Vilnius, for the city stands at the crossroads of the continent. In 1989, scientists at the French National Geographical Institute located the centre of Europe at 54°54' North and 25°19' East. At this point, straight lines stretching from the cartographical extremes of Europe – Spitsbergen Island in the north, the Canary Islands in the south, the Azores in the west and the Arctic Urals in the east – meet at the unremarkable mound of Bernotai, some twenty-five kilometres north of Vilnius. The mathematical computation of Europe's focal point coincided with the disintegration of the Cold War continental divisions, but it was overshadowed by revolutionary political and social changes following the collapse of the Soviet Union and the re-establishment of Lithuanian independence in 1990. For more than a decade, the centre-point of Europe was a hidden secret of Vilnius. Its symbolic profile increased only on the day of Lithuania's accession into the European Union. On May 1, 2004, a white granite column, crowned with a wreath of stars – the symbol of the European Union – was ceremoniously dedicated on the site.

Europe is not actually a continent, but part of the much larger geographical entity called Eurasia. The name of Europe comes from the ancient Greeks, who gave it the luscious body of a young daughter of the king of Tyre. The princess Europa fell prey to the wiles of the Olympian gods: she was seduced and then abducted by Zeus, who, for the purpose of the tryst, had transformed himself into a dazzling white bull. On his strong bovine back, Zeus took startled Europa across the sea from her native shores in Asia Minor to Crete, where, after voluptuous love making, he made her the queen of the island. The geographical separation between Europe and Asia was born from this legend of divine transgression. While the myth gave Europe its identity, history (or, rather, a particular plotting and reading of it) bestowed it with specific geographical features. Because of the lack of any detectable physical boundaries, the delineation of Europe as a separate continent has evolved primarily as an idea of geographical distinctiveness. The map of Europe, then, speaks more about the powers of historical imagination than any force of nature. Accordingly, a search for the centre of Europe is first and foremost a journey through the mindset of Europe.

The quest for the centre always starts with the demarcation of peripheries, for no middle point can be found without first identifying and then measuring the margins. Borders uphold the centre, they give it a sense of gravity, keep it alive. A centre without borders collapses and becomes a contested space. In other words, it turns into frontier. Finding the cartographical centre of Europe faces another challenge, since it requires measuring the exact spatial parameters of an idea. Distilling a geographical vision into a series of numbers and giving it a mathematical expression turns this project into a kabalistic interpretation of the universe. There is, however, no secret formula to be discovered behind this scientific mapping of Europe. The extreme peripheries of Europe are determined by the geographers themselves, who use history and geopolitics as their guiding stars. The French computation of Europe, which included Madeira and the Canary archipelago – technically parts of Africa but historically and politically associated with the European states – is no different. Thus, indirectly, history through geography placed the heart of Europe next to Vilnius. Yet this placement should come as a reminder that history and geography are never written by the same people. For centuries, Vilnius has lived under the shadow of Europe, and even its newly found continental significance only restates its peripheral location within Europe. The freshly demarcated and sealed off boundary of the European Union runs some thirty kilometres east of the Lithuanian capital, situating the centre of the continent very close to Belarus, at whose border the current political project of "Europe without borders" comes to a halt.

Yet the centre-periphery relationship is never just about the power of the centre and the subjugation of the periphery. The margins bleed into the centre, thereby constantly undermining its influence by bringing their own uncertainties and insecurities into play. It is the same with the marginalised centrality of Vilnius: the city gathers the history of Europe and streams it into uncharted channels. In this sense, Vilnius is more like a threshold than either a centre or periphery. The threshold, to paraphrase Walter Benjamin,

2. Wilno by J. Bułhak.

is not a border or a point, but a zone where time and space swell. It is not a place but a condition, "a fluid breaking or splitting with extremist tendencies" that "can be neither measured nor localized."[1] Sentiments about *Wilno* (the Polish name for Vilnius) as a threshold site were expressed by Jan Bułhak, a celebrated Polish photographer of the twentieth century, who spoke of and, in his mesmerising black-and-white prints, attempted to capture its sinuous nature. Bułhak placed the city onto the fluid landscape of a human soul, and made it a challenge to the hardened, familiar parameters of European time and space. Wilno, in the photographer's words, is a suspension of disbelief:

> True Wilno remains closed and silent to snobs. Is it worth it to reveal your real treasures to souvenir-hunting vandals and ignorant blockheads? The city speaks softly of simple and noble things, and does not open up for everyone. It does not shout like a hawker or brag about its own merits – it simply leads an open-minded traveller to a discovery. There have been many visitors from distant lands who have succeeded in finding the authentic Wilno and, to many, the encounter with the city has been a great spiritual experience. These guests remain loyal to the city to the end of their lives, praising it intelligently in the languages of art. Of course, there have been plenty of indifferent guests who left the city with a mocking sneer. But they saw only its simplicity, its shortcomings and its imperfections, and they

will never know that a meeting with Wilno is a trial of the soul, a test of human perception. Such a test is alluring to some, but to others, the unenlightened ones, it is a perilous trap.

So here is our Wilno: some say the city is dirty, poor and dull; others assert that it is a lovely, exceptional and noble place. What can we say about it today? From which side we should begin our investigation of our Wilno, sunken deep in a two-river valley, surrounded by mountainous greenery and cragged with graceful church towers in the shape of spiral-like poplar trees of an old country manor?

Let us not hurry inside the city, and linger for a moment at its threshold. Wilno dwells between the hills, allowing the pleasure of a distant observation. So let us enjoy this pleasure of viewing the city from a distance.[2]

This book is about distance, suspension and discovery, about the threshold moment – an uncharted zone – that separates Vilnius from its foreign visitors. It is a narrative of the city from a stranger's point of view, with its history detailed by the geography of intimate reflections, official accounts, private letters, journalistic reports, military observations and the travel narratives of its various guests. Therefore, this book is not only about Vilnius, but also Europe. It is a map of the continent walked through the streets of Vilnius.

Vilnius has always offered a critical link between different components, nations and interpretations of Europe. The town has often been depicted as a bridge between East and West, but, as with any strategically ambiguous site, it has also been a highly contested place. As a result, the city has never possessed a single identity. The place speaks of Jewish *Vilne*, Polish *Wilno*, Russian and French *Vilna*, German *Wilna*, Byelorussian *Vilno* and Lithuanian *Vilnius*. These different topological realms might share the same terrain, but they lead to strikingly different experiences and memories of the place. Initially, my goal for this book was to parallel, compare and, if possible, synchronise different articulations of the city. As a historical and cultural geographer, I wanted to map out the cityscape by finding the specific narrative threads that cross its various linguistic, religious and ideological boundaries. For this purpose, I read and walked through a whole array of official and personal narratives. Yet with each new linguistic or ideological excursion, I was driven towards a different geographical trajectory of the place. My research site – the city of Vilnius – dispersed in front of my eyes, and instead of coming to the point of the city's representational intersections, I found myself exiting the city through different narrative gates.

Somewhere in the midst of my investigation, I came to realise that what I was encountering was not so much disparate interpretations of Vilnius, but centrifugal depictions of Europe. The reason I could not find the central

3. Vilnius in many languages: *Widaw* in German, *Vilna* in Italian, *Wilenski* in Lithuanian (Old Byelorussian?), *Wilna* in Polish, *Vilne* in French and *Vilna* in Latin. Detail from a map of Lithuania published in Venice in 1696.

historical theme within all these urban narratives was very simple: I was searching for the unity of the city within different maps of Europe. So, instead of leaving Vilnius by mapping out the separate trajectories of dispersed local narratives, I decided to enter the city from the different cultural points and linguistic angles of Europe. Subsequently, the epicenter of my investigation shifted from a search for the narrative nexus of Vilnius to questions concerning the changing idea of Europe.

While the analytical alteration modified the course of my research, it did not change the intention of my explorations. Vilnius, with its multilayered cultural landscape, remained the focal point of my interests, but I oriented my research towards the interplay between the geography of Europe and history of Vilnius, making it a story of interaction between local meanings and their foreign interpretations. Nonetheless, this reversal of the investigative flow inevitably changed the expositional terrain of the city: from a native, familiar and mundane place, Vilnius was turned into a foreign, strange and even exotic locale. Still, I believe that some characteristics of my indigenous comprehension of the city survived this transposition, simply because my initial analytical goal and personal knowledge of the place positioned me, so to speak, on the native side of the representational mirror. This native search for Europe in Vilnius shed a new light on the local implications of various political battles, ideological frictions and cultural collisions of continental proportions. It also led me to new theoretical and narrative frontiers of geographical investigation by allowing me to trace and pace the experiences of travellers in a more dynamic and imaginative fashion. The book is based on written records of Vilnius, which by no means result in a verifiable map of the place. But what it does is no less real, for it enlivens local history with the voices, experiences and fantasies of travellers who made the city a stopping point on their journeys of self-discovery. In short, my narrative of Vilnius is a travel story, a history of the city charted as a passage from a familiar world into an unknown realm.

Vilnius has never been a city of travelers, and, unlike the more celebrated cities of Europe, such as Rome, Paris, London, Berlin, Vienna or Moscow, it has never acquired a narrative and representational canon which could guide foreign visitors through its history and geography. The history of Vilnius mirrors that of Europe, but only as an altered, distorted echo of its grand story. Of course, every place in Europe has its own voice, capable of setting the unifying rhythm of the continent slightly off-key. But in this polyphony of resonant variations, Vilnius comes in with its tune altogether offbeat. Although the city's history is full of dramatic and often tragic changes, local events and personalities rarely enter the shared historical vocabulary of Europe. And to this day, Vilnius stands as a continental outsider, an unfamiliar character – a trespasser – within a well-crafted storyboard of Europe.

This absence of European familiarity does not mean that Vilnius has lacked encounters with outsiders. On the contrary, during its centuries-old history the town has experienced countless invasions of strangers, mostly passing through it in times of war and foreign occupations. Because of the frontier-like character of these encounters, Vilnius has rarely been envisioned and experienced as a destination on its own – instead, it has been viewed as a gateway site, a place that leads to other ends, in other words, a threshold. The transient and inadvertent nature of Vilnius's visitors shaped the foreign knowledge of the place. Foreigners in Vilnius are more like gleaners (or, worse, foragers), who see, imagine, and often experience the place as a leftover of a far greater – European – historical harvest. Although I have used foreigners as narrators of the city, this book is not so much an attempt to change this notion, as to expose another side of it. While the opinions of foreigners tend to marginalise Vilnius, their narratives, often unwittingly, position the idea and practice of Europe at the centre of local history. In other words, what the strangers saw as peripheral, I made central.

The inversion of the representational hierarchy allowed me to ease the separation between foreigners and locals, which, in a way, corresponds with the historical transformation of Vilnius. History and geography made the city a place of migrants, fusing the experiences of strangers and locals, newcomers and residents, and expatriates and natives into a myriad of intertwined narratives and memories that can easily transgress different temporal and spatial orders. In a way, everyone in Vilnius can be a stranger, not because of her or his foreign origin, but because the city possesses so many names and histories that a single human identity can hardly embrace it all.

Different foreign voices and native tongues make it difficult to place Vilnius within a single orthographic world. Throughout the text, I tried to use the name of Vilnius as it is found in the original sources; hence, the name of the city alternates between its contemporary Lithuanian version to more historically, linguistically and personally accurate versions, such as *Wilna*, *Vilna*, *Vilne* and *Wilno*. The same goes for all other local names of places and peoples. To help readers to sail more smoothly through this archipelago of different orthographical imprints, an index with all versions of place-names is provided at the end of the book.

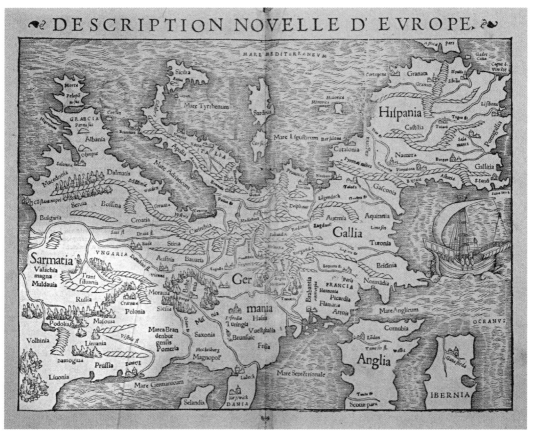

4. "New map of Europe," from *La cosmographie universelle,* 1556. Europe is oriented to the south: Lithuania, along with Livonia and Prussia, is located on the lower left of the map, on the southeastern coast of the *Mare Germanicum,* or Baltic Sea.

CHAPTER ONE:

The Brink of Europe

> Perhaps coming from an area which for a long time has been considered the
> Eastern marches of Rome-centered Christendom makes one more sensitive
> to shifting points of gravity, symbolized by the very fluidity of such terms
> as *the West* and *the East.*
>
> Czesław Miłosz

Vilnius was born into Europe as a spiritual anomaly – a pagan city in a sea
of Christianity. An epistle, received in 1323 by the pope in the southern city
of Avignon, heralded Vilnius's nativity. Brought by an austere monk from the
Baltic port of Riga, the letter arrived at the grey-stoned papal palace with the
first shivering gusts of the mistral. The arrival of the mistral usually coincided
with the coming of Advent and the beginning of a new cycle in the Catholic calendar. The letter, purportedly authored by Gediminas, the self-styled
"king of the Lithuanians and many Russians," promised a new beginning as
well. In a diplomatically crafted Latin script, the Lithuanian king asked the
pope – "the highest priest of the Roman throne" – to accept his royal sub-
mission and take him and his countrymen into the Christian communion
of saints. The request delighted Pope John XXII, who had unsuccessfully
attempted to convince Gediminas to take Catholic baptism for many years.
The letter, however, was unsigned, undated, and had no obvious markings of
its geographical origin or return point. This lack of epistolary courtesy made
it look less convincing, if not altogether false, and the pope read its message
with a guarded sense of political uncertainty. [1]

There were plenty of reasons to mistrust Gediminas. For one, he was a
heathen – the last remaining pagan ruler in Europe. Worse, his patrimony –
Lithuania – was an apostate state. In the middle of the thirteenth century its
ruler, Mindaugas, took baptism from Pope Alexander IV, only to renounce
the faith two years later. For more than a century, Lithuanians had been the
mortal enemies of the Catholics, assaulting their castles, looting their newly
built towns, burning churches, slaughtering priests and enslaving neophytes
at the Baltic frontiers of Christianity. The popes repeatedly called for a holy
war against them. The Teutonic Order, dislodged from the Holy Land after
the loss of Jerusalem, spearheaded the Nordic Crusade.

The Order was a monastic institution, whose members took a vow of chastity in repentance for their sins. The Teutonic knights, as they came to be known, built a brotherhood of penitent warriors who took the cross with a sword in hand, thus ensuring their own personal salvation with the blood of unbelievers, heretics and apostates. After travelling from the Mediterranean to the Baltic shores at the turn of the thirteenth century, the Teutonic Order had become an efficient military machine with an apostolic mission to spread and uphold the Catholic faith among the indigenous pagan peoples. A succession of popes blessed them with absolution, ensuring their devotion to the Mother Church, and various Holy Roman emperors granted them vast territories, making the Order one of the greatest feudal domains in Europe. As a sign of their privileged social and religious position, multilingual European aristocracy showered them with financial donations and a growing surplus of idle sons. Despite its cosmopolitan support, the Teutonic Order drew its numerical strength from the populous aristocratic class of the German-speaking realm; hence its name. As a result, its missionary zeal was tinted with the colours of feudal expansionism, social oppression and cultural change. Together with the cross, the knights brought German advances to the Baltic region, building mighty castles, merchant towns, baronial manors and Catholic parishes in exchange for their domination. The warrior-monks were followed by lay German settlers from the Hanseatic towns, making the religious mission a colonial movement, which was christened in the Romantic, nationalist era of the nineteenth century as the "Drang nach Osten," the drive to the East.

The knights, empowered by the tripartite support of the church, emperor and aristocracy, built a fortified state in Livonia and Prussia, the conquered territories located at the northern and western borders of Lithuania, thus in effect isolating the pagan country from Latin Europe. Within a generation or two of accumulated wealth and prestige, the Order became increasingly independent of its benefactors. The monks ruled the conquered Baltic lands without any fealty to the imperial or ecclesiastical authorities. Emboldened by their political success, military prowess and commercial shrewdness, they showed little respect for the complex hierarchies of Latin Europe. The Order's arrogant ways did not go unnoticed. While Pope John XXII often called the knights the beloved sons of the Catholic church, they received little affection from the king of France, the paymaster of the papacy.

Pope John XXII, a Frenchman of poor origins, was elected in 1316 to serve the needs of the French crown, which had brought the previous pope from Rome to Avignon, a town located in the southern region of France. Despite his age – John XXII was almost seventy years old at the time of his election – the pope showed no signs of lethargy. In Italy, he led a long and brutal crusade against local states opposing the French-dominated papacy. During this war, he excommunicated Ludwig of Bavaria, a restless challenger to the throne of the Holy Roman Empire and the main instigator of the anti-papal league in Europe. Pope John XXII was also busy in cleansing the church of various dogmatic diversions. The defining edict of his papacy was the excommunication of an influential branch of the Franciscans brothers, known as the Spiritualists, for their adherence to principles of evangelical poverty based on the assertion that Jesus and the Apostles had no material possessions. In an opposing stroke, in July of 1323, he made Thomas Aquinas, the "Angelic Doctor" of theological wisdom, a saint.

Soon after receiving the first letter from Gediminas, the pontiff was visited by a delegation from Riga, which brought another epistle from the Lithuanian ruler. Gediminas blamed the aggressive policies of the Teutonic knights for the stubborn rejection of the Catholic faith by the Lithuanians. Still, the pope need not have doubted Gediminas's intent to take baptism. Pope John XXII also learned from the delegates that Gediminas had trumpeted his yet-to-be-consecrated conversion to the rest of Europe. The king had dispatched several other letters, addressed to "all Christians, men and women, scattered around the world," in which he announced the expected arrival of papal legates in Lithuania. Strategically, the key destinations of this important broadcast were narrowed down to the "renowned cities of Lubeck, Stralsund, Bremen, Magdeburg, and other commendable towns from Cologne to Rome." Gediminas also informed the largest Catholic monastic houses – the Franciscan and Dominican Orders – of his desire to become a Christian and invited members of their brethren to come to his realm to spread the word and good deeds among his subjects. Following the customary practice of important public notices, Gediminas asked the anonymous recipients of his messages to duplicate the letter and, after a copy had been nailed on the front door of the nearest church, to pass it down the postal chain of medieval Europe to the next town or monastery. This way, declared the author of the message, "the glory of God" will be shared with everyone. Gediminas's holy intentions were highlighted by the carefully chosen dating of the communiqué. The first pack of letters was signed on January 25, the day celebrating the conversion of Paul the Apostle, who was responsible for spreading the Christian faith among the gentiles. The second round was sealed on May 26, the day of Corpus Christi, honouring the sacrament of the Eucharist and the transubstantiation miracle of the body of Christ. [2]

Before these letters reached their intended Christian audience, the city of Vilnius was an unknown, nameless place. A human settlement must have existed on the site a long time before Gediminas came to power around 1315, but his conciliatory words to Latin Europe encoded the existence of the place within the historical record of Europe. Accordingly, Vilnius's age is dated from 1323, putting it at the same age as the sainthood of Thomas of Aquinas.

The recorded birth of Vilnius is supported by a local myth. Usually, legends are much older than documents, yet, in Vilnius's case, the temporal distance between myth and archive is negligible. Indeed, the myth of the city's origins might have been invented in response to its documented founding. This might explain the fact that the legend and the record have the same main protagonist, Gediminas, confronting the same geopolitical dilemma of how to make Lithuania an acknowledged and accepted nation of the world. Both the myth and the historical records – the letters – seek to establish a link between local and foreign worlds through a construction of Vilnius as a meeting ground of the two realms.

Vilnius, according to the legend, was born out of a dream. While hunting in the heavily forested environs of the future city, the exhausted Gediminas took a rest. In his sleep, he had a vision of a ferociously howling iron wolf. Puzzled by the unusual apparition, Gediminas asked the chief pagan priest for an explanation. The oracle interpreted the royal dream as a challenge to his civic duty. The priest instructed the king to build a town on the spot of his dream, which would bring world fame to his name and to Lithuania. Gediminas wasted no time and immediately turned the vision into stonework. A towering castle was built on the highest hill overlooking the confluence of the two rivers, around whose winding courses the city was laid out.

Vilnius most likely took its name from the smaller of the two rivers, the *Vilnia,* which connotes a wavy, rippling and meandering stream in Lithuanian. The name also hints of the proximity of the place to the other world. The Lithuanian words for the departed (*velionis*), ghost (*vėlė*) and devil (*velnias*) share the same etymological root with Vilnius, which was one of the most sacred sites of pagan Lithuania. The word Vilnius points to the exceptional and perhaps even magical characteristics of the place. It denotes a bond between different, opposing realms of the universe, making Vilnius a pulsating place – more like a moment in time than a physical location – linking the living with the dead.[3]

Vilnius's etymology (name), legend (narrative), and history (factual record) convey its native origins. Many towns built on the Baltic frontiers of

5. Gediminas builds a castle on the site of his dream: a romantic nineteenth century representation of the founding myth of Vilnius.

Christendom, such as Riga, Tallinn and Königsberg, were founded to advance and strengthen foreign hegemony over the conquered lands and indigenous peoples. In spirit and body – that is, legal wording and social functioning – they were colonial towns. Vilnius was different – autochthonous, pagan and unconquered, it strengthened local traditions. The place was made the capital of Lithuania *in response* to foreign intrusions. So if pagan spirituality was the godmother of Vilnius, then the long and exhausting war with the Catholic world was its godfather. Gediminas chose Vilnius as his royal residence because it was located deep in the heartland of Lithuania, protected not only by pagan gods, an efficient army, and a well-placed warning system, but also by vast forests, winding rivers, unsettled swampy terrain and capricious weather – all making a foreign passage to the city a strenuous proposition.

Despite the geographical isolation and defensive qualities of the place, Gediminas envisioned Vilnius as a meeting ground of Europe. In his letters of promised conversion, he invited the Catholics of Europe – merchants, knights, churchmen and artisans – to come and settle in the newly consecrated capital of Lithuania. He promised the newcomers exclusive religious, legal and cultural privileges, but with an important demand for their loyalty and respect for local pagan traditions. Hence, the only people explicitly excluded from this generous offer were the warrior-monks of the Teutonic Order.

In the militant zeal of their missionary activity, the knights, of course, were the most vociferous opponents of the diplomatic, peaceful conversion of Lithuania. Having chosen the path to salvation through warlike evangelism, they were determined to keep Lithuania pagan. The knights saw the establishment of a Christian community in Vilnius without their participation as a direct challenge to their political and personal survival. Without the menacing presence of the Lithuanian heathens, the Order could have faced the possibility of a violent end, just like the one met by the Templars, whose brotherhood was brutally crushed by the preceding Pope Clement V following fatal accusations by the French king. Fortunately for the Teutonic brotherhood, the new king of France, the young and boisterous Charles IV, was scheming once again to liberate Jerusalem from the Muslim rule and showed little interest in Baltic affairs. The French left the question of the Lithuanian conversion in the hands of the pope, who still kept in his heart the residue of a loving attachment for the missionary zeal of the knights.

In order to stress its earthly necessity, the Teutonic Order dedicated the unconquered Lithuania to the Virgin Mary. The devotional gesture made political hegemony over the country a spiritual matter. The Holy Roman Emperor sanctioned this celestial bargain, yet the pope disagreed, since he was not eager to share the honours of spiritual conquest with the political entitlements of the knights. Pope John XXII was willing to keep Lithuania sovereign as long as its rulers accepted Catholicism. From distant Avignon, he sent two letters: one to Gediminas, praising him for his decision to accept Catholicism, and another one to the Teutonic knights, lecturing them for their insubordination. The pope angered the knights by pursuing a six-year peace treaty between pagan Lithuania and the surrounding Catholic powers in order to achieve his goal of conversion. Reluctantly, the Teutonic Order conceded to a diplomatic defeat.

In the first part of the fourteenth century, the state of Christendom was far from ideal. Irreconcilable doctrinal differences between Catholic and Orthodox believers kept Christians permanently divided. Among the Catholics, theological divisions and feudal animosities were no less detrimental. The papacy became nothing more than a religious commodity to be bargained, bought, usurped and fought for, or simply married into. The Vicar of Christ was kept under the watchful eye and controlling purse of the French crown in a gilded exile in Avignon. In matters of politics, the pope must have felt himself a spent force. Providentially, the conversion of Lithuania offered a unique opportunity for the restoration of papal spiritual

6. Pagan Lithuanians worshiping fire, the oak tree and the garden snake, from *La cosmographie universelle*, 1556.

authority and social standing. Lithuania was located at the junction of various European religious, military and trade orbits, in the region where the interests of different political powers and religious authorities intersected. While the Lithuanian rulers were pagans, they had expanded their political control deep into the Christian Slavic provinces. In the west and north, this growing state was shouldered by Catholic countries; in the east and south, it merged with the Orthodox provinces of Russia; and on its extreme southeastern edges, it crossed into the tributary domains of the Mongol-Tartar khanates. Latin baptism would have inevitably made Lithuania a bulwark of Catholicism in a region of unstable religious loyalties, and it could have created the perfect environment for a desirable union between the Greek and Latin-rite adherents under the auspices of the papacy. The pope could not but think that his path to a beatific, or even saintly, afterlife might lead through the baptismal immersion of the distant pagan king of Lithuania.

For such a crucial mission, Pope John XXII selected three legates: two prominent French theologians, a bishop and an abbot, both members of the Benedictine Order, and the archbishop of Riga, the expected spiritual godfather of Gediminas, who was also sent to take up his distant see after years of exile due to the continuous confrontation between the Teutonic Order and local Catholic church hierarchy. After arduous land and sea journeys, the legates reached Riga, the capital of Livonia, in the early fall of 1324. They found the city in turmoil. A low intensity war was brewing between the Teutonic knights, who had assumed political and ecclesiastical control of Livonia, and the burghers of Riga, who were trying to protect the civic privileges and business interests of the growing mercantile class. The archbishop sided with the merchants, who in their turn, looked for military help from the pagan Lithuanians. Before a peace treaty was signed in Vilnius, a blasphemous alliance between pagans and Catholic burghers emerged against the Teutonic brothers. Faced with the new crisis brought on by this ungodly union, the legates immediately sent an envoy to Vilnius to prepare the ground for the ceremonial conversion of Gediminas.

In the Baltic region, the best time for land travel was in the middle of winter, when swamps, lakes and rivers froze solid. But such was the urgency of the matter that the apostolic scouts left Riga before the onset of winter and reached Vilnius in early November, on a Saturday following All Saints Day. They were the first known foreigners who travelled to the Lithuanian capital and left a written record of their visit. Nothing is known about the personal traits – names or national origins – of these earliest visitors, but a detailed report of their mission, written by the delegates themselves, was later sent to the pope.

According to their report, upon their arrival in Vilnius the papal envoys were greeted courteously by Gediminas, who personally offered them a nourishing meal and comfortable lodgings. The next morning, the messengers joined a small community of (foreign) Catholic monks for an early Mass, thanking God for their safe arrival and praying for success in their mission. Afterwards, they went to see Gediminas at the reception hall in the castle. To their displeasure, the diplomats found Gediminas surrounded by numerous councillors, representing all the clans and religious creeds of his domain. While pagans dominated the assembly, there were also some Russian Orthodox representatives and possibly a Catholic monk among the royal advisers. The assembled crowd greeted the delegates with mistrust, and, without any polite prologue or diplomatic courtesy, Gediminas asked the chief envoy for the reason of their visit. The diplomat gave an unwavering answer: they had come to Vilnius on behalf of the Holy Father to discuss Gediminas's baptism. Impatiently, Gediminas asked if they knew what was written in the letters sent to the pope. "Yes," replied one of the messengers, "it expressed your desire to become a Christian." "Rubbish," Gediminas responded, "I never meant to, but if you understood it that way, then it must have been the fault of brother Berthold. He wrote the letter, and should take full responsibility for the error. And if I ever thought of conversion," thundered the Lithuanian ruler, "let the devil himself baptise me!"[4]

After this ominous rebuke, a recomposed Gediminas confirmed the wording of the letter, except for his acceptance of Christianity. He explained his rejection of the Catholic faith by invoking the idea of religious tolerance and equality. In Lithuania, proudly declared its ruler, all creeds are accepted: the Poles, Germans and other Catholics worship in the Latin manner; the Russians follow their unique Orthodox traditions; and "we, the pagans, venerate god according to our ancient rituals." Yet in the end, summed up Gediminas, "we all love one god."[5] The papal diplomats argued otherwise and defended the idea of the benevolent supremacy of the Catholic faith. Once again, their dogmatic stand angered the pagan king, who ended the reception with an impromptu lecture about the double-faced character of the Catholic faith. "Why do you always talk about Christian love? Where do you find so much misery, injustice, violence, sin and greed, if not among the Christians? Especially among those crusaders, who put on the robes of pious monks but only spread evil everywhere."[6]

The humiliated delegates spent the remaining days of their failed mission in the cloistered seclusion of the tiny Catholic community of Vilnius. Their frequent prayers for the lost soul of Gediminas bore no welcoming results. The pagan ruler, citing the arrival of a distinguished Tartar delegation, refused to see them again. Instead, the delegates were visited by several of his councillors, who advised the visiting Catholics to find the culprit among their own people. This cryptic remark of the pagans unleashed a wave of accusations and incriminations. The Dominicans blamed a Franciscan monk – a scribe employed by Gediminas – for writing the erroneous words in the letter sent to the pope. In return, the Franciscans accused the Dominicans of setting Gediminas against the pope by suggesting he should take baptism from the hands of the powerful king of Bohemia and Hungary instead of from the distant and weak pope. Both sides pointed a finger at the Teutonic knights, accusing them of bribing various pagan chiefs with expensive gifts to oppose the conversion of Gediminas. In the end, old Father Henekin, Gediminas's translator, summed it all up: "I know for sure that the king wrote the named letters in sincerity and was determined to take baptism. Why he changed his mind – I cannot know, but between you and me, I am sure it must have been the work of an evil seed planted by Satan himself."[7]

Upon learning of Gediminas's renouncement of his baptismal intention, the pope wasted no time in calling for a new crusade against the Lithuanians. The holy war, which offered a full remission from all sins to its participants, was planned for 1329, in the first year after the expiration date of the signed six-year peace treaty. The massive crusade was led by King John of Bohemia, who denounced the pagans as "the pestilential enemies of Christ" and praised the Teutonic knights for their "memorable holiness of life" in turning

7. A Teutonic knight, from *La cosmographie universelle*, 1556.

"themselves into an unbreakable wall to defend the faith against the Lithuanians and their partisans, whoever and whatever they may be."[8]

As a rule, a military excursion into Lithuania was a regularised and routine affair. Known across Latin Europe by its German name, *reysa*, it became a crucial part of medieval chivalric culture. *Reysa* was foremost a social event, a masculine pageant of chivalric tournaments, hunting parties, feasts, drinking rounds and ceremonial displays of wealth and piety. In between these pageants, and weather permitting, the crusaders would usually make a several week foray through the wilderness into pagan land. Often, a particular *reysa* – the northern crusade – carried specific national colours, since the knights had a tendency to arrive in waves, not unlike modern-day tourists. Hence, Lithuania was invaded by "Bohemians in 1323, Alsatians in 1324, Englishmen and Walloons in 1329, [and] Austrians and Frenchmen in 1336."[9] Chaucer captured its English scope in a passage of *Canterbury Tales* depicting the adventures of the knight: "Full often time he had abroad bygonne/Above all nations, to Prussia./ In Lithuania had he reysed and in Russia /No Christian man of his degree more often."[10] A French contemporary referred to *reysa* as *belle guerre*, "a grand affair" with a "great assemblage of knights and squires and noblemen, from both the kingdom of France and elsewhere."[11] But while the desire for personal salvation and social display drove European crusaders into pagan Lithuania, the modus operandi of the holy war was determined by the forces of nature.

On average, there were two expeditions a year – the *winter-reysa* and the *sommer-reysa* – each calling for specific military objectives and tactics. The ultimate goal of every *reysa* was the capture of a pagan fortress; yet the success of each expedition very much depended on the changeable climatic conditions of the season and, in most cases, the crusaders were content with a large booty of slaves, farm animals, supplies and trading goods. The Lithuanians responded in kind, plundering the territories settled and colonised by the Teutonic knights. So despite their pageant-like atmosphere, the crusading raids were not without fatal consequences. An untold number of people were killed, enslaved or driven from their homes, which essentially turned the vast territory that buffered Vilnius from the incursions of the Order into a depopulated wilderness. Royalty also fell victim to the war. The king of Bohemia lost his eyesight during the *reysa* and returned from the Lithuanian forest with a new royal epithet – John the Blind. And Gediminas died in battle against the crusaders in 1341. The descendants of Gediminas continued the fight against the Teutonic knights well into the fifteenth century, but the decisive victory against the Order was achieved in 1410, when its army was defeated by combined Lithuanian and Polish forces, led by his grandsons Vytautas and Jogaila. By this time, Jogaila (Jogiełło, in Polish) was the King of Poland and his cousin, Vytautas, ruled over the vastly enlarged Grand Duchy of Lithuania. In combination, the two countries became one of the most powerful forces in Europe.

When Lithuania appeared for the first time on the map of the world, it still carried the stigma of a heathen title. In 1375, Abraham Cresques, a Jewish-Spanish cartographer, together with his son, was commissioned by the ruler of Aragon to create the most detailed map of the universe as a gift to the young king of France. Known as the Catalan Atlas, the map projected the unity between cosmographical and nautical matters of the universe, charting the known world through the prism of a Mediterranean seaman. As a result, most of the distant and cold Baltic Sea region was poorly delineated, leaving plenty of empty space to be filled by the phantasmagorical imagination of a medieval mind. Laconically, yet, evocatively, Cresques summarised the place inhabited by the Lithuanians as *Litefanie Paganis* – Pagan Lithuania.

The Lithuanian pagan elite finally accepted the Catholic faith in 1387, under conditions included in the marriage contract between the forty-year-old Jogaila and the twelve-year-old Queen Jadwiga of Poland. With the marriage came the purge of heathen relics from the sacred landscape of Vilnius: the Catholic Cathedral was built on the site of the destroyed pagan shrine. As a wedding gift to Lithuania, Jogaila granted Vilnius municipal rights based on the civic charter of the German town of Magdeburg. Still, the conversion did not end the tradition of the annual *reysa* against Lithuanians. The Teutonic knights had besieged Vilnius in 1383, but because of infighting among the descendants of Gediminas, assaults on the city continued for another decade. Ironically, one of the most successful attacks of the knights on Vilnius in the centuries-long history of the crusades against Lithuania was led by Vytautas (the most revered ruler in Lithuanian history), who opposed the patrimonial rights of Jogaila to the city.

The first person to leave a known description of Vilnius was an abortive crusader named Guillebert de Lannoy, a patrician from Flanders with an archetypal aristocratic pedigree and cosmopolitan loyalties. Lannoy was born in 1386, the year of Jogaila's marriage to Jadwiga. War was in his blood, and at thirteen he became a wandering knight. After fighting in England, Burgundy and Spain, he arrived in Prussia in the winter of 1413 for the *reysa* against the "Saracens of the North." He came a few years too late, for after the 1410 defeat, the Order was in a state of collapse. The *reysa* was called off, leaving Lannoy with nothing chivalric to do. Restless for an adventure, the Flemish knight made himself a diplomat. First, he went to the northern Russian principalities of Novgorod and Pskov, where he was expelled for being a spy. Next, he came to neighbouring Lithuania, where, in a stark contrast to Russia, he was greeted as a dear friend. Eight years later, Lannoy (this time in the official capacity of ambassador for Henry V of England) passed through Lithuania on his way to Syria and Egypt on a secret mission to resurrect the Kingdom of Jerusalem, the failed state of the early crusaders.

A journey from England to Egypt through Lithuania might seem improbable, but at the beginning of the fifteenth century, the vastly enlarged and politically stable Grand Duchy of Lithuania connected Latin Europe with the Islamic world as no other continental power did. Still, finding and reaching Vilnius had its challenges. Once he approached the frontiers of Lithuania, Lannoy remembered wandering through "an exceedingly empty countryside covered in great woods, rivers" and frozen lakes, without seeing a living soul for two days and nights. The first signs of human activity appeared only near Vilnius, inhabited, in the words of the diplomat, by "Christians who were forced into the faith by the Teutonic Order." Only after meeting Grand Duke Vytautas in Vilnius did travelling through Lithuania become more comfortable for Lannoy, since the Lithuanian ruler saw "a great honour in ensuring freedom and comfort to all foreigners passing through his domain." All the same, Vilnius was yet to resemble the stone-built and well-fortified town of a powerful European state. The enormous timber castle, built on "a very steep, sandy hill, reinforced with stone, dirt and bricks," dominated the site. The town itself, squeezed into "a long, narrow" stretch of "disagreeably assembled wooden houses with a few stone churches in between" was an open place with no protective walls or gates. Local inhabitants spoke "their own language" with "men sporting shoulder-length, untied hair, but young women dressed in a simple fashion, just like in Picardy."[12]

Lannoy was most intrigued by Trakai, a lakeside town "seven miles" west of Vilnius. In 1391, the old town of Trakai was destroyed by the crusaders.

Jttaw ist auch ein waitte gegennt gegen dem auffgang an die Poln stossende schier alle seeig vnnd weldig Vitoldus ein bruder Vladislai hat daselbst geregiert vnnd nach verlassung der abgötterey das sacrament Cristi mit dem Polnischen königreich empfangen vnd zu seinen zeitten ein grossen namen gehabt. Den fürchteten seine vnderthanen also sere weil sie von ime gehaissen warden sich zeerhencken. so wolten sie ime lieber gehorsam erscheinen denn in sein vngnad fallen. Welche ime widerspennig waren die liess er in ein beernhawt neen vnd den lebendigen beern zerzereissen fürwerffen vnd auch mit andern grawsamen peynen verfolgen. wo er ritte so füeret er alweg einen gespannten bogen. wenn er dann ymant ersahe der anderst geparet denn ime gefiele so schosse er ime also pald mit einem pfeil. vnnd tödtet vil menschen durch spil diser plätig wüettrich. Sindugal sein nachkomen neret ein beern die was gewenet prot auss seinen henden zenemen. offt in die welde zelawffen vnnd widerkomende bis an des fürsten schlafkamer zegeen vnd an allen thüren zekratzen vnnd mit den füessen anzeklopffen so yne hungret so tete ime den der fürst auff vnd gab ime die speys. Etlich edel iungling macheten einen anschlag vber disen fürsten vnd komen mit gewappenter hand für des fürsten schlafkamer an der thür nach weise der beern an klopffen de. Sindugal mainet die beern wer da vnd eröffnet die thür vnnd wardt alspald von den edel lewten erstochen. Darnach geläget die herrschfug diss läds an Casimirü. zu sumer zeite ist vor wassern zu de Littawen mit leichtiglich zekome. zu winterzeit fert man vber die gefrorne see. Die kaw flewt zyhe auff de eyse vn schne vn füere speyss auf vn tag mit inn. Alda ist kein rechter gepannter weg. so sind auch alda selte stett vn wenig dörffer. Bey de littawin

8. "Lithuania," a phantasmagorical portrait of the country, from *Weltchronik*, 1493.

Vytautas, who was born there, had built a new, well-protected ducal castle on the lake. Showered with monarchical privileges and attention, the new town became a cosmopolitan centre of Lithuania, where "Germans, Lithuanians, Russians and many Jews, all speaking their own separate tongues, live together." Among the Jews and Christians of all denominations, there were many Tartars living in Trakai. "The Tartars," stressed Lannoy, "are genuine Saracens, having no knowledge of the teachings of Jesus Christ." Yet Vytautas embraced this local diversity, which was, in part, created by his own policies of allowing peoples of various creeds to settle in and around Vilnius. Twice baptised – once by the Teutonic knights and again by the Polish primate – Vytautas was extremely practical in religious and cultural matters. With no hesitation, Lannoy described Vytautas as "a very powerful monarch who had conquered twelve or thirteen kingdoms" and a wealthy prince, "owning no less than ten thousand saddled horses." In a more cautionary tone, he commented on his laxity in spiritual matters, finding him dining together with the "Saracen infidels," with both fish and meat being served on Fridays. As a sign of the ruler's pagan upbringing, Lannoy pointed out Vytautas's enthusiastic support of the Hussites, the excommunicated heretics of Bohemia and sworn enemies of the papacy.[13]

Although Catholicism became the religion of the Lithuanian rulers, the Latin church failed to impose its dominance over Vilnius. In the first part of the fifteenth century, the civic and religious rights of its Catholic and Orthodox residents were equalised, making the city an effective meeting point of the two streams of Christianity. The Jews must have started to settle in Vilnius in the middle of the century, for the Jewish community already had its own cemetery by the 1480s. In 1495, the Jews were ordered to leave Lithuania by the less tolerant Grand Duke Alexander, who, following the example of the Spanish royals, was eager to prove his Catholic credentials by expropriating Jewish properties. The ban, however, was short-lived: by 1501, the Jews were allowed to return and had all their properties restored to them.

Alexander was keen to make Vilnius an international trade centre. He issued a decree prohibiting foreign merchants travelling through Lithuania from bypassing Vilnius where, conveniently, they were allowed to build residences. This obligatory sojourn generated urban growth and prosperity, but it also brought a new malady. In 1498, less than four years after it was first recorded in Naples, a syphilis epidemic swept through Vilnius. For better protection and control of the city, Alexander commanded a wall with nine gates to be built around its perimeter. It took two decades to encircle the city with a three-kilometre stretch of brick wall several meters in height. By the time it was finished, advances in weaponry and novel military strategies made the city wall a weak defence. Once again, relative geographical isolation offered the best protection local residents could pray for.

Almost two centuries after the first foreign diplomats reached Lithuania, another papal legate, Zaccharia Ferreri, a nominal bishop of Sebaste, the lost Catholic See in the Holy Land, visited Vilnius. Born in 1479 in northern Italy and educated in Padua, Ferreri belonged to the generation of clerics who embraced the spirit of Renaissance ideas. In 1513, he was excommunicated by the pontiff for supporting a reformist approach to the Catholic church and fled

9. Ostra Brama (in Polish) or Aušros Vartai (in Lithuanian), 1924. The gate is the only surviving structure of the town's defensive wall and has become one of the most recognisable landmarks of modern Vilnius.

to France. He was restored to prominence the following year with the election of Leo X, a scion of the Medici family, who lavished Rome with endless spectacles of aristocratic wealth and artistic imagination.

In 1520, Ferreri was assigned by the pope to persuade King Sigismund (brother of Alexander and the subsequent Grand Duke of Lithuania) to join a new crusade against the Ottomans, whose rapidly expanding empire had already reached the southern limits of Lithuania. In order to unite the warring Christian parties against the Muslims, Ferreri was sent to make a permanent peace between Poland-Lithuania and the Teutonic Order. He was also expected to go to Moscow to "save" the tsar from the schismatic – Orthodox –

beliefs by asking him to join the crusade. Ferreri failed on both accounts: the peace treaty between the Order and Poland was negotiated by the Holy Roman Emperor (an old adversary of the pope), and the trip to Moscow was averted by King Sigismund, who showed little faith in Ferreri's missionary qualifications and diplomatic skills.

Ferreri, a fanatical Catholic, was more successful in convincing the Polish king to wrestle against the rising wave of Protestant thought. In Poland, he organised a public *auto-da-fé* of Luther's books (one of the first such acts in Europe) and pushed for an edict banning Lutheran publications. Overwhelmed by his initial success, the legate ignited a fiery campaign against Orthodox believers, which included a majority of Lithuania's population. In this two-fronted theological war, Ferreri found an accomplice whose life story led him to Vilnius. For some time, the papal office in Rome had been receiving requests from the highest secular and clerical authorities of Poland-Lithuania to initiate a canonisation process for Prince Casimir, the older brother of Alexander and Sigismund. Pope Leo X took the request seriously and instructed Ferreri to collect materials and eyewitness accounts about the saintly deeds of the deceased prince.

Casimir was a grandson of Jogaila and a fourth-generation offspring of Gediminas. He was born in 1458, the second son of the king, and was groomed to become a ruler himself. After his older brother took the throne of Bohemia, the thirteen-year-old Casimir was sent by his father to Hungary to claim that country's royal title. The war quickly turned sour: the unpaid and demoralised mercenary army ran away, leaving the defenceless young pretender in disgrace. Humbled by the failure, Casimir returned from the war a different person. He rejected the luxuries and easy-going life of the court, devoted his youthful energy to celibacy and asceticism, and turned his princely attention to charity and evangelical work. Despite the prince's troublesome piety and ill health (he was suffering from consumption), Casimir's father had chosen him as his successor to the Polish throne. With paternal encouragment, Casimir became active in governing Poland and, during his regular visits to Lithuania, called on his father to strengthen the Catholic church in the region by restricting the religious freedoms of the Orthodox population. Yet in defiance of his family's plans, the prince refused to marry the daughter of the Holy Roman Emperor. It was rumoured that Casimir, in his angelic beauty, spent his nights in prayer, and completely rejected sex and procreation, even as a family and royal duty. When the doctors, with the blessing of his parents, prescribed sex with a beautiful woman as the most effective antidote to his consumptive (and presumably impotent) condition, he declared a preference for death and the heavenly afterlife over the restorative pleasures of the sinful act. He was found dead in a prayerful pose on the cold morning of March 4, 1484, at age twenty-six, on the doorstep of a church in a Lithuanian town. His body was brought to Vilnius and buried in the royal crypt of the Cathedral.

Pious acts and a celibate life were not enough to make Casimir a saint. Miracles were needed for a successful canonisation, and so Ferreri went to Vilnius in search of them. During a month-long trip from Poland to Vilnius (which, according to some contemporaries, was located very close to the North Pole), Ferreri became increasingly aware of the celestial guidance of Casimir. All through his journey, torrential rains savagely pounded the earth with thundering storms announcing the imminent end of the world. The legate, however, never felt a drop. The daily deluge only started at night or as soon as the travellers reached a shelter. In fact, the stormy weather, in the words of the legate, made the trip easier, for "during day, the clouds veiled us from the hot sun. And the night rains seemed to us a heavenly blessing, since it washed away the dust (which makes travel here so torturous) from the sandy roads, so it could do no harm to our eyes. Surprised by our luck, we understood it to be a reward from God for our research work on the accomplishments of Blessed Casmir, whose saintly life story we lovingly took to our heart."[14]

The atmospheric drama reached its climax at the gates of Vilnius, where, after "travelling through primeval forest, uninhabited and swampy terrain," the legate was met by a crowd of exuberant locals. At the end of a thanksgiving Mass and dinner, Ferreri, "with a welcoming party of the bishops of Vilnius, Kiev and Kaffa, magistrates, clergy and a countless number of the Catholic and schismatic (Orthodox) population" was ready to enter the city. Once again, the sky took on a menacing colour. A squall rumbled in the distance. The patricians, all garbed "in silk, precious stones and gold," and an inestimable number of plebeians nervously looked at the heavens. Fortuitously, the storm broke loose only after the ceremonial procession gathered at the high altar of the Cathedral. For Ferreri, this was a sure sign of the unblemished sainthood of Casimir.[15]

Ferreri must have heard about the visit of another papal envoy, Jacobus Piso of Transylvania, who had passed through the city six years earlier, in 1514. Piso had come to Vilnius for the celebration of the most recent Polish-Lithuanian victory over a Russian army at Orsha. This defeat of Moscow was not attributed to any divine interventions: the shared honour of victory went to the hetman of the Lithuanian army and the king of Poland, the brother of Casimir. Piso stayed in Vilnius for five days and wrote a sixteen-line verse, entitled "De Lithuania" (published in 1533 in Vienna), describing each day of his visit. On the first day of the visit, the exhausted traveller, scorched by heat, is revived by the refreshing waters of Vilnius. The next day, he pays his respects to the hetman, and a day later, the news of the victory is publicly confirmed. On the fourth day, he attests "to the glory of the king" by observing the procession of enemy prisoners. Finally, on the fifth day, "a happy hour has arrived" when the gracious king finally allowed the weary diplomat to leave town. "What else is there to say?" Piso ends the poem in answer to his own rhetorical question: "Farewell, the land of Lithuanians, and be strong, for I would not want to live here, even if I was treated like a god."[16]

Ferreri's experience of Vilnius was different. He was treated, if not like a god, then at least as the revered messenger of the Holy Father. He stayed in the city for six months, from September through February, and very much enjoyed the ceremonial social character of his visit. Ferreri vigorously exploited his high ecclesiastical status, calling a synod and railing against the new and old heresies: Luther's teachings and Russian Orthodox preaching. Winter cold, however, threatened to spoil his spiritual work. For the Italians, writes Ferreri, "who are used to the Roman climate, even a mild cold can be hazardous." But in "Lithuania, which is an arctic country where even wild animals freeze to death, and trees and house logs crack apart from cold," one could easily get frostbite and perish very quickly. But the Almighty showed his mercy; the winter was the mildest in memory. At Christmas, the Italians could stay outdoors all night and day, going from church to church while "preaching against the heresies of the Russians," without doing any harm to their sensitive dispositions. And while Ferreri thanked Casimir for the agreeable weather, "the Lithuanians were unanimous that only we, the Italians, could have brought the warmth of Rome" to Vilnius.[17]

The locals were quick to point out miraculous interventions of Casimir experienced amidst their own people. Deaf, blind, crippled and sick devotees were routinely cured of their conditions at the site of his grave. A girl was resurrected from death. Indeed, the future of the entire country was said to be in the hands of the deceased prince. A year ago, Fererri was told, a miracle, "rarely known in ancient times and unseen in our times," had saved Lithuania from complete annihilation. The army of Muscovy – sixty thousand in strength – poured into Lithuania, which could muster only a force of two thousand volunteers. All hope was lost. Vilnius was left defenceless, its inhabitants ready to die or live in captivity. With tears in their eyes, the Lithuanian soldiers asked Casimir for protection and forgiveness for failing to venerate him as a saint. The prayer restored their courage and, "shielded by the faith," they mercilessly attacked the enemy. The Lithuanians won the battle without losing a soul.[18]

10. Saint Casimir, 1749. This iconographic image of the saint portrays him on a background of three Vilnius landmarks: the Casimir Chapel at the Cathedral, Castle Hill and Three-Cross Hill.

Ferreri painstakingly collected various testimonials about the miracles, including his own accounts of the "blessed" weather conditions, and completed the first hagiography of Casimir while still in Vilnius. The book, *Vita S. Casimiri,* published in 1521, described the saint's life in a humanist fashion, intertwining the miraculous curriculum vitae of Casimir with more mundane descriptions of the royal family, national history, geographical facts and ethnographical details. Vilnius had already brought three saintly martyrs to the world, but they were dismissed by the Catholic church as heretics. In 1347, three local converts to the Byzantine Orthodox faith, members of the ducal court, were tortured and killed by a pagan mob in Vilnius. Thirty years later, their relics were taken to Haghia Sophia in Constantinople, the patriarchal church of the Byzantine Empire. The worship of the three martyrs survived the Ottoman conquest of Constantinople and was strengthened by the Metropolitan of Moscow, who, in 1549, added them to the universal list of the Russian Orthodox saints. This Orthodox hagiology made Vilnius a part of the Byzantine world, and Ferreri was determined to make it irrelevant by sanctifying Casimir as a progeny of the Latin universe.

In the book, the legate was keen to establish a familial connection between Vilnius and Rome by pointing to the orthographical similarity of the name Lithuania to Italy (*Lituania* and *Italia*, respectively). Indeed, he amalgamated the two names into *Litaliania,* a notable, if completely imaginative country, whose "ancient past was made famous by the colonies established by the supporters of great Pompeus."[19] Despite this genealogical affiliation, Lithuania, "a country of bitter cold where summer is a rare visitor," was the antithesis of Italy. Instead of being sheltered by the Mediterranean and the Alps, Lithuania is "from all corners surrounded by vast plains overgrown with forests and filled with lakes and swamps." There are no "vineyards and orchards," but the forest is full of "many little animals prized for their warm and luxurious fur."[20] Still, by blending Italy with Lithuania, Ferreri put Vilnius on the Renaissance map of the antique world. Like ancient Rome, Renaissance Vilnius stands at the crossroads of various trade routes bringing wealth "from the German [North], Sarmatian [Baltic] and Pontus [Black] Seas and even some more distant lands – Armenia, Schytia, Thracia, Greece and Mysia [Asia Minor]."[21]

Ferreri praises Casimir as the embodiment of the ancient unity between Lithuania and Italy, and ends the hagiography with a celebration of Vilnius as a city poised to become a beacon of Christian solidarity:

> Rejoice glorious and beautiful Italy, for giving birth to the honourable Litalinian and Lithuanian nobilities, who gave us Casimir. Rejoice vast and spacious Sarmatia for conquering frost, cold and your own bareness as you nurtured this most beautiful and blissful tree of life, yielding the sweetest fruit of virtue and honour. Rejoice the holy and pious Mother Church, for bringing into the light Casimir as a true son of Christ and a warrior for the faith. ... Above all, rejoice Vilnius – the glorious city, where Casimir's white bones, his beloved body and holy relics will be kept for posterity as a guarantee of his immortality and glory. Let us share this news with every Christian ecclesia and let God's name be honoured in every temple with music: here in songs, there in organ hymns!"[22]

The laudatory salutation to Casimir was a century premature. The Vatican found no flaws in the saintly life of Casimir, but Pope Leo X died in 1521, and, soon after his return from Lithuania, Ferreri expired, too. The sack of Rome by the Imperial troops in 1527 and the swelling religious controversies of Europe put the beatification of the pious Sarmatian prince on a long hold. So while the Protestant doctrine fervently purged Heaven and Earth of idolatrous worship, Catholic Vilnius, for the time being, was left without a patron.

11. "Sarmatia, the threshold province of Europe," from *La cosmographie universelle*, 1572.

CHAPTER TWO:

Mapping Sarmatia

> While the cartographical frame within which [Renaissance] men could
> think of themselves as Europeans became more clearly defined, and
> while those of one country came to learn more of those of others through
> increased travel and reading, there was a counter-tendency at work: to
> know was not necessarily to like. Information opened minds; it also fed
> prejudices.
>
> John Hale

One of the earliest known mappings of Vilnius was made in 1513 on a chart
entitled *Tabula moderna Sarmatie Europa* published in Strasbourg.[1] According
to the cartographic legend, the map was a revision of an earlier one made by the
cardinal and governor of Rome, Nicolus Cusanus (1401-1464), who attempted
to place ancient geographical knowledge on the political terrain of fifteenth-
century Europe. The Grand Duchy of Lithuania appears, for the first (known)
time, on the 1491 copy of the Cusanus chart; yet its capital city is indicated only
as a nameless town. The 1513 copy demarcates Lithuania by sprinkling its territory with several named and well-marked towns. Ironically, this time around
the mapmaker was so enthusiastic in populating Lithuania with numerous cities and castles that he recorded Vilnius twice on the same map. The first label
correctly identifies the Lithuanian capital as the town of Wilno, situating it at
the confluence of two unnamed rivers. The second label incorrectly marks the
city as *Bilde*, located south of the original Wilno. The name *Bilde*, which has
no known historical equivalent, appears to be a corrupt version of the place
name *Wilde*, which was used to identify Vilnius in several German-language
descriptions of Lithuania of the fifteenth century. The German usage of *Wilde*
as a name for Vilnius (as in *die statt Wilde, für die Wilde, zur Wilde*) stems from
old chronicles of the Teutonic Order, yet it continued to be used sporadically
in many records and maps up until the eighteenth century.[2]

Geographical misnomers were not unusual in early European chronicles,
and in the frontier-like environment of Lithuania, vernacular names were
subject to a great variety of misspellings and linguistic alterations. Yet the
orthographic affinity of *Wilde* to Wilna (or Vilnius) probably has something

to do with the ideological and, in this case, geo-religious struggle over control of Lithuania. The German word *Wilde* has very specific connotations: *der/die Wilde* means savage or wild. The vast forested territory which separated Vilnius from the Teutonic Knights' possessions in Prussia was depopulated due to the endless raids of the crusaders, and was simply referred to in German as *die Wildnis* – the wilderness. This made the idea and practice of the annual *reysa* into Lithuania inseparable from the experience of the country as a wild frontier of the known world.

In Lithuania, the intimate relationship between urban and wild – culture

12. Lithuanian moose, from *La cosmographie universelle*, 1556.

and nature – reached a level rarely encountered in western Europe, where cities were more a part of a rural (rather than forest) environment. Even after the end of the Teutonic raids, reaching Vilnius inevitably involved crossing long stretches of wilderness, where surprises and dangers lurked around every corner. A late fifteenth-century cosmography describes:

> "the famed forest [that] runs throughout Sarmatia [has] nothing superior to it in all of Europe. The forest extends to Krakow [the capital of Poland], and it is possible to hike through it to Lithuania and Scythia. The great forest runs through the entire region like outstretched arms, giving shelter to very large herds of wild animals. In the northern part of the forest live ferocious bisons, huge beasts who very much hate the sight of humans; as venison they are quite tasty, the color of their skin resembles lemons; the forehead is white with protruding horns; it requires enormous efforts to hunt them."[3]

From the perspective of any European adventurer brave enough to step into this northern wilderness, Vilnius must have appeared as a tiny urban island lost amidst a sea of endless evergreens. But Vilnius, with its exclusively wooden houses, was not only engulfed by the forest; it grew out of it. The town, in contrast to its western European cousins, stood not in opposition to wilderness, but had a symbiotic relationship with it.

This perception was no doubt augmented by the religious beliefs and practices of the local pagan people, who worshiped natural phenomena such as the sun, the moon, thunder, animals and especially trees and forests. The most important pagan Lithuanian shrine was located at the historical heart of Vilnius – the confluence of the Neris and Vilnia rivers – and was protected by a sanctified oak grove. The oxymoron of calling a city *Wilde* positioned it outside of urban Christian Europe, where the boundary between the natural and civic realms was more clearly defined, if not always marked by a stone wall. So it should not come as a great surprise that Vilnius became European (that is, Catholic and Latin) with the help of an axe blade. The 1387 baptism of Lithuania was consecrated by the formalised destruction of the holy oak grove, which stood in the sacred valley beneath the Castle Hill. In the clearing left after the spiritual purge, the first Catholic Cathedral of Vilnius – a stone building – was built.

During the Renaissance era, the relative geographical isolation of Vilnius turned into its greatest cultural asset. Located at the frontiers of every spiritual milieu of Europe – Catholic, Protestant, Byzantine Orthodox, Judaic, Islamic and even pagan – the city nurtured a landscape of religious tolerance and cultural cross-pollination. Humanist thought and Renaissance aesthetics came to Vilnius relatively late. The Gothic style reached its height in Vilnius only with the construction of the elegant Saint Anne's Church in 1500, when the Renaissance century was already dawning further south. The first printing press in the city was set up only in 1522, almost seventy years after Gutenberg printed the first book in Mainz. But the first book published in Vilnius was *A Little Itinerary Book,* a collection of religious hymns and a church calendar for laymen of the Byzantine Orthodox faith, lavishly set in Cyrillic in the Slavic (Old Byelorussian) language by the Catholic-educated humanist scholar, Francis Skaryna. A few decades later, religious tolerance took on a more formal character: in 1563, amidst the brutal religious conflicts in Europe, a law guaranteeing religious freedom in Lithuania was passed by an assembly of nobles in Vilnius. The following year, the grand duke issued a decree forbidding local authorities from charging Jews with the crime of ritual murder unless based on the testimony of three Christians and three Jews. Such equality was rare in Europe, where religious segregation was enforced by the rule of mob and often supported by law.

The Lithuanian ducal court, now decisively based in Vilnius, became even more cosmopolitan, with royal marriages that spanned Christendom. Foreign diplomats came to Vilnius not only to discuss matrimonial matters, but also to work on issues of war and peace. In 1517, Sigismund von Herberstein, one of the most successful diplomats of his time, passed through the city on his way to Russia to negotiate a truce between Lithuania and Moscow, which was finally signed in 1522. He returned to Lithuania in 1526 to renew the treaty. Herberstein served the Habsburgs, the most powerful ruling family of Europe, and his personal involvement in the Russian-Lithuanian conflict attests to the growing geopolitical significance of the two (still peripheral) countries within the context of the European balance of power. Lithuania, a predominantly Orthodox country ruled by a Catholic royal family, was unique in its position as a mediator between the two religious camps. Any potential alliance between the two creeds, and hence the possibility of the reunification of the Christian world, would need to go through Lithuania and its capital, Vilnius.

At the end of his diplomatic career, Herberstein published a book, *Notes upon Russia*, which became a canonical treatise on Russia and the surrounding countries. Two chapters were devoted to Lithuania: one about the geography, history and social nature of the country, and the other, in the words of the author, was left to a survey "of their wild beasts." Heberstein's description of Vilnius must be read in the light of his diplomatic mission, which tried to establish a common political, if not cultural, ground between Moscow and Lithuania as the best guarantor of peace.

"Vilna," wrote Herberstein, "is surrounded by a wall, and contains many temples and houses built of stone. ... It has also a parish church and several monasteries, with a convent of Franciscans, which was constructed at immense expense, and is remarkable for the strictness of its discipline. The Russian churches in it are much more numerous than those which have been built for the observance of the Roman ritual."[4] The mighty militia of the grand duke "wear a long dress, and carry bows like Tartars; but they also have a spear and shield, like the Hungarians."[5] Outside the city, "the people are miserable, and oppressed with heavy servitude; for when any man who is attended by a host of servants enters the house of any husbandman, he is at liberty to do with impunity whatever he thinks fit, to seize and consume any of the necessaries of life, and even cruelly to beat the husbandman himself." Yet corruption and servitude cut through all social levels: "the husbandmen are not on any account allowed access to their masters without bringing presents, and when they are admitted, they are referred to the stewards and officials, who, unless they receive presents, will make no arrangement, nor give any decision to the advantage of the applicant. Nor was this the case only with the poor, but also with the nobles, whenever they wished to obtain any favour from their official superiors. I once heard a certain youthful minister, of high rank about the king, say that the only word in Lithuania is 'gold'. "[6] But most scandalous was what went on deep in the Lithuanian forest, where "horrible sights may occasionally be witnessed; for in them there dwell a considerable number of idolators, who cherish, as a kind of household god, a species of reptile, which has four short feet like a lizard, with a fat black body, not exceeding three palms in length."[7]

At the time of Herberstein's diplomatic involvements, the Grand Duchy of Lithuania included the territories of contemporary Lithuania, Belarus, the Ukraine and the western part of Russia. In the north, the Grand Duchy neighboured new strongholds of Lutheranism: Sweden, Prussia and Livonia (contemporary Latvia and Estonia). In the east, the dukedom's frontier reached deep into the Russian Orthodox principalities of Novgorod and Smolensk, bordering the state of Moscow. In the south, it created a vast buffer zone with the Ottoman world through its changing borders with the Muslim-ruled Crimean Khanate and the Byzantine Orthodox-dominated Moldavia. The country encompassed many European geographical divisions: it stretched from the woody and marshy lowlands of the Baltic Sea region to the virgin steppe plateau of the northern coast of the Black Sea. It also included the fertile area of the Carpathian piedmont regions of Volhynia and Podolia, and the heavily timbered territory of the Russian forest.

This vast land was inhabited by a great variety of peoples: Poles, Lithuanians, Ruthenians (Ukrainians), Byelorussians, Russians, Jews, Germans, Latvians, Armenians, Tartars, and other minority groups. Six languages – Polish, Latin, Old Byelorussian, Hebrew, German and Armenian – were used for legal purposes. Religious profession was equally diverse. On a basic level, there were three major Christian communities in the dukedom: Catholic, Greek Orthodox and Protestant. In 1596, a fourth element was added – the Uniate church, which attempted to resolve the dogmatic and liturgical schism between the Greek and Latin churches. Most of Lithuanian Jewry was Ashkenazi (western European) in origin, except for the Karaites, who were brought to Lithuania by the grand dukes in the fourteenth and fifteenth centuries from their Crimean homeland on the Black Sea. The Karaites are thought to be descendants of the Khazars, a semi-nomadic people who accepted Judaism in the ninth century. The Ashkenazi Jews practised the rabbinical form of Judaism, wrote in Hebrew and, in most cases, spoke vernacular Yiddish; the Karaites followed the Babylonian version of the Judaic faith, used the Arabic alphabet for Hebrew scripture and spoke a Turkic language. There were also Muslim Tartars, who, like the Karaites, came from the Crimea.

The cultural vastness and heterogeneity of Lithuania was hard for foreigners to grasp. This was further confused by the ambiguous geographical definition of Lithuania, which carried two spatial meanings: first, as the political state of the Grand Duchy of Lithuania, and second, as an ancient province belonging to the original patrimony of Gediminas. Between the two definitions, there was a difference of continental proportions. At its height, in the first part of the sixteenth century, the Grand Duchy was roughly the size of

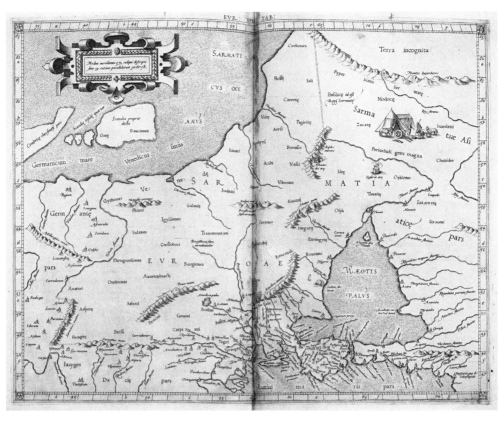

13. Sarmatia in Europe and Asia, from *Geographia*, 1513.

the Holy Roman Empire and was the largest political body in Europe after the rapidly expanding Russian state. In contrast, the province (or country) of Lithuania, only partially inhabited by Lithuanians, covered a much smaller territory surrounding Vilnius. To complicate matters, Lithuania (the Grand Duchy and the province) was invariably allied with its monarchical partner, Poland. This political partnership was deepened by the Union of Lublin, which, in 1569, created an amalgamated state of Poland-Lithuania, or, as it was known constitutionally, the Commonwealth of Both Nations.

Neither the Polish nor Lithuanian identities or nations could accurately embody such geographical and cultural diversity. The only country capable of encompassing this union of differences was the elusive Sarmatia, whose cartographical origins could be traced back to the geographical and historical works of the ancient Greeks and Romans. Reputedly, the Greek geographer

Ptolemy situated the barbarian tribe of the Sarmatians somewhere in the steppes between the Azov and the Caspian seas. Historian Herodotus and other commentators moved the semi-nomadic Sarmatians westwards to the area of the Black Sea and the lower basin of the Dnieper River. Some time later, this tribe of permanent wanderers was moved further north, to the region where the vast southern steppes and plains of Eurasia meet the northern forest and marshlands of the Baltic Sea littoral. According to the Roman scholar Tacitus, this was an unexplored land somewhere near the "Suabian Sea" (most likely the Baltic Sea), where "our knowledge of the world ends."[8] Renaissance geographical thinkers discovered this imperfect spatial knowledge of the ancient scholars and laid it out on the contemporary map of Europe. The Baltic Sea became *Mare Sarmaticum* and the lands stretching ad infinitum southeast from the sea were identified as Sarmatia, split into two dominions: *European Sarmatia* and *Asian Sarmatia*.

At the dawn of the Renaissance era, European Sarmatia was described as "an extremely large and desolate region, uncultivated and located in wilderness, in a rigid climate. It is bounded on the East by Moschos [Muscovy] and the river Don; on the South by Dacians [Romania] and Pannonians [Hungary]; on the West by Bohemians, Moravians, Silesians and the Teutons, and on the North by the German [Baltic] Sea and the Harbor of Gdansk."[9] This confusingly vast cartographical existence of Sarmatia was made more corporeal by the emergence of Sarmatism, a peculiar socio-cultural milieu that found fertile ground among the Polish-Lithuanian nobility of the sixteenth century.

Sarmatism resulted from a fusion of regional patriotism with the rediscovery of classical Greek and Roman texts. Although it was based on ancient geo-mythology, Sarmatism "was a unique variation of what might be called Renaissance national self-definition. In the Renaissance spirit of a return to sources, the peoples of Europe searched for or created their own (mythic) origins. Sarmatism expressed for the Poles the idea that, like other European nations, they too had their origins in the peoples discussed by the authors of antiquity, but their ancestors were even older than some of those claimed by many other Europeans."[10] After the Union of Lublin, the antiquated myth of Sarmatia effortlessly annexed Lithuania, as the cultural perimeter of the Sarmatian identity "was gradually altered to embrace the non-Polish nobility in the Commonwealth. Any nobleman of the Commonwealth who defended the political liberties and privileges of his class was considered a Sarmatian. Out of this myth, or point of view, arose a doctrine which, by the end of the sixteenth century, was an apologia for the political and social status quo." Through the steady assimilation of the Polish-Lithuanian upper

SARMA-
TIÆ EV"
ROPEÆ DESCRI,
ptio, quæ Regnum Polo-
niæ, Lituaniam, Samogiti-
am, Rufsiam, Mafouiam,
Prufsiam, Pomeraniam, Li-
uoniam, & Mofchouiæ,
Tartariæ̃ partem com-
plectitur.

Alexandri Gwagnini Vero-
nenfis, Equitis Aurati, pedi-
tumq̃, præfecti, diligentia
confcriptæ.

Typis Matthiæ Wirzbietæ.

14. Frontispiece from A. Gwagnini's *Sarmatiae Europeae Descriptio,* 1578.
The full title of the book indicates Sarmatia as a region which stretches
from Poland, Lithuania, Samogitia, Russia, Prussia, Pomerania, Livonia and
Mazovia to the western parts of Muscovy and Tartaria.

classes, "Sarmatism became, in essence, the 'historical' documentation for
the existence of the nobility and its political authority."[11] The royal family of the Jogaila lineage was considered the embodiment of the Sarmatian
heritage: for instance, Grand Duke Alexander (who resided in Vilnius) was
"judged to be the ornament of Sarmatia" because "all of Sarmatia has hardly
anyone equal to him in courage and sublimity of mind."[12]

One of the first extensive scholarly works on Sarmatia was written by Alexander Gwagnini (1538-1614), an Italian officer in the service of the Grand Duke of Lithuania. Gwagnini became interested in the history and geography of Lithuania, and in 1578, in Kraków, published a book in Latin entitled *Sarmatiae Europaeae Desciptio*. Subsequently, the manuscript was republished in several different editions and translated into Polish. Gwagnini explicitly equated Sarmatia with the Grand Duchy of Lithuania, which he described as a "very expansive" country with "a definite location" covering "many duchies, states and provinces of different names" under its title.[13]

Vilnius, at the time of the Lublin Union, was depicted as being a chaotic and rough metropolis of the Sarmatian frontier. The first bird's-eye view of the city projected in the 1576 edition of *Civitates Orbis Terrarum* (the famous atlas of world cities designed by the Flemish artist Franz Hogenberg and cartographer Georg Braun, a dean of the cathedral in Cologne) gives an impression of a large town built almost exclusively out of wood. The lengthy description of the city summarises the exotic character of the place:

> Vilna is a large, densely populated city, center of the Grand Duchy of Lithuania and the diocese. Called *Wilenszki* by the local population, but *die Wilde* by the Germans, it takes its name from the local river, which starts in Lithuania and, then, by joining the river of Niemen, reaches *Mare Prutenicum* (the Prussian Sea). The city is surrounded by a brick wall with several gates that are never closed. … Most houses are wooden, small and low, without bedrooms and kitchens (often, without barns, although many residents keep farm animals), built sporadically in a chaotic fashion. Yet some streets, such as German and Castle Streets, are lined with beautiful stone houses, built by foreigners who come here on business. Vilna has two royal palaces: one of them is large and beautiful, with many chambers; the other one with towers is built on the hill. Although Lithuania has no mining industry, there is an arsenal containing weapons of all sorts at the foot of the hill. The churches are mostly brick, but there are also some wooden ones. Different confessions have their own houses of worship. Renowned for its kilned brick architecture, the Bernardine monastery is the most elegant. The Ruthenian Hall, where goods from Moscow, such as finest furs of wolf, white fox, marten sable, ermine, leopard and other beasts are displayed, is also fascinating. There are numerous fountains in the streets for the residents to use, but they are all connected to a spring near the German Gate.
>
> There are many extramural settlements, like in all well-designed cities, each with its own name. One of them, engulfed by the Vilna River, stands out from the rest because of its poverty. Since there are no streets, tiny houses are built without any system, as if by magic or chance, guided only by the wishes of its barbarian residents. Anyone who desires can bring few pine planks and build a primitive hut. Beyond the gate of the royal palace, King Sigismund Augustus constructed a

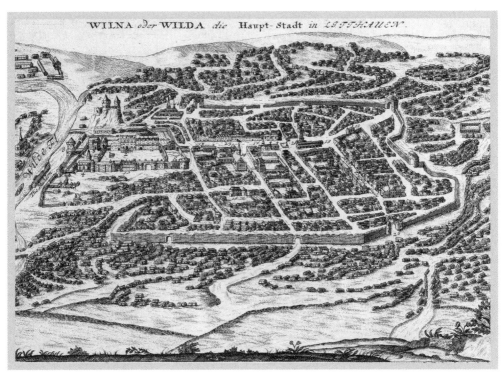

15. "Wilna or Wilda, the capital city of Lithuania," circa 1720. This map is based on an earlier plan of the city, first published in the sixteenth century in G. Braun's atlas of famous world cities.

wooden hunting lodge to escape the hassle and troubles of city life. The grounds of the lodge contain a copse with a vivarium for various exotic, expensive beasts.

The residents of Vilna, especially those living in suburban hovels, are uneducated, sluggish, lazy, idle and subservient, with no knowledge or liking of arts and sciences. They are true slaves of their masters, without a desire for freedom. Surprisingly, they are very much pleased with their miserable existence and show love and obedience only to those masters who scold and beat them mercilessly. Meanwhile, they usually run away from those masters who treat them well.

Locals make no grape wine, but love to drink. They drink mead and beer, and have a great liking for warm wine, and eat onions and garlic. Their houses are always full of smoke, because they are built without chimneys. As a result, people turn blind. Nowhere in the world are there so many blind people as here. Their homes are free of any decorations or expensive utensils. Parents together with their children, cattle, and beasts live together in a dirty hovel. The wife of the master of the house, who has just given birth, lies nearby on a hard bench, and on the third and fourth day after labour, resumes her domestic duties and outside work. In the entire city, nobody has a bed, and if that is not enough, sleeping softly is considered to be a sin. There are plenty of wealthy people who sleep on benches, covered only in bearskin. The life of the aristocrats is not much better, only that they wear fancier clothes embroidered in gold and silver. The wealthy burghers, too, happily dress their wives attractively, while country folk always wear simple clothes of the same cut and colour.

... The Tartars live mostly in the suburbs. They tend land or work as coachmen and porters; in winter, they help local merchants to transport goods throughout the countryside. ... In general, it is possible to travel to and from this city only in winter, since Lithuania is completely surrounded by swamps and woods. The insufferable roads leading to the city become passable only after the lakes and marshes are covered by ice. Local pack animals are like their owners: strong and brutal.

... The townspeople observe strange religious customs. They piously attend every sermon, intensely following every gesture of the priest, such as the raising of a chalice or consecrating of sacraments, full of admiration. They pray obsessively with pounding on their chests and faces. Those who had illicitly copulated or debauched themselves the previous night do not come inside the church, but remorsefully stay outside the doors eagerly staring at the priest attending the mass. This custom is so widespread that it is very easy to spot every errant youth and sinful maiden in town. ... When death finally releases them from their miserable servitude ... they are buried in good clothes and with money for the afterlife journey. The dead also carry letters from their relatives or dear friends, addressed and written to Saint Peter, so that he – being the gatekeeper of Paradise – would let the deceased into Heaven. This and other superstitious customs are so pervasive that even those who still reject the Christian faith [local Jews and Muslims] follow them unquestioningly. One can never forget that in the past, locals worshiped snakes, sun, thunder and fire as their gods.[14]

Overall, foreigners were cautioned about visiting Vilnius. "This large city," warns the guide, "has no hospital or hospice for the poor and sick where they could recover at the mercy of benevolent people." Worse, "the residents, intoxicated by mead, warm wine or strong beer, easily get into arguments, brawls and savage fights, which lead to serious injuries. Killing a foreigner is not considered to be a mortal sin and the criminal can get away with the fine of sixteen thalers. But if a Lithuanian gets killed and the killer escapes, the victim's family embalm the body of the deceased and keep it unburied until the criminal is caught and put on trial. If the victim is buried before the trial, the criminal might go free for lack of evidence."[15]

Now and then, Sarmatians were depicted in various world cosmographies as "cruel and sluggish people."[16] This distressing picture of the region was reinforced by the Spanish priest, lawyer and poet Petrus Royzius (known as Mauro), co-author of the Second Lithuanian Statute (1566), who lived in Vilnius for several years. He was the first to paint a grim Sarmatian portrait of the city in verse:

Terrible famine, morbid disease and no less dangerous robberies
Vanquish Vilna folk at homes, churches and streets.
When these wrongs come together, they leave corpses everywhere.
Can anyone overcome this evil?
Famine could be fought with plenty of food, grave illness with medicine.
But the robbers go free, for there is no justice in this town.[17]

16. Saint Christopher as the emblem of Vilnius.

The citizens of Vilnius fought the damaging foreign reports (and, no doubt, the grim reality) with the help of Heaven. While the case for the sainthood of Casimir was still adrift, they put Saint Christopher on the seal of the city. It was a thoughtful choice – Saint Christopher was the patron saint of travellers, and by the end of the century reports of the city grew more positive. In Mercator's atlas of the world, Vilnius is described as a well-travelled town inhabited by hospitable people: "Except for government officials, all burghers are innkeepers, selling beer, mead, and warm wine. They welcome strangers into their houses, seat them near the hearth and invite them to have a cup of each drink. Only after the guest has tasted the drinks will the hosts let him go. If the guest asks for more, or decides to dine with the family of the host, he will be charged a small fee."[18]

Historical records are scanty on how foreigners responded to this overwhelming hospitality, because very few of them left any written impressions. Within the cultural context of Sarmatia, travellers tended to compare Lithuanians to Poles, finding Lithuanian society much more lax in social discipline, cultural sophistication and sexual morals than its more westernised counterpart. Lithuanian nobles were periodically portrayed as reckless drunkards who enjoyed endless hunts and feasts. An occasional traveller noted the unusually relaxed sexual atmosphere found in the households of the Lithuanian elite. The wives and daughters of the Lithuanian noble families were sometimes depicted as sexual predators, being interested in amorous affairs as much as their husbands or fathers. According to some reports, many unmarried women were openly sexually active with multiple partners, and even after marriage were permitted to keep lovers, with the consent of their husbands. Early printed accounts detailing the Lithuanian practice of *mat-rimoniae adiutores* appeared in Polish and German manuscripts of the late medieval period and, in later centuries, piquant stories about local women regularly surfaced within various cosmographies of Europe. An English version of such an account was reprinted in 1611 in a text entitled *The manners, lawes and customs of all nations*, where it was noted that Lithuanian women "have their chamber-mates & friends by their husband's permission, & those they call helpers or furtherers of matrimony, but for a husband to commit adultery is held disgraceful and abominable: Marriages there bee very easily dissoluted, by consent of both parties, and they marry as oft as they please."[19] The Amazon image of the Lithuanian woman fitted the ideal profile of a Sarmatian female, depicted in 1516 in Latin verse, "Sapphic Ode," published in the German city of Augsburg:

> There is a land with wide and spreading plains,
> That stretches far away towards the north,
> Where with a thousand oxen tills the soil
> The hardy Sarmatian.
>
> ....
> Here Venus teaches the loveliest of girls,
> Who shall be worthy of the bed of Jove,
> And who alone deserves to hold the golden
> Apples of Atlas.[20]

While the mapping and foreign knowledge of Vilnius proceeded in tandem with charting the contours of Sarmatia, the spatial visibility of Sarmatia became eclipsed by the cartographical discovery of Europe. The entwined cartographical history of Sarmatia and Europe reveals the intimate relationship between geography and mythology. The metaphor and name of Europe has its origins in an ancient Greek myth, but the idea of Europe as a geographical unit places its origins in the visualisation of Christendom in the Renaissance period. With time, in John Hale's words, "from myth and map, chorography, history and survey, Europe passed into the mind."[21] By the 1600s, the mythological name of Europe had become inseparable from its geographical body: surrounded and safeguarded by water on three sides, Europe gradually dissolved into the vast landmass of Asia. This cartographical concept of Europe grew with advancements in mapping techniques and colonial discoveries of the globe. At the beginning of the Enlightenment, Europe's continental distinction was firmly implanted in the minds of the educated elite of the western world. Sarmatia was the opposite: born in the minds of ancient scholars, it faded away into the realm of phantasmagoria with the passing of time. By the middle of the eighteenth century, Sarmatia retreated back to its mythological origins and left the map of Europe.

In general, early imprints of Europe did not show bias towards the western parts of the continent. The Renaissance maps, devoid of "indications of political frontiers ... were not devised to be read politically. And the busily even spread of town names did not suggest that western [Europe] had any greater weight of economic vitality than eastern Europe. This even-handed appearance of uniformity owed something [not] to the cartographer's *horror vacui*, but more to their places of work and the networks of correspondents ... radiating from them." Most maps were produced in the northwestern corner of Europe, which had intense commercial, religious and political connections with the Baltic Sea region. As a result of these networks, neither "cartographers nor traders thought of Europe as comprising an 'advanced' Mediterranean and a 'backward' Baltic, or a politically and economically sophisticated Atlantic West and a marginally relevant East."[22]

Vilnius, the capital city of one of the largest political entities in Europe, was recognised as equal to any important urban centre of western or southern Europe. The city's cartographic visibility was also sharpened by the relative representational emptiness of its hinterland. There were fewer towns in Lithuania than in other parts of Europe, and except for vast forests and swamps, there were no other significant topographical elements – mountains, large rivers or lakes – to be mapped out. Indeed, the cartographers of the early Renaissance often exaggerated the topographical features of Lithuania. The rolling, undulating landscape around the city was portrayed in a similar fashion to the mountainous regions of the Carpathians; swampy areas of the Lithuanian-Byelorussian lowlands frequently appeared as immense lakes equal in size to uncharted seas; and minor rivers were delineated as gargantuan waterways.

Vilnius's magnified presence was also directly linked to the political conception of Lithuania as a geographical frontier of European civilisation. In western Europe, the dynastically unified state of Poland-Lithuania became widely recognised as "a steadfast fortress, not so much against the Turks and Crimean Tatars but against those other westward-pressing 'barbarians', the peoples of Russia, from the Muscovite heartlands around the capital to the semi-independent Cossacks of the South."[23] This newly acquired location of Lithuania as the *antermurale christianitatis,* the bulwark of Christendom, stimulated not only the western European geographical imagination (which populated the country with exotic natural phenomena, strange peoples and bizarre local history), but also contributed to the propagation of the art of geography. A masterpiece of cartographical precision was created in 1613 with the production of the map of the Grand Duchy of Lithuania, commissioned by Mykolas Radvila (Mikołaj Radziwiłł in Polish), a cosmopolitan scion of one of the wealthiest families of the Lithuanian nobility. This detailed map depicts the vast region stretching from the shores of the Baltic Sea to the central areas of Ukraine. Its elaborate design delivered the Renaissance practice of accurate cartographical workmanship into the era of Baroque spatial exuberance. Accordingly, the geographical narrative attached to the map depicts Vilnius as a "famous and great city" with many "splendid public and private buildings ... and numerous extravagant Roman Catholic and Russian Orthodox churches."[24]

Baroque came to Vilnius directly from Rome, bringing the eminence of Casimir back from its grave. The pope finally sanctified local worship of Casimir with a declaration of sainthood in 1602. Two years later, Jesuits laid the foundation stone – a massive boulder brought to the city by a procession of seven hundred people – for the Saint Casimir Church in Vilnius. Modeled on the *Il Gesù* in Rome, the church was one of the first Baroque edifices erected outside Italy. At first, it appeared that the spirit of Saint Casimir delivered the promised success, bringing wealth and glory to the city. In 1610, a united Polish-Lithuanian army occupied Moscow and crowned the son of the Polish king a tsar. With the help of the Jesuits, Saint Casimir was made the patron saint of Lithuania, Poland and Russia. Ten years later, as a token of the Catholic victory over Russian Orthodoxy, his feast day, celebrated on March 4 (the day of his death), was extended to the entire Catholic church.

Although the Polish-Lithuanian victory was short-lived, the enormous loot brought from Moscow enriched Vilnius, furthering the architectural ambitions of the Jesuits. The consecration of the massive Saint Casimir Church in 1618, however, coincided with the beginning of the Thirty Years War, which left most of Central Europe in ruins. And by the time the relics of Saint Casimir, encased in a silver sarcophagus, were placed in the elegant Baroque chapel of the city's cathedral in 1636, Lithuania was on the brink of annihilation. In Poland-Lithuania, several decades of war were followed by a disastrous period of internal and external discords, later known as the Deluge (1648-1667). Muscovite forces ransacked Lithuania and, from 1655 to 1661, occupied Vilnius, where the Russian Tsar Alexei Mihailovich declared himself the grand duke of Lithuania. While the body of Saint Casimir was

17. The resurrection of Vilnius under the patronage of the princely Radvila (Radziwiłł) family after the devastation of Lithuania by the Muscovite army.

being spirited away by the retreating Lithuanian forces, the Russian army desecrated the city's many Catholic and Uniate churches.

Yet amidst the ruins of the wars, the Baroque style flourished, enriching Sarmatism with the metaphysical theatricality of the era. More specifically, the allegorical apogee of Sarmatism corresponded with the glorious delivery of Vienna from a Turkish siege by the Polish-Lithuanian army, led by King Jan Sobieski in 1683. Still, for the Commonwealth, the political spoils of victory were short-lived. A never-ending parade of destructive foreign invaders, from the Swedes to the Ukrainian Cossacks and from the Ottomans to the Muscovites, marched through the country. The exposed frontiers of the Com-

18. The triumph of Poland. This celebratory print from the seventeenth century commemorates the Polish-Lithuanian battles against the Commonwealth's adversaries from the east. On the top of the picture, in the celestial realm, the Polish eagle overpowers the two-headed Russian (Byzantine) eagle, while on the ground, the Polish-Lithuanian forces, armoured in western European fashion, defeat the turban-wearing Ottoman army.

monwealth nonetheless played an important role in shaping the peculiarities of Sarmatian culture. And while many local "practices stemmed from the expressiveness of the pan-European Baroque ... they developed unique forms in the Polish-Lithuanian Commonwealth in part because of its extensive contact with the Russian and Ottoman civilizations."[25]

This continental porosity was counteracted by local isolationism. In the face of political annihilation, nativism took over cosmopolitism and, having "lost all hope of salvation, Polish society turned in on itself and, bewitched by the imaginary ideals of 'Old Sarmatia', began to lose sight of elementary realities."[26] During the so-called Saxon era (1697-1764), when the Commonwealth was ruled by two foreign monarchs (the electors of Saxony), Sarmatism acquired its explicit qualities of nostalgic inwardness and sentimental nativism. The Polish *szlachta* (nobility) filled Sarmatia with real and fictionalised memories of the past. In this sense, Sarmatia was more like a palimpsest than a country, an imaginable and readable realm – a recognisable topos – pieced together by the familiar elements of mythology, genealogy, history and geography. It was real because it was decipherable. The representational reality of Sarmatia was supported by the theatricality of the Baroque imagination, which freely mixed ancient epics, biblical scenes, exotic locations, fantastic motifs and contemporary European political events into an unfolding everyday drama.

Various daily rituals, official ceremonies, habitual gestures, oratorical diatribes, and, of course language, kept the Sarmatian nation of the Polish-Lithuanian nobility apart from other surrounding nations. The Polish *szlachta* wore specific Sarmatian garments, followed unique Sarmatian social and religious practices, and even suffered from a bizarre medical pathology, explicitly identified in Latin as *plica Polonica*, which was once described by an eighteenth century Swiss physician as "an acrid viscous humour penetrating into the hair" with the general symptoms of "itching, swelling, eruptions, ulcers, intermitting fevers, pain in head, languor, lowness of spirits, rheumatism, gout, and sometimes even convulsions, palsy, and madness." The disease, just like membership in the nation of Sarmatia, was thought to be hereditary, but, to the horror of foreigners, was also "proved to be contagious when in a virulent state."[27]

It is difficult to say how Sarmatian Baroque-era Vilnius was. The composition of the municipal officials reveals a pattern of ethnic fragmentation, with Poles comprising roughly fifty per cent, Ruthenians thirty percent, Germans eight per cent, Italians four per cent, and some tiny minorities of Lithuanian and Hungarian origins. The general population was even more diverse, since the Jews, Tartars, lower class Lithuanians and foreigners could not participate in local government. Members of religious orders or noble households were also excluded from the ranks of urban citizens. Even after the Jesuit-led Counter-Reformation, the urban elite remained religiously divided: Catholics dominated urban politics, but only slightly, since they comprised about sixty percent of the elected officials; second were Uniates – about thirty percent; then Protestant and Orthodox, each comprising about three percent of the elite. (One should point out that after 1666, Protestants and Orthodox believers were banned from holding municipal office, significantly altering the demographic picture of the city's ruling class.)[28]

In the immediate environs of the city, the diverse communities of Christians, Jews, Karaites and Muslims lived in close proximity to each other, and so Vilnius became the meeting ground for a whole array of languages: Lithuanian, Slavic (Polish, Ruthenian, Russian, Old Church Slavonic), Latin, German, Yiddish, Hebrew and Turkic. Foreigners were quick to find its biblical equivalent in the infamous Babylon. Such allusion carried a double-edged meaning, since it implied both a great fascination with and a harsh condemnation of the local reality. In the eyes of many foreigners and some locals, especially the Jesuits, the city's multiculturalism was perceived as a curse rather than a blessing.

Sarmatism was the social privilege of the nobility, with the countryside manor being its main cultural domain. Vilnius, despite its diminished political status, reduced wealth, shrinking population and deepening provincialism, was still, by far, the largest town in the region. In 1645, Vilnius, excluding its suburbs, had about 300 brick buildings and 200 wooden houses, with a population of about fifty thousand people.[29] Still, local nobility dominated the city, both culturally and politically. In general, the *szlachta*, which comprised about ten per cent of the Polish-Lithuanian population, was one of the most privileged social groups in Europe. The nobles had a right to assembly with the duty to elect the ruler of the country. They also determined the issues of taxation, foreign policy and war, and even enjoyed the right of revolt against unpopular state policies. With such enormous power in their hands, the country gentry treated the city as their backyard. Indeed, the local nobility owned many buildings in the city and funded the construction of many fine Baroque churches. The Sarmatian facade of Vilnius was also coloured by the determination of the upper crust of Lithuanian nobility to keep the allegorical associations with Rome alive. Ever since the Renaissance, the most powerful families had traced their genealogical roots back to lost tribes of ancient Roman warriors, visualising the city as a Sarmatian duplicate of Rome. However imperfect, such a vision prolonged the artistic vitality of the Baroque style beyond its western European lifespan.

Peace and concord in Vilnius were scarce in the eighteenth century, as waves of foreign armies brought more destruction. In 1702, a Swedish army looted Vilnius; in 1705, a Russian army led by Peter I occupied the town – it was soon followed by a Saxon force. In 1710, plague killed about thirty-five thousand inhabitants (certainly more than half of the population), and in 1720, a violent rebellion of the lower classes swept through the city. Devastating fires occurred regularly: in 1715, 1737 (three-quarters of the city was affected by this fire), 1741, 1748 and 1749. Economically and politically, the

19. The plague in Vilnius in 1710.

city could never fully recover from this march of social and natural disasters. Despite these and other cataclysmic events, or perhaps because of them, this was precisely the period of Baroque splendour in Vilnius. In a broad time-line of aesthetic evolution, the year 1750 marks the dividing moment between Baroque and Neoclassical sensibilities. By this time, the cult of Enlightenment rationality had reached and begun remaking every major capital city of Europe: Paris, London, Vienna, Berlin, Naples and Saint Petersburg. Yet in provincial Vilnius, old modes reigned supreme, and by the 1770s the "architects in Lithuania developed their own original forms, that can also be regarded as an extraordinary extension of the Baroque or Rococo traditions."[30] This was a period when the so-called Vilnius Baroque matured, and ever more elaborate churches were commissioned and built in the city by rich Lithuanian magnates, who drew their wealth from vast rural estates. As a result of this architectural proliferation, at the end of the eighteenth century, in a city of no more than forty thousand inhabitants, there were thirty-two Catholic churches with fifteen monasteries, five Uniate churches with three monasteries, and one Russian Orthodox, one Lutheran and one Calvinist church.[31]

Vilnius Baroque reversed the clock of European urban evolution, and rather than moving the townscape towards the Neoclassical sense of spatial order, it seemed to reorder the city back to its medieval origins. Hence, there are no straight axes, symmetrical squares or framed street vistas – characteristic of Baroque cities – in Vilnius. In other cities, Baroque space expands horizontally, in Vilnius it shoots vertically, like smoke from a sacrificial fire that tries to appease, rather than compete, with the heavens. Of course, the local persistence of Baroque was also an illusion, because Vilnius, along with the rest of Poland-Lithuania, was not immune from the intellectual, aesthetic and political changes of the time. The splendid autumn of Vilnius's Baroque was a short-lived elegant gesture of the city's delayed aesthetic development, a gracious farewell to its phantom golden age.

The longevity of local Baroque did not amuse those visitors of Vilnius whose ideas about the world and art were already framed by modern methods of scientific observation and the Enlightenment values of secular judgment. When the term "Baroque" was first introduced in the middle of the eighteenth century in France, it carried extremely negative, if not derogatory, meanings. The *Dictionare de l'Académie française* (1740) defined Baroque as something "irregular, bizarre, [and] uneven" which implied a lack of separation between real and imagined spheres.[32] The rationalised thought of the Enlightenment era, in contrast, "made it possible to separate what in the Baroque had been perceived as united: art, society, morality, mores, in brief, the Baroque assumption of the conjunction of reality and appearance. The enlightened mind penetrated appearances to reveal the fiction of Baroque society, and so drew distinctions between art and luxury, taste and fashion, morality and aesthetics, subject and object."[33] As the European society built on theatrical illusions and metaphysical allusions gave way to one constructed on natural science and public scrutiny, Sarmatian alchemical desires of transforming impoverished reality into rich phantasmagoria were devalued as frivolous and socially irresponsible cultural and political experimentations.

20. Roads to Vilnius. Detail from "Neueste Karte von Polen und Litauen," 1792.

CHAPTER THREE:

Enlightenment Shadows

Where barbarous hordes of Scythian mountain roam,
Truth, Mercy, Freedom, yet shall find a home…
Oh, bloodiest picture in the book of Time,
Sarmatia fell, unwept, without a crime.

"Poland," Thomas Campbell

When the renowned traveller and naturalist Johann Georg Adam Forster settled in the Lithuanian capital in 1784, he found the Baroque city in decline. "A hundred years ago," wrote Forster to his best friend in Germany, "Wilna had 80,000 inhabitants. Today, if one includes 12,000 Jews – it has only 20,000."[1] Forster's statistical observation was more than just the passing comment of a dispassionate scientist. It was a lament, a grieving evaluation of the human condition. Wilna, thought Forster, was an antithesis to human progress, a provincial backwater not worthy even of the title of a town, not to mention a capital city of a European country. At best Forster envisioned Wilna as a place of exile – a purgatory in the scientific age of the Enlightenment – where unlucky, ignorant souls of Europe are kept in the dark ages of superstitions and barbarism. The city no longer denoted the uncultivated peripheries of Europe; it was a wild frontier where urbane civilisation reverts back to its feral state.

Forster's antipathy towards the chief city of Lithuania (still a large if impoverished country) was formed through the prism of his cosmopolitan upbringing, a life-altering experience unusual even for his age of academic internationalism and extensive European travelling. Forster never went on a Grand Tour of Europe, a social affair which became extremely popular among the aristocratic and intellectual youth of the eighteenth century; instead he circumnavigated the Earth. A voyage around the world led Forster to Wilna. In 1772, at the age of seventeen, he had joined his father, also a scientist, on the *H.M. S. Resolution* during Captain Cook's second expedition to the South Pacific. At a time when Europe could barely imagine the far side of the world, young Forster surveyed, documented and fraternised with the inhabitants of Tahiti, New Zealand and the desolate islands of Tierra del Fuego. Afterwards,

Forster published a book, *A Voyage Round the World*, detailing scientific discoveries and personal impressions of the trip. The two-volume and 1,200-page manuscript, conceived, in the words of its young author, as "a philosophical history of the voyage," was published in English and German.[2]

Forster was a scientist with the soul of a revolutionary artist, who, according to his contemporaries, "demonstrated his universal receptivity and education by combining French elegance with popular forms of presentation, and English utility with German depth of feeling and spirit."[3] The expertly illustrated book – one of Forster's responsibilities during the expedition was to make drawings of various discoveries – became the talk of the enlightened salons of Europe. And while more vigorous academics objected to the author's subjectivity, the tone of the book perfectly fitted the emerging spirit of the Romantics in their quest for the unity of rationalism and imagination. Some decades later, Alexander von Humboldt, a leading geographer and aesthete of the modern age, thanked Forster for introducing into science the "descriptive powers of the observer, the enlivening of the descriptive element of nature, and the multiplication of views."[4]

The book launched Forster's professional career as a "natural-born" scientist, leading to his teaching appointment at the Carolineum College in the Hessian town of Kassel. The ambitious naturalist was deeply unsatisfied with this minor academic post and was hoping to reach the same scholarly status as his father, who had became a professor at the prestigious University of Halle under the patronage of the enlightened monarch, Frederick the Great of Prussia. In the fall of 1783, Forster received an offer from the University of Vilnius and, seeing no future prospects in Germany, decided to move to Lithuania.

Wilna is located roughly 1,100 kilometres northeast of Kassel. At the end of the eighteenth century, with good weather conditions, this distance could be leisurely covered in a matter of a few weeks. Forster's trip to Wilna lasted almost six months. He wanted to see more of the German lands in order to deepen his professional contacts and acquire some valuable academic knowledge. During the trip, Forster happily explored the social pleasures of his literary fame. In the Saxon mining town of Freiberg, the naturalist met Prince Stanislaw Poniatowski (junior), nephew to the king of Poland and treasurer of the Grand Duchy, who, in Forster's words, "portrayed Lithuanians in a most positive light."[5] While young Poniatowski acknowledged the social and economic problems of the country resulting from having "too many heads with too many opinions," he also made encouraging remarks about the expansion of "the Enlightenment [*Aufklärung*] in Poland." The prince cautioned Forster about the slow penetration of progressive ideas into Lithuania, but described

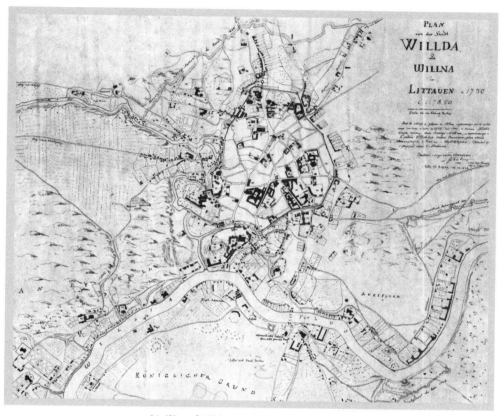

21. "Plan of Willda or Willna in Lithuania," 1737.

Wilna as "the most pleasant place in Poland and the university as having a much better reputation than the University of Kraków."[6]

After a brief detour to Saxony, Forster came to Vienna, where he lingered for a few months enjoying dinner parties, salon gatherings and aristocratic soirées. Viennese society relished Forster's piquant tales of the customs and habits (including sexual mores) of Pacific Island societies. Forster, in turn, thought Vienna was a paradise, and felt miserable at the thought of his inevitable departure. When the day came, wrote Forster, "all my friends and [Prince] Kaunitz have encouraged me to hope that I can come back here when I leave Poland. Even the Emperor said to me: 'I think we will see you soon in Vienna again, because you won't be able to stand it long among the Poles.' "[7] The emperor also showed some scepticism about the prospects of spreading the Enlightenment in Lithuania: he could not believe there was a university in Wilna, nor did the prospect of teaching natural sciences to locals make any sense to him. Before learning anything about science, the Poles, remarked the emperor, need to be taught an alphabet.

22. The great courtyard of the university in Wilna, 1786.

At the end of the eighteenth century, the University of Vilnius was in transition. The old Jesuit Academy, established in 1579 to advance the Catholic Counter-Reformation, was the material and, in many respects, the intellectual foundation of the university. After the papal closure of the Jesuit Order in 1773, the academy was taken under the direct patronage of the Lithuanian state. In 1781, the academy became the supreme school of the Grand Duchy of Lithuania, supervised by the newly created Education Commission, which attempted to build the first integrated pedagogical system in Europe. Despite this progressive thinking, financial resources and the political will to implement the project were limited. Most of the university faculty consisted of its former professors, secularised ex-Jesuit priests and monks, and the new curriculum differed little from the dogmatic program of the old college. The Educational Commission, headed by the bishop of Płock (the brother of the king of Poland) actively sought to lure various European academic celebrities to Wilna. The chair of natural sciences at the university was first offered to Forster's father, who had a much wider academic reputation. When Forster *père* declined the offer, he skilfully proposed his son. The Commission agreed to employ the younger Forster, with the stipulation that he would receive a doctoral degree within the first year of his arrival in Wilna. Besides strenuous teaching responsibilities, he was also expected to set up a botanical garden of Lithuanian flora, establish an agronomy program and proceed with research on the possible industrial and mining potential of local natural resources. Unfortunately, young Forster was poorly trained to meet those expectations. While he had received a doctoral degree from the University of Halle, he knew very little about the natural world of Lithuania, contemporary husbandry practices, or industrial methods of economic development.

Forster saw his position in Wilna as a professional move solving his personal problems. He was unsatisfied with his bachelor life in Kassel, where he had frivolously joined the Freemasons, partied a great deal, and acquired many debts. In order to make his life in distant Wilna more comfortable and productive, he searched for a wife. Just before leaving for Lithuania, Forster proposed to Therese Heyne, the daughter of his friend and colleague, Christian Gottlob Heyne, a professor of classical philology at the University of Göttingen. There is little evidence of love sparks between the betrothed. Forster was not a very good-looking man, and, for his age, was in poor health. During three years at sea he had lost most of his teeth due to scurvy and suffered from various digestive problems, recurring infections and rheumatism. Therese, who was ten years younger, beautiful and an exceptionally well-educated woman, responded to Forster's kindness, intellectual reputation and potential academic prospects. Once agreed, the marriage was postponed for a year, until Forster would be firmly settled in Wilna. In the interim, the two became intimate correspondents, showering each other with long detailed letters (alas, not love ones) on a weekly basis.

Forster's earliest impressions of the place are captured in his confidential correspondence with Therese and his closest friends and family. The Commonwealth was not a foreign land to Forster, who was born in 1754 in the village of Nassenhuben in the region of the Vistula Delta, where Polish and German languages intermixed freely. The scientist grew up in a German-speaking Protestant household, even though the Forster family had ancestors who had come to Poland in the 1640s from Scotland and England. But since the area around his birthplace remained in Polish possession until 1793, Forster, nominally, was a Polish subject. Yet his reaction to Poland-Lithuania was generally that of a complete stranger. In general, the German attitude towards Poland-Lithuania was condescending. The country was understood to be a political anachronism with no value to the culture of the Enlightenment. Goethe, who made a week-long trip from Weimar to Kraków in 1790, laconically recapped this German view of Poland: "In these eight days I have seen much that is remarkable, even if it has been for the most part only remarkably negative."[8]

Other Europeans had a more dramatic view of the country. Forster travelled to Wilna on a well-established road via Warsaw, Białystock and Grodno, in the middle of autumn. A month or two later, precisely the same route was taken by Count Louis-Phillipe de Segur, an envoy *extraordinaire* of Louis XVI to the Russian imperial court in Saint Petersburg. Segur described a disturbing feeling of displacement resulting from the passage over the border from Prussia into Poland:

> In traversing the eastern part of the estates of the king of Prussia, it seems that one leaves the theatre where there reigns a nature embellished by the efforts of art and a perfect civilization. The eye is already saddened by arid sands, by vast forest. But when one enters Poland, one believes one has left Europe entirely, and the gaze is struck by a new spectacle: an immense country almost totally covered with fir trees always green, but always sad, interrupted at long intervals by some cultivated plains, like islands scattered on the ocean; a poor population, enslaved, dirty villages; cottages little different from savage huts; everything makes one think one has moved back ten centuries, and that one finds oneself amid hordes of Huns, Scytians, Veneti, Slavs, and Sarmatians.[9]

Segur was the same age as Forster and, like him, was also a seasoned traveller (he had spent some time in North America). But the count was the offspring of some of the wealthiest families of France and, in contrast to the scientist, could enjoy all the comforts of travelling. He sleighed through the Commonwealth in winter, and, despite the gloomy opening, experienced the trip as a jovial ride through "an inconceivable mélange of ancient centuries and modern centuries, of monarchical spirit and republican spirit, of feudal pride and equality, of poverty and riches."[10] Nevertheless, misfortune caught up with him somewhere between Białystok and Riga where, because of a heavy snowstorm, he was forced to leave his luggage behind. The diplomat never recovered his belongings, and months later, in response to official inquiries, he received a strange report from local authorities stating that everything he owned was lost in a fire in the middle of frozen Lithuania.

William Coxe (1747-1828), a well-versed Englishman, traversed Lithuania en route to Russia in 1778 on a Grand Tour of Europe as the tutor-companion to a young English aristocrat. Coxe comments on the monotony and repetitiveness of the road, resembling an uneventful passage through the sea: "I never saw a road so barren of interesting scenes as that from Cracow to Warsaw. There is not a single object throughout the whole tract which can for a moment draw the attention of the most inquisitive traveller."[11] But if passing through Poland was a dull activity, then trekking through Lithuania was a protracted adventure with a picturesque ending. "The roads in this

23. Jewish merchants near Wilna.

country," remarks Coxe, "are quite neglected, being scarcely superior to by-paths winding through the thick forest without the least degree of artificial direction: they are frequently so narrow as to scarcely to admit a carriage; and are continually so obstructed by stumps and roots of trees, and in many parts so exceedingly sandy, that eight small horses could scarcely drag us along."[12] As the fatigued traveller pushed deeper into the woods, the scenery around became even bizarre: "the towns and villages were long and straggling; all the houses and even the churches are of wood; crowds of beggars surrounded our carriage whenever we stopped; Jews made their appearance without end."[13]

In Lithuania, in contrast to most of Europe and Russia, the traveller's day-to-day communication with the passing local world was brokered through Jews, who managed most of the mercantile and travel necessities of the country. "If you ask for an interpreter, they bring you a Jew; if you come to an inn, the landlord is a Jew, if you want post-horses, a Jew procures them and a Jew drives them; if you wish to purchase, a Jew is your agent: and this is the only country in Europe where Jews cultivate the ground: in passing through Lithuania, we frequently saw them engaged in sowing, reaping, mowing, and other works of husbandry."[14] The Jews were not only essential in making the trip more comfortable, but their "unfamiliar appearance" enlivened the jaded mind of the traveller:

> We found ourselves in the middle of a large barn or shed, at the further end of which we descried two large pines, branches and all, in full blaze upon an hearth without a chimney: round it several figures, in full black robes and with long beards, were employed in stirring a large cauldron suspended over the flame. A belief in witchcraft, or a little superstition, might easily have represented this party as a group of magicians engaged in celebrating some mystic rites; but upon nearer inspection, we recognized in them our old friends the Jews preparing their and our evening repast.[15]

Incidentally, Coxe was one of the few foreigners who tried to identify the pathogenesis of *plica Polonica*, naming three main causes of the disease, such as the erratic and unhealthy "nature of the Polish air, the unwholesome local water and the gross inattention of the natives to cleanliness."[16]

This depressing or phantasmagorical portrayal of Lithuania was disputed by other travellers, who found it a fanciful exaggeration of reality. In a direct response to Coxe's account, Friedrich Schulz, a minor German writer, made a corrective report. "Those travelling to Russia, who recall or find out how boringly monotonous the roads to and from Berlin are ... will thank me for it. The road [through Lithuania] is not much longer than the road to Berlin, but travelling here is much cheaper and faster, through countryside that is more pleasant, bountiful and inhabited by polite people. Do not believe the rumours about the dangers. I crossed this road three times and many of my acquaintances have done the same, and none of us saw anything suspicious either during the day or the night."[17] Schulz's report was not all dry facts; he, too, relied on his artistic knowledge in order to capture the feeling and colour of an everyday scene. Once, he stayed in a Jewish inn until the early morning hours in the "unlikely company of Russian soldiers, half-naked Lithuanians, inebriated Poles and a large family of Israelites. Many patrons of this inn could be in the paintings of Fielding or Hogarth. But I was so overwhelmed by them, that I will never seek for a similar camaraderie."[18]

Forster was a more morose traveller. Initially, he was deeply offended by the poverty and oppression of the local people and responded to their misery with humility. "It was the dilapidation, the filthiness in the moral and physical sense, the half-wildness [*Halbwildheit*] and half-civilisation [*Halbkultur*] of the people, the sight of the sandy land everywhere covered with black woods, which went beyond any conception I could have formed. I wept in a lonely hour for myself – and then, as I gradually came to myself, for the so deeply sunken people."[19] Later, his emotions changed. "This was another moment of foolishness on my side," remarked Forster to his friend Friedrich Heinrich Jacobi, a German sensualist philosopher, "but now I am fully recovered to recognize the ridiculousness of my behaviour."[20]

With every day of his journey, Forster becomes more and more accustomed to Lithuania. He sends a sociological report to Therese from Grodno, where, during the Sejm (Parliament) meeting, "the entire Polish and Lithuanian nobility" is assembled. "I am slowly beginning to acquaint myself with the customs of this original nation... the initial shock is gone and I can observe things without any bitterness...[and] despite some deficiencies in the liberal Constitution of this kingdom, I am extremely delighted to see that freedom is enjoyed here by every noble Pole."[21] Locals, reports Forster to his other correspondents, adore everything French and hate everything German. This has, in Forster's opinion, a negative cultural effect: "In Poland to call somebody a German – is the worst insult; as a result, the education of the upper nobility is entirely in the hands of degenerate French barbers and *modistes*."[22] And since "the Polish aristocracy follows the French spirit, they still look at everything in the superficial and encyclopaedic fashion."[23]

A few days later, on the road to Wilna, Forster participated in a forum of a different kind. In one of the humble inns, he joined the party of a jolly Catholic priest drinking vodka with an ancient Jewish postmaster. The cronies amused the scientist with their raucous conversation, during which every form of authority was dethroned. The two cursed everyone: from the Holy Roman Emperor and the Polish king to the bishop of Wilna and the local abbot. A day or two later, a barely sobered Forster reached his final destination, ending his travelogue of Lithuania at the gates of Wilna:

> Thursday, November 18 [1784] At 5 a.m. I leave from a very poor Jewish inn and arrive at 9 a.m. (4 miles) to Gostki or Swetnik, at another Jewish-run post station, where I change my clothes and continue the trip to Wilna (3 miles), which I reach at one o'clock. One mile before Wilna, the environment near the Wilia River becomes very beautiful: steep sandy hills and chalk cliffs crowned with splendid forest greenery. The location of Wilna is unexpectedly wondrous; once you come closer to the city, the view from surrounding hills into the valley, where this entire great city, graced with so many towers, is located, is truly impeccable and magnificent. Inside the city – narrow dirty streets and numerous ruins – still, among them, one can encounter one or two impressive buildings. *Finis viaeque chartaeque.*[24]

The naturalist turned his concluding remark – the end of the road and this story (a satirical phrase from Horace implying a lack of narrative interest) – into a premonition. He immediately sent a warning to his fiancé concerning their future prospects in the city. He had little encouragement to share:

24. Wilna: the city wall, 1785.

"In Wilna, you will find the once populous city in rapid decline: abandoned buildings and heaps of refuse are everywhere. Here you will meet weakened people who are simply oblivious to their tragic condition; and finally, you will witness the nightmarish results of the coupling of a half-cultured nation with half-feral vices."[25] He fell short on details, remarking that "it would take an entire volume to describe what in the German borderlands is so ingeniously referred to as the *polnische Wirtschaft* [*Polish economy*]."[26]

Despite his German origins, the young professor was welcomed by the city's social elite. He enjoyed local hospitality, but saw in it signs of cultural regression. "People's generosity here, like in all uncultured countries of the world, is overwhelming; people socialise without any *gene* [modesty] and even their appearance is less restrained than in other places. Tolerance rules absolute!"[27] Soon the prudish scholar became alarmed. "The Poles behave in such a way that it leaves me with no doubt about my sensual presence among them; oh yes, I do sense my physical being in this pitiful world, surrounded by cruel, half-civilized and half-wild people of this land with dishevelled, sad forests....

In such a country I must say goodbye to my illusions..."[28] More than anything else, he was irritated by the social (and sexual) intimacy of Vilnius's elite. Flirtatious sensuality drove Foster insane, because he felt powerless and speechless in the face of local mores. "Nowhere are people more sensual than here. Nobody is interested in anything else except in the discovery of physical pleasures. The only pleasure I can have here is corporeal: if I want to socialise with women, I have to flirt endlessly; sometimes I even have to fondle them because they all want to be stimulated only in a carnal way. The society fully sanctions this sort of behaviour. Here, you can kiss a maiden's bosom in public without causing a scandal!"[29] Forster refused to acclimatise to local mores and soon after his arrival became infatuated with the idea of an escape. "Wilna," declared the desperate naturalist to his best friend in Germany, "is certainly not a place where I can stay forever!"[30] Impulsively, he decided to leave his position at the university and, in disguise, run away to the more exotic and warmer Constantinople. Poor health and lack of funds, rather than teaching commitments and professional rationale, cured Forster's nomadic impulses.

Admittedly, Wilna was not such a dreadful place, especially after the arrival of Therese. While "the city is in a terribly deplorable state," remarked Forster, "*meo judicio*, it still looks much better than Kraków and overwhelmingly surpasses Grodno."[31] And after a summer vacation in Germany, the professor confessed that Wilna was a far greater city than most provincial German towns. He took the city's intellectual isolation as a professional challenge. "After all," Forster wrote to his father-in-law in Göttingen, "Wilna is probably the best place in the world to be left in peace, where I can patiently, thoroughly study a number of interesting subjects; this fact eases my otherwise terrible condition."[32] And in a letter sent to Johann Gottfried Herder in Weimar, he summarised his role in Wilna as that of a lonely missionary of the Enlightenment: "Nonetheless, I have achieved more here than I could have achieved anywhere else in the world; I see myself as planting a seed of hope."[33]

Yet there was no harvest from Forster's seeds of hope. This was, in part, because Forster concluded that Wilna, in spite of his best intentions, was unworthy of his talent:

Here, where science is covered by the silence of the night, where scientific achievements are not rewarded, even by a simple honorary prize, where the most renowned and celebrated people are only those who own the most serfs or gamble the most money – here, a foreigner, because of the apathy of his compatriots, gradually starts to feel abandoned by the better part of civilised society. ... Local society is marked by sluggishness, constant postponements and indifference to anything virtuous; here, a traveller will encounter the tolerance and masking of elementary wrongdoings, the persistence of habitual moralising nonsense, lack of modern forms of education, and, at times, a remorseless contempt for learning; in addition, the country is gripped by a senseless patriotism, an irrational governing structure and a sickly state constitution. Here, French opulence conjugates with Sarmatian bestiality, and in order to survive and stay vigorous and mentally alert, one has to become static, remorseless and turn his eyes away from all this non-sense. ... In Wilna, there is not a single bookstore, and in Warsaw – there are one or two bankrupt book dealers, who trade only in indecent novels.[34]

After Forster's death, Therese expressed a more balanced view of the situation:

They didn't keep their word [in Wilna] but now, after more than forty years have gone by, I believe that, in a certain sense, Forster, too, didn't keep his word, and I am surprised that Heyne [her father], at the time, did not give him a piece of advice for which I had neither the experience nor the insight. Forster waited for the fulfil-ment of the promises made to him, so that he could accomplish something great, whereas he would have improved his position substantially if he had accomplished the little that was possible with the small means available to him, and had kept insisting, at the same time, on the fulfilment of their promises to him.[35]

Forster's inability to learn the Polish language (the local vernacular) made his life in Wilna less communicative. Although he was supposed to teach in Polish, he continued his instructions at the university in Latin, which nei-ther he nor his students knew well. Soon the naturalist turned his linguistic frustrations into a hatred of everything Polish. He decided to prevent his daughter, who was born soon after Therese arrived in Wilna, from even hear-ing the language. "I hope that my daughter will not need knowledge of the Polish language, though we shall stay here for seven years. But even if her tongue becomes more flexible, it would not outweigh the potential harm that extensive Polish conversations with various ignorant natives, local priests and other fools will inflict on her mind."[36]

Forster showed even less interest in the (larger) Jewish side of the city. He often negatively fused the two worlds together, especially in matters of local trade, which he described as "completely dominated by Christians with Jew-ish virtues"[37] who charge "*unchristlich* [unchristian] rates"[38] because they are "more greedy than the Hebrews."[39] Still, one of the few people Forster came to respect in Wilna was a Jewish doctor with whom he shared the discovery of the German-Jewish philosopher Moses Mendelssohn.[40] The German pro-fessor joined a small philosophical salon held regularly at the doctor's house.

He credited the hostess of the salon – the doctor's wife – for its enlightened ambiance. But despite warm feelings, the Forsters never became good friends with this Jewish couple.

Lithuania, in general, posed an awkward representational challenge to Forster, not because it was "an unfortunate country ruled by fierce anarchy," but because, in his own words, he needed to use "entirely different colours and metaphors" in order to capture it.[41] Consequently, Forster was constantly searching for that perfect descriptive stroke that could magically transform the chaotic scene of Lithuania into an orderly picture. In the end, he found Lithuania to be trapped by the two contrasting poles of cultural development:

> You would find ample material to laugh at in this mishmash of Sarmatian or almost New Zealander crudeness and French super-refinement … or perhaps not; for one only laughs about people whose fault it is that they are laughable; not over those who, through forms of government, rearing (such should education be called here), example, priests, despotism of mighty neighbours, and an army of French vagabonds and Italian good-for-nothings, become spoiled already from youth, and have no prospect for future betterment before them. The actual people, I mean those millions of cattle in human form, who are here utterly excluded from all privileges of mankind … the people are at present through long-habitual slavery truly sunken to a degree of bestiality and insensibility, of indescribable laziness and totally stupid ignorance, from which perhaps even in a century it could not climb to the same level as other European rabbles.[42]

Forster, a self-appointed expert on human races, showed no interest in the intermediary cultural location of Lithuania as a place between civilisation and savagery. Instead of looking around and finding something new or interesting in Lithuanian nature (as he was expected to do by his colleagues), he turned inwards, concentrating on his own development. In the naturalist jargon, he described his life in Wilna as that of the maggot ready to emerge from its cocoon and spread its wings.[43] In more a classical term, he called it *Ulubris Sarmaticis*.[44] In ancient times, Ulubris was a far-off town where, reportedly, the first Roman emperor Augustus (Octavius Caesar) spent his adolescence before he was adopted by his great uncle Julius Caesar. It was a place of exile, but also anticipation, and Forster was hoping for a royal commission to rescue him. As always, his wife was more pragmatic. "Our climate is severe," wrote Therese, "the environment is harsh and infertile; food, in general, is cheap, but nobody keeps a fixed price. The nation is feral and local people do not belong to humanity. But enough about them; I pity them, but can not wait to become a loyal subject of Russia, Austria or Prussia, when the next partition of this country will start again."[45] Both of their wishes came true.

In the summer of 1787, Forster was approached by the Russian ambassador with an offer. The Russian Admiralty was planning a journey around the globe, including an extensive scientific investigation of the Pacific Ocean coastline in Asia and North America. Forster was recommended to the post of chief scientist of the voyage, with a promise of unconstrained research freedom and substantial financial reward. He was thrilled by the opportunity to go "beyond Japan and Kamchatka," and immediately notified Herder about his prospective rescue from Sarmatia: "My dearest and beloved friend! ... You are probably aware, that thanks to the *Deus ex machina*, I am released from my Wilna Pontus [*Wilnaschen Pontus*] and as a Russian subject, I am going on the South Sea expedition again."[46] There was, however, a major obstacle in Forster's plan – the University's Senate was unwilling to release him from his seven-year contract. Russian Empress Catherine II interfered and through her ex-lover, the Polish King Stanislaw Poniatowski, she bought out Forster's contract with the university.

The Forsters left Wilna at the end of the summer of 1787. The naturalist went to London, his wife to her parent's home in Germany. Meanwhile, war broke out between Turkey and Russia, and the expedition was indefinitely postponed. In London, Forster was asked to reassume his teaching position at the university in Wilna, but, unburdened from his financial obligations, he refused to go back to "exile." Notwithstanding, he was enchanted that he was still needed in the backwoods of Sarmatia:

> My happiness increases every day, because I get so many letters from Poland. Since the expedition around the world has been cancelled, I am requested to return to Wilna. I am wanted at the local university, and I am asked to submit my conditions of employment. I must admit, this is not just pleasing – it is the hour of my triumph – the only one victory that should make any honest and determined individual satisfied. Before, I was scorned, because I was leaving; now, they are eager to reward my diligence by inviting me back in the most honourable manner. This request doubles my satisfaction, since there is no need for me to go back. Once in a lifetime, there could be Wilna, but never twice. I believed I followed responsibly in my duties, and everyone was content with me; but I was not gratified with the situation. I should have been content with my time spent there ... a bachelor might have been satisfied with it, but the married man has to worry about the happiness of his wife and the education of his child. Still, it makes me joyous to know that my chair is still empty and the University cannot find anyone more suitable than me.[47]

25. A view of the university's botanical garden. The garden was set up by Forster's successor, professor S. B. Jundzila, only a few years after the German naturalist left Lithuania.

As the next years passed, his hopes for the resurrection of the Pacific voyage dimmed, and Forster shifted his aspirations to the promises of universal human emancipation offered by the French Revolution. He arrived in Paris at the height of the revolutionary euphoria as a delegate to the National Assembly, representing the German territories captured by the French. But in a movement where even revolutionaries of French blood came easily under suspicion, Forster's mixed Germanic background pushed him perilously to the margins of the revolution. At age thirty-nine, on January 10, 1794, Forster died of pneumonia in Paris, during the worst months of the Terror. His sickness and early death almost certainly saved him from the guillotine. But he died an isolated man. Forsaken by his estranged wife and his own father, ostracised by most of his German compatriots and largely forgotten by his French revolutionary comrades, Forster expired in despair, in his "safe harbour of resignation."[48] Even humanist Goethe, who had befriended Forster some years earlier and greatly valued his inquisitive mind, expressed only a reserved sympathy about his death in Paris. "Then poor Forster," lamented the famous writer, "had to pay for his mistakes with his life after all, even if he did escape a violent death! I pitied him sincerely."[49]

Forster's death in Paris coincided with the political dismemberment of Sarmatia. In 1793, Russia and Prussia proceeded with the second partition of Poland-Lithuania, provoked by the adoption of the liberal constitution of the Commonwealth in 1791. During the 1792 Russian invasion of Poland-Lithuania, the tsarist army occupied the Lithuanian capital. On April 24, 1794, local rebels liberated Vilnius and established a Lithuanian revolutionary committee. The Russian army besieged the city until the rebels capitulated some four months later. The defeat of the rebellion led to the final partition of the Commonwealth in 1795, making Vilnius a Russian provincial town.

26. Erasing Sarmatia from the map of Europe. This allegory represents three enlightened rulers – Catherine II of Russia (with her foreign minister Nikita Panin), Joseph II of Austria and Friedrich II of Prussia – initiating the first partition of Poland-Lithuania in 1772.

CHAPTER FOUR:

Napoleon's Curse

> In 1789 there was a ferment in Paris: it grew and spread, and found ex-
> pression in the movement of peoples from west to east. Several times that
> movement is made to the east, and comes into collision with a counter-
> movement from east westwards. In the year of 1812 it reaches its furthest
> limit, Moscow, and then, with a remarkable symmetry, the counter-move-
> ment follows from east to west; drawing with it, like the first movement,
> the peoples of Central Europe. The counter-movement reaches the start-
> ing-point of the first movement – Paris – and subsides.
>
> *War and Peace*, Leo Tolstoy

On September 11, 1804, on the eve of the day of the Most Holy Name of Mary,
one of the best doctors in Vienna, Johann Peter Frank, left his hometown for
the Russian city of Vilna. Doctor Frank was joined by his son, Josef Frank
(also a medical doctor), his daughter-in-law – the elegant and talented Italian
opera singer Christine Frank née Gerhardi, his two unmarried daughters,
Carolina and Lizete, and the housekeeper Frau Janisch. In addition, three
male servants, a chambermaid and a cook accompanied the extended family.
The elder Frank handed the responsibilities of navigation over the dangerous
pathways of wartime Europe to his son and became the first casualty of the
road: after a cold night in the open, he caught a chill and had to stay in bed for
a week. At the end of September, the caravan finally reached Lithuania at the
border post on the Bug River, where the three great powers of Europe – Russia, Austria and Prussia – had established their new frontier after dividing
Poland-Lithuania.

"In Tiraspol," recalled Josef Frank, "we said goodbye to the Austrian Kingdom. After crossing the Bug River, we came to Brest-Litovsk; the Cossacks
very politely opened the gates of the Russian empire for us. I had seen these
bearded Cossacks some years ago, when the Russian army led by Suvorov was
stationed near Vienna [in 1799], and their strange appearance did not surprise
me a bit. I also realised very quickly that these Cossacks were not as fierce as
one might expect them to be. In truth, they were more reasonable than most of
the Russian customs officials."[1] The Russian empire also pleased the travellers

with its effective road demarcation. "As soon as we entered Russia, we were very surprised by the neatly painted green poles that marked every passing *verst* and accurately noted the distances between the border and the two Russian capitals, [Saint Petersburg and Moscow]. Since seven *versts* roughly equals one German mile, we found it strange that the biggest empire in the world uses the smallest units of geographical measurement."[2]

The freshly painted border and road postings were signs of a new era. When the Russian, Austrian and Prussian monarchs three times (1772, 1793 and 1795) divided the Polish-Lithuanian Commonwealth into three portions, they initiated a period of unprecedented territorial rearrangement. The dismembering of the Commonwealth was presented by the absolutist regimes as a necessary and beneficial act of the Enlightenment spirit: the anarchy of Sarmatia replaced by imperial order. The spirit of youth took over the age of traditions. As Frank noted, in Russia under young Tsar Alexander I, who came to the throne in 1801, "changes occurred all the time. Young empires, like Russia, essentially differ from old monarchies. New administrative methods are tested continuously making every year unlike the previous one. A new order replaces the old one, moving local society from one system to another. In the Russian empire, where everything changes all the time, the only sure thing is instability itself."[3] Yet even the tsarist form of political originality, cultural change and social flexibility could not compete with the continental ambitions of Napoleon, who garnered the uncontrollable energies of the Parisian streets and turned them into an efficient state-making apparatus driven by revolutionary ideals and war profit. Napoleon's spectacular rise to imperial heights made every map of Europe obsolete. Under the pressure of the French army and local revolutionaries, old states crumbled as never before, while new ones, adorned with ancient names or novel labels (such as Etruria, Helvetia, Illyria and Batavia, or the Cisalpine Republic and Confederation of the Rhine), were created overnight with a swift stroke of the conqueror's pen. Europe, along with the Franks, was on the move, shedding its old way of life for new beginnings.

However, the Franks soon discovered that travelling through the changing imperial realm was no less challenging than rambling around chaotic Sarmatia. The newly charted road was depopulated and lacked most elementary conveniences. "We moved as fast as we could through these sandy Lithuanian roads. The endless forest we passed through had some sense of majesty. But the frosty fields that opened up between these woods looked as if winter had already arrived. The northerly wind, too, came as an early reminder. We drove day and night without finding any shelter or food. ... The hunger soured our

27. Vilna: the city cordon.

glorious arrival in Vilna, which we entered on October 4, 1804, at ten thirty in the morning."[4] Two months later to the date, in Paris, Napoleon crowned himself an emperor.

Vilnius, or as Russians and French called it, Vilna, had become the third largest city in the Russian empire after Saint Petersburg and Moscow. The total population of the (former) Grand Duchy of Lithuania was about four and half million people, and the census held in 1795 found 17,690 inhabitants of the Christian faith living in the city. Among its residents, there were 2,471 noblemen, 568 Catholic priests and 107 priests of other confessions, 238 teachers and professors and 860 craftsmen organised into 38 guilds. The Russian authorities also counted 32 Catholic churches, 15 monasteries, 5 Uniate churches with 3 monasteries, one each of Russian Orthodox, Lutheran and Reformist (Calvinist) churches, along with 10 large palaces.[5] The local Jewish population – perhaps a majority of its inhabitants – was simply left uncounted by the tsarist bureaucrats. Frank, in his memoirs of Vilna, imbued this statistical picture of the city with more lively details:

> Vilna looked chaotic – many palaces were surrounded by hovels. Although there were plenty of brick buildings, most houses were built of wood. Beneath Castle Hill, the city that stretched along the confluence of the two rivers was extremely dirty. The excellent Italian-style Town Hall building stood on a vast pleasant square completely filled with unsightly huts of various tradesmen. The streets leading to the majestic Cathedral were unpaved and full of garbage, and during rain they rapidly turned into swamp. Pigs were running everywhere, and outside the town all one could see and smell were enormous piles of dung. The suburbs were literally sinking in sand and dirt, and the natural beauty of the surrounding landscape could not hide it.[6]

Despite its deplorable appearance, the town possessed the aura of a ancient cosmopolis. "The Lithuanian capital," recounted Frank, "had more than 35,000 residents: among them there were about 22,000 Catholics, 600 Greek Orthodox, 500 Lutherans, 100 Reformats, 11,000 Jews and 60 Mohammedans. The local aristocracy, university professors and burghers were mostly Catholics. Among the Greek Orthodox, one could find government officials, merchants and Russian peasants. The Lutherans and Calvinists (mostly Germans) were involved in arts, crafts and trade." The Jews "comprised a separate community" whose local history was "lost in time." The Jewish people came to western Poland from Germany, but, noticed the doctor, "to the eastern part of the country [Lithuania], they came from the region of the Caspian Sea. Other experts also count the Karaites as Jews, even if they do not speak a German-influenced language. In Lithuania, though, the German-origin [Ashkenazi] Jews greatly differed from their compatriots in Germany: in Vilna, they dressed like Don Basilio from the 'Barber of Seville.' Jewish women wear exclusively Oriental fashions, but their garments – expensive or cheap – are almost always very dirty."[7]

The Franks fit well into the imperial world of this provincial metropolis. The father-son team moved to Vilna at the invitation of Alexander I to head the Faculty of Medicine at the local university. Soon, the older Frank was called to Saint Petersburg to become a personal doctor to the tsar's family, but his son stayed in Vilna for almost two decades. (During his long and eventful life, the elder Frank had the privilege and challenge of serving as a medical advisor to three imperial families of Europe: the Habsburgs, the Romanovs and the Bonapartes). In 1803, the University of Vilnius was reorganised and modernised once again. Under the auspices of the Polish-Lithuanian aristo-

28. The Imperial University of Vilna in the first part of the nineteenth century.

crat Adam Jerzy Czartoryski (1770-1861), Curator of the Lithuanian School District and a close friend and chief adviser to the tsar, the university was transformed into a progressive European academy. During the two decades of Czartoryski's supervision, "which spanned the turmoil of Napoleon's collapse and the post-Napoleonic settlement, *Wilno* carried the torch of Polish culture, salvaging many of the ideals of the old Educational Commission and sowing the seed for the most brilliant intellectual harvest of the century."[8] Despite its Polish national character, the university received the title of the Imperial University and became a leading academy of Russia. The Franks were its shining scientific stars.

The younger Frank was born in 1771 and studied at the university in Göttingen, but spent most of his youth in Italy, where he met his wife. In the small world of the European academic elite, the professional pathways of

29. Street scene in Vilna.

the Frank and Forster families intersected on several occasions. The Franks were fully aware of Forster's luckless life in Wilna two decades earlier and of his tragic death in Paris, but they shared neither his gloomy attitude towards Lithuania nor his revolutionary zeal. The Franks were true members of the Viennese bourgeoisie: they took life's pleasures with gusto. Through his wife, the younger Frank became attached to the European musical and theatrical milieu and his homes, both in Vienna and Vilna, were always open to people from the academic and artistic worlds.

Most local residents of Vilna opposed tsarist rule, if not directly then at least in private, and Frank's loyalty to the Russian and Austrian imperial regimes should have made him an unwelcome foreigner. Yet the Frank family, housed at their comfortable home on Great Street, led the salon life of the city.[9] This was, no doubt, achieved with help of the social grace, professional etiquette and cultural sensibilities of the hosting couple. Frank was a good, non-discriminatory doctor with a reputation of being a zealous practitioner of modern medicine. His diagnostic principles and therapeutic methods might have angered some of his colleagues and local herbalists, but they gained him enormous popularity among the novelty-obsessed patients of the Vilna elite. The doctor also made stylish, benevolently arrogant and flirtatious advances towards local society, which made him the object of all kinds of gossip, amorous obsessions and social requests. His wife, Christine, was a charming diva, too: a prima donna with a heart of gold, who not only tolerated her husband's indiscretions, but also had a brilliant career of her own. In provincial Vilna she was a musical Italian-Viennese treasure of European magnitude. A few years before the family's arrival in Lithuania, Franz Josef Haydn composed his masterpiece oratorio, *The Creation,* specifically for Christine's voice. After the first public performance of the composition in Vienna in 1799, the critics described her as a graceful beauty with the most sumptuous of all soprano voices. In spite of her operatic success in the Habsburgian capital, she followed her husband to Vilna, where the two tried to benefit the local world with shared responsibilities: Christine organised and performed recitals for the doctor's charitable works. This generous arrangement defeated all local resentment – the Franks became the darlings of society, with their salon becoming the unifying heart of the culturally and politically divided city.

For the Franks, life in Vilna offered a certain degree of comfort. "There was no lack of food in the city," remembers the doctor, "especially in winter when the frozen roads made the transportation of goods reliable. Beef, veal and pork were of the highest quality and twice cheaper than in Vienna. There was enough excellent poultry, in particular, succulent chicken. The local market was usually full of game and fish. Common people eat mostly potatoes, cabbage and beets, but rich homes served asparagus, Brussels sprouts and artichokes. Bread and beer were superb; however, wine was very expensive and had to be brought from Riga."[10] In volatile, wartime Europe, the availability of inexpensive food supplies was no small matter, especially during the years of the Napoleonic continental blockade.

In Vilna, a predominantly Catholic and Baroque city, the Franks felt at home. Frank, in contrast to Forster, was eager to integrate into the local world. He first learned Polish and then Russian. The family adopted an abandoned baby (rumoured to be an illegitimate son of the doctor). Subsequently, while visiting the elder Frank in Vienna, the child became a playmate to Napoleon II, the son of the deposed Napoleon and the grandson of Franz I, the emperor of Austria. Even after this acquaintance with the imperial offspring, Frank insisted that his only son should receive a local – Catholic and Polish – education. Still, the liberal doctor was mildly shocked by the informality of local religious customs:

> In Vilna, we found more monks and nuns than in Vienna. Apart from the Cathedral, Saint Casimir and Saint John (which belonged to the University), all other churches were owned by various monasteries. It was impossible to attend the popular masses at the Dominican Church, especially on Sunday, when people were constantly coming in and out, endlessly wandering around the aisles,

greeting, kissing and loudly gossiping with friends and acquaintances. There were also Greek, Lutheran, Reformist [Calvinist] churches, a Jewish synagogue and a mosque. In general, the Catholics did not celebrate the Sabbath, because it was a market day when peasants sold their produce. In contrast, the Jews strictly observed their Sabbath and other religious holidays. On those days, they would never engage in any trade, even if you offered them all the treasures in the world. The Muslim Tatars scrupulously observed Friday, their holy day. I was very much impressed by the concord, and even brotherhood, found among the members of various confessions. During the official dinner in honour of the emperor's [Alexander I] birthday, given by the Russian governor-general in his palace, I found the Catholic bishop, Greek archimandrite, Lutheran pastor and Calvinist minister sitting at the same table. All pleasantly engaging in friendly conversation.[11]

Frank, however, was not oblivious to the changing social and ethnic stratification of the city's population. When the family settled in Lithuania, Vilna "had plenty of fancy shops, mostly owned by Germans, who led opulent lifestyles and soon all went bankrupt. With time, the German owners could not compete with the Jewish merchants, who live frugally and were satisfied with small profits, and could charge much lower prices for the same goods."[12] During the years of the Napoleonic wars, when smuggling and illegal trade became rampant, the most challenging competition for the Jewish trade arose from the protectionist policies of the Russian state and its corrupt local representatives. "We should not forget," remembers Frank, "that the wives of the high-ranking Russian officials took anything they wanted from the Jewish stores without even thinking of paying for the requisitioned items. The merchants could not complain to the authorities, because if they were caught with contraband goods, they needed protection from the officials."[13]

Frank was one of the first non-Jewish visitors or locals of the city to enter the Jewish part of it with a sense of professional duty. For the doctor, the Jews of Vilna offered a unique opportunity to test some of the earliest theories of medical ethnography. At the entrance of the Jewish Quarter, he imagined himself travelling into exotic – Oriental – parts of the world:

As soon as I arrived in Vilna, Jews started coming to me, because they always pay a visit to a newly arrived foreign doctor. The medical practice among the Jews was very profitable, but the financial rewards could not outweigh the unpleasantness of the practice. However, I had a much higher goal. I wanted to study the habits and lifestyle of this mysterious nation. Local Jews should not be mistaken for the Jews from other parts of Europe, where they look more or less like the Christian population. The Polish Jews have nothing to do with them. So I told myself: if so many doctors have to brave long sea journeys in order to study various diseases in distant and exotic lands, then I must not be afraid of lesser dangers posed by treating Vilna Jews. After this professional resolution, I was ready to enter the dilapidated courtyards full of garbage, climb the hazardous stairways leading to shabby, dirty apartments, and be exposed to unhealthy air and lice.

At first I could barely understand their language, since they spice up the German language with many Polish and Hebrew words. In contrast, the Polish Jews understood me perfectly, but kept me asking questions. I quickly got irritated by having to repeat the same things all the time. After a while, I realised that I needed to tell them everything in detail: how to drink medicine and how to follow a special diet. It worked! And I started to use this method of explanation for all my [Jewish and non-Jewish] patients.

I have to admit that the Polish Jews take very good care of their patients – everything is provided for them. Undoubtedly, the Jews have to take care of themselves because they live their lives constantly battling various diseases. According to doctors Friedlander and Tainer, who wrote medical monographs about the diseases of the Polish Jews, the feeble constitution of the Jews is a result of their lifestyle. From the earliest childhood, the Jews are forced to study intensely the so-called religious scriptures, which essentially is some sort of rabbinical gibberish. They marry very young, at the age when the northern [European] children are still in puberty. And we should also remember their inadequate diet, which consists mostly of herring and onions; their screeching religious ceremonies in stuffy badly ventilated synagogues; and the practice among their women to wash themselves with cold water after menstruation and intercourse. On top of it, there is zealous fasting, rigidly observed by almost all Jews, and unsanitary home conditions. We cannot forget the illegal trafficking of goods, which makes the Jewish life so stressful and results in so much heart disease; in addition, there is the cruel attitude of other local inhabitants, police and army towards them. I won't annoy the reader with an additional long list detailing their unhealthy lifestyle. Nonetheless, I should say that the people of this nation have preserved a peculiar, almost Oriental, complexion, which makes them more resistant to certain medical pathologies. The course of chronic diseases, for instance, is much less variable among the Jews than people of other nations, who, in general, need more medical attention and care. In general, the Polish Jews exemplify many medical hypotheses of Hypocrite, especially his observations about the course of the crisis. The medical treatment of the Jews would have been more scientifically interesting and professionally beneficial had they allowed post-mortem autopsy. Yet the ancient Jews happily accepted the embalmment of their dead.[14]

The professor failed to produce any substantial work on Jewish "clinical conditions," but his attempt to record and systematise "Jewish diseases" was one of the first attempts to racialise medical knowledge. At least on one occasion, Frank's interests in Jewish bodies were driven by more tantalising objectives:

One of my patients, merchant Simpson, was ill with rheumatism and showed some epileptic symptoms. He did not care about Jewish superstitions and allowed his pretty wife to dress in the French fashion, but he told her to cover her hair in the

Jewish tradition. She kept a carriage and was free to make social visits; she could even flirt a bit with other men. This kind of liberty made the merchant a pariah within the Jewish community, and when he died, the Kahal (the Jewish communal authority) advised against his corpse being buried in the Jewish cemetery. The Jewish poor were ready to desecrate his body and Madame Simpson panicked; fortunately, everything ended only in tears. She respected me unquestionably, and one time, she uncovered her head in front of me. This was a gesture of extreme intimacy and I admired it more than any other act of gratitude. How smart are the Oriental women, I told to myself, that they only appear in public wrapped from head to toe in shawls![15]

By the time of Frank's arrival in Vilna, European ideas about the Orient had acquired new connotations. The Orient became Europe's martial, mercantile and aesthetic playground: it was not just to be conquered, but unveiled, seduced and exposed. European empires were made in the Orient, and Napoleon was eager to take its most prized trophy, India. He saw two obstacles on his way to India – the British navy and the Russian expanses. Unable to overpower the former, he concentrated on the latter.

In 1807, at the height of his military triumph, Napoleon signed the Tilsit peace treaty with Alexander on the Niemen River. The peace treaty strengthened the Continental System and established the Grand Duchy of Warsaw from the remains of the greatly reduced Prussian kingdom. Although peace between France and Russia prevailed for some time, both sides were preparing for a new war. While Vilna was outside the Grand Duchy, the resurrection of the Polish-Lithuanian state was on everyone's mind. In the spring of 1812, Napoleon started to assemble a massive army for the invasion of Russia. He envisioned the impending war as "his 'Polish war', and in crossing the frontier of the Russian Empire, the Grande Armée was in fact restoring the historic border of Poland and Lithuania, annulled in 1795."[16]

For the Franks, the year 1812 also brought significant changes. Sensing mistrust and hostility – after all, Austria was on the side of Napoleon – the family left Vilna in May of 1812, just before the start of the military campaign. Throughout the war, the Franks safely stayed in Vienna. But a misfortune struck Christine Frank: she lost her voice in front of the entire Austrian imperial family during a performance of Mozart's *Le nozze di Figaro*, conducted by Salieri. Her voice came back, but without its former strength and clarity. She never performed again.

For his Polish war, Napoleon took along the newest and most detailed charts of Lithuania, but, just in case, he also picked up some maps of India.[17] The emperor showed very limited cartographical understanding of Russia, and when one of his generals, Narbonne, asked him about the strategies of war, he merely gave a rhetorical answer: "Let destiny be accomplished, and Russia be crushed under my hatred of England! At the head of four hundred thousand men ... with a Lithuanian corps of the same blood as some of the population we'll be passing through, I don't fear this long road fringed with deserts. After all ... this long road is the road to India. Alexander the Great set out to reach the Ganges from a distance no less greater than from Moscow. ... It'd be a gigantic expedition, I admit; but possible in the nineteenth century. At a blow, France will have conquered the independence of the West and the freedom of the seas."[18] In this grandiose scheme of global domination, Vilna stood as a portal to the Orient.

To secure "the independence of the West," the six hundred thousand men of the Grande Armée gathered on the left bank of the Niemen River, a Lithuanian river that, after the imperial remapping of Europe, had become the border of Russia. The Grande Armée – the largest army ever assembled in the history of Europe – was truly a babel of nations:

> From right to left, or from south to north, the army was drawn up along the Nie-men. At the extreme right, coming from Galicia, Prince Schwartzenberg with thirty-four thousand Austrians; on their left, coming from Warsaw and moving towards Bialystock and Grodno, the king of Westphalia at the head of seventy-nine thousand two hundred Westphalians, Saxons, and Poles; farther to the left, the Viceroy of Italy who had effected the junction of his seventy-nine thousand three hundred Bavarians, Italians, and French near Marienpol; next, the Emperor with two hundred thousand men commanded by Murat, the Prince of Eckmuehl and the Dukes of Danzig, Istria, Reggio, and Elchingen. These troops had marched from Thorn, Marienwerder, and Elbling; and on June 23 all were gathered in one compact body near Nogarisky, about a league above Kovno.
>
> Everything was ready. From Guadalquivir and the shores of Calabria to the banks of the Vistula, six hundred and seventy thousand men (of whom four hundred and eighty thousand were already present), six companies of engineers, one siege train, several thousand wagons of provisions, innumerable droves of cattle, one thousand three hundred and seventy-two pieces of canon, and thousands of artillery and hospital wagons, had been mustered and were now stationed a short distance from the Russian river.[19]

Count Phillipe-Paul de Segur, who described this impressive convention of Napoleonic Europe, was following in the footsteps of his father, who had crossed Lithuania on his diplomatic mission to Saint Petersburg in 1784. In imperial France, the Segur dynasty made the most of its *ancien régime* pedigree. Segur the Elder had served as the Grand Master of Ceremonies during Napoleon's coronation, and his son joined the 1812 expedition as the

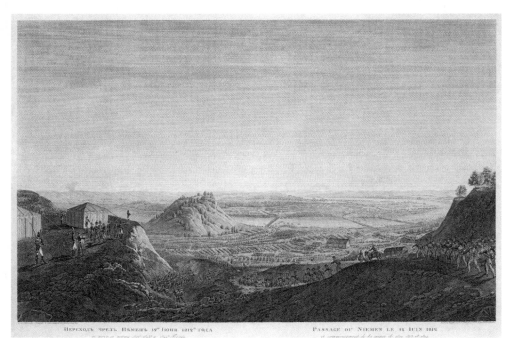

30. The Grand Armée crossing the Niemen (Nemunas) River.

Quartermaster-General. The yonger Segur adored Napoleon and, like most military men, was seduced by the ambitious orientation and force of the campaign. "Through the gloom our eager eyes strained to see into this glorious promised land. We imagined we heard the joyful shouts of the Lithuanians at the approach of their deliverers. In our mind's eye we saw the river lined with their imploring hands. Here we had nothing, there, everything would be lavished on us … [and] we should be surrounded by love and gratitude. … Day would shortly appear, bringing its warmth and illusions. … Day did appear! And it revealed to us only barren stretches of sand and dismal black woods. Then our disappointed eyes turned back upon ourselves, and we felt pride and hope swell again in us at the impressive sight of our assembled army."[20]

Baron Louis-Francois Lejeune, the future painter of the Napoleonic battlefields, witnessed this sense of pride from the hilltop where Napoleon set up his observation point. This was, in the artist's words, "the most extraordinary, the most pompous, the most inspiring spectacle imaginable – of all sights the one which, by exaggerating the extent of his power, both material and moral, is most capable of inebriating the conqueror. … The salutes of thousands of trumpets and drums – the enthusiastic shouts acclaiming the emperor whenever he appeared – so much devotion and discipline, shortly to set in motion this multitude whose immensity lost itself on the horizon, where its weapons twinkled like so many stars—all this exalted everyone's confidence in the chief who was leading us."[21] Less imaginative or privileged participants of the campaign, such as Lieutenant Heinrich August Vossler from Württemberg (who kept a diary of the events), saw a different picture. "On the 22nd and 23rd of June a veritable torrent of troops at last rolled forward across the immense plain to the very banks of the river, which formed the frontier with Russia, and there awaited the order to cross. For days past the French army had left a swath of pillage and destruction in its wake as it moved through friendly territory. Heaven only knew what it would do on enemy soil!"[22]

The first sentries crossed the river without a fight. In Segur's memory, only "a single Cossack officer commanding a night patrol" appeared on the shore. "He was alone, and seemed to think he was in the midst of peace, wholly unaware that all Europe in arms was at hand. He asked the intruders who they were. 'Frenchmen,' they told him. 'What do you want?' he questioned further. 'And why have you come to Russia?' One of the sappers answered bluntly, 'To make war on you! To take Vilna and set Poland free!' "[23] Following the battle call of the first troops, Napoleon crossed the river twice on the same day: the first time wearing the French colours, and the second time, sporting the gallant uniform of a Polish hussar.

The only enemy encountered by the liberating troops on their way to Vilna was sent by the heavens. The frontier city of Kovno was already partially destroyed by the evacuating Russian forces. The liberating Napoleonic troops despoiled what was left of it. "Camp fires were still smoking in the market place, the furniture had been taken out of the houses and the windows shattered. At most a Jew was seen to be here and there. One glance was enough. Kovno was a totally plundered town."[24] After a calm morning, the suddenly darkened sky ambushed the Grande Armée with a fireball of thunder. "The threatening sky," recalls Segur, "in this land without visible shelter, threw a gloom over our spirits. ... This thunderstorm was as grandiose as our undertaking. For several hours the clouds grew thicker and blacker over the entire army. From one end to the other, for fifty leagues around, the troops were everywhere endangered by the lightning and overwhelmed by the downpour. Roads and fields were flooded. The unbearable heat changed suddenly to disagreeable cold."[25]

With the unpredictable Lithuanian weather as its main adversary, the army laboriously moved forward. "To sum up," wrote Vossler, "our situation was this: we were embarked on a strenuous campaign entailing frequent forced marches along abominable roads, either smothered in sand or knee-deep in mud and frequently pitted by precipitous gulleys, under skies alternately unbearably hot or pouring forth freezing rain."[26] At least Vossler's division was following the road to Vilna – the elite Imperial Guard, muddled by the weather, went astray. A veteran of the Guards, Sergeant Bourgogne, remembers being "lost, and [I] did not know which way to turn. I ran to take shelter in the direction of the village where the General was lodged, but I had only the lightning to guide me – suddenly, in one of the flashes, I thought I saw a road (it was unfortunately a canal, swollen by the rain to the level of the ground). Expecting to find solid earth under my feet, I plunged in and sank."[27]

It was convenient for everyone to blame the weather and treacherous terrain for slowing down the advance. But to a large degree, the chaotic march on Vilna was a symptom of French geographical ignorance of the region. The French maps of Lithuania were seriously flawed: they were outdated, inappropriately scaled, and topographically incomprehensible. The French orthographic transcriptions of the Lithuanian place-names were so defective that it made basic communication with the local population impossible. The natives could not give directions simply because they could not understand the foreign pronunciations of the names of their own hamlets, villages or towns. It did not help that the retreating Russian army had removed all the milestones from the roads: nobody seemed to know how far Vilna was, or which direction the army should go. At the imperial headquarters, Polish count Roman Soltyk immediately realised that "the geographical notion of the Muscovite empire entertained in Napoleon's office was about as imperfect as could be, and likewise of its topography. At all hours Napoleon kept interrogating the Polish General Soholnicki about such matters. On my offering to rectify the place names' orthography, I was ordered to write them in on the map, so that Napoleon could have a better idea of his whereabouts."[28] For the rest of the army, the sun rather than a map became the most reliable guide for moving eastwards. "Every day," wrote General Compans home to his young bride: "I am becoming aware of the inadequacy of the maps we have, so I've bought a compass to guide me. Although I'm not used to this instrument I'm not unhopeful that it'll enable me to find Saint Petersburg or Moscow."[29]

Meanwhile, the tsarist administration and local population in Vilna were also preparing for the war. The headquarters of the Russian army, led by the emperor, was placed in Vilna. From the beginning of June, Alexander, and with him the Russian imperial court (except for its ladies' quarters), moved into the former palace of the bishop, which, at the time, functioned as the official residence of the governor-general of Lithuania. While the preparations for war included some military drills and inspections, for the most part it consisted of endless parades, processions, pageants, visitations, salon-parties, dinners, theatre performances, musical concerts and extravagant balls. Although in

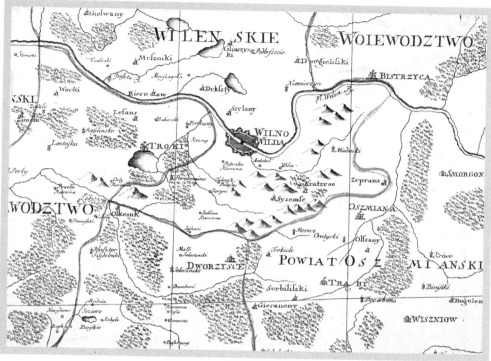

31. Poland and Lithuania, circa 1770. Most maps used by the Grand Armée during the 1812 campaign depicted Vilna as a mighty fortress, even though the last remains of the city's defensive wall had already been destroyed by the Russian administration.

general, local nobles, especially the younger generation, were leaning towards Napoleon, the Lithuanian nobility happily joined the Russian imperial court. Everyone in the city expected the tsar to grant Lithuania autonomy as a countermeasure to Napoleon's promises to restore the old Commonwealth.

Napoleon expected a battle over Vilna, but Alexander denied him that. He left the town swiftly after hearing the news of the beginning of the campaign. The Russian troops and officials soon followed the tsar. Evacuated Vilna prepared for the arrival of the Grande Armée. On June 28, the Polish Lancers entered the city and were greeted by a patriotic crowd. "Our entry," remembers one of the participants, "was a triumph. Streets and public places were full of people. All the windows were adorned with wildly enthusiastic ladies. Valuable carpets hung on the façades of several buildings."[30] An "immense white and sky-blue flag, said to be the colours of the Jagiellonian [dynasty], ancient sovereigns of Lithuania," was raised on the ruins of the ancient castle overlooking the city.[31] Segur echoes the same sentiment: people in the streets were "embracing and congratulating each other. Old men appeared again in their former costume, with its memories of honour and independence. They weep with joy at the sight of the national banners being followed by innumerable crowds."[32] The disgruntled Napoleon showed no interest in this public display of joy. For him, taking provincial cities was a matter of strategic importance; so, in the first instance, he wanted to know everything about the military and topographical features of the place. Before entering the city, the French emperor sent an emissary to fetch the rector of the university, Jan Śniadecki, an aged professor of astronomy and meteorology. Śniadecki tactfully reassured the emperor of the city's (and the university's) loyalty to him rather than to his imperial nemesis, Alexander. In return, the rector was made a member of the provisional government of Lithuania. After the interview, according to General Caulaincourt (a former French ambassador in Russia), "the Emperor passed through Vilna without making himself known. The town seemed to be deserted. Not a face showed at a single window, not a sign of enthusiasm or even curiosity. Everything was gloomy. Passing straight through the town, he inspected the burnt Vilia bridge, the terrain beyond the city and the magazines the enemy had set fire to and which were still burning. Hastening on the repairs to the bridges, he gave orders for defensive outworks, and then returned and went to the palace."[33] In a bold gesture, Napoleon took the same rooms in the same palace that just two days earlier had been occupied by Alexander. As one court replaced the other with phenomenal speed, Vilna's role changed as well. Before the invasion, it had been the nominal war capital of Russia; now, it was the first city of Napoleonic Europe.

Perhaps fear gripped the city, but none of the French, including the emperor, failed to notice the difference in the local attitude towards the Polish and foreign liberators: the Poles and Lithuanians were greeted as family members, the French and other Europeans as complete strangers. Even when Napoleon set up his Imperial Headquarters in the palace of the Russian governor-general and his arrival was made public, there was still no jubilation in the town. "The Emperor," noted Caulaincourt, "was struck by this. Entering his study, he remarked: 'The Poles hereabouts aren't like the ones in Warsaw. They're cooler than Poles [in Warsaw] and much more reticent.' "[34]

Despite the strategic success, Napoleon was not satisfied with the tactical outcomes of the French occupation of the city. Napoleon wanted to humiliate Alexander and simultaneously carve a road to the Orient. The Russian retreat annoyed him greatly, for it deprived him of an epic launch for his campaign. When Napoleon received a letter from Alexander proposing the negotiation of a peace agreement under the condition of immediate withdrawal of the

32. The palace of the governor-general in Vilna, where Alexander I and Napoleon stayed during the 1812 war.

Grande Armée to beyond the Niemen, Napoleon, according to Caulaincourt, became enraged:

> Alexander's laughing at me. ... Does he imagine I've come to Vilna to negotiate treaties? I've come to finish off the barbarian colossus of the North, once and for all. They must be thrust back into their snow and ice, so that for a quarter of a century at least they won't be able to interfere with civilized Europe. The sword is drawn. The Tsar sees his army has been cut in two. He wants to come to terms. The acquisition of Finland has turned his head. If he must have victims, let him defeat the Persians; but don't let him meddle in Europe's affairs. My manoeuvres have disconcerted the Russians. Before a month has passed they'll be on their knees to me.[35]

While waiting for the next move, the French and their allies turned Vilna into Europe's social and political playground. As soon as Napoleon had settled his expeditionary court in the city, the ambassadors of Austria, Prussia and the United States of America arrived from Paris. Once again, the city was consumed by a festive mood, and the swift transition from Russian to French rule only accelerated the intensity of the celebrations. Duke Fezensac remembers arriving in a city where: "assemblies, balls and concerts succeeded one another uninterruptedly. Present at these celebrations, we could hardly recognize the capital of a country ravaged by two enemy armies, and whose inhabitants were reduced to misery and despair; and if the Lithuanians themselves seemed sometimes to remember this, it was in order to say that no sacrifice was too great for Poles when it came to the reestablishment of their country."[36] Once again, the local nobility joined the growing party of Europe's old and new aristocracy with the passion of a rekindled love affair. At nightly balls, Captain Fantin des Odoards recalls having "a better opportunity of judging the fair sex of Vilna, of whose charms I'd formed a favourable opinion at the religious service. This time I was filled with quite another sort of admiration when I saw them animated by dancing, pleasure and patriotism and noticed how white and rounded were the objects rising and falling under the national colours during the gentle embraces of the waltz."[37]

The gathering of the European elite could not conceal the fact that Vilna was the easternmost place conquered by the French. In part, it already belonged to the mysterious cartography of the Orient. On his arrival in the city, Captain Francois Dumonceau, for instance, noticed near the Ostra Brama gate "a kind of cloister with a chapel. Its bell tower was a parti-coloured striped ball, the first bizarre Russian bell tower we'd see. Its walls were placarded all over with lengthy proclamations in Russian we'd have liked to decipher."[38] A fairy-tale Oriental setting even took over the French army's headquarters, located next to the palace, where Carabinier-Sergeant Bertrand came across:

> ... two townsmen and two other persons in turbans seated around a well-lit table, on which was a good dinner. Valets dressed in the Emperor's livery were waiting on them. Stupefied, I didn't know whether to advance or retreat. But not yet knowing how to beat a retreat, I go in, raising my hand to my shako. 'What do you want?' says one of my turbans. 'A corner where I can get some rest. But I see this isn't the place, excuse me.'—'If there's only you,' replies the turban, whom I'd recognized as Roustam, the Emperor's mameluke, 'come in. Your division has been in the advance guard all day. You must be dead beat.' Amazed at my lucky windfall, I valiantly plant my fork in a chicken wing, followed by an iced ham, the whole washed down with the finest vintages. The second turban, Murat's mameluke, orders up a square-shaped bottle wrapped in straw, and we drink the healths of the Emperor, of his worthy spouse, of the Prince Imperial, of King Murat.[39]

The nightly escapes into the street and the social maze of Vilna had a detrimental effect on discipline. Thousands of soldiers and officers went missing, and "all around the city and in the countryside," according to Countess Tiesenhausen (a native of Lithuania), "there were extraordinary excesses. Churches were plundered, sacred chalices were sullied; even cemeteries were not respected, and women violated."[40]

The pillaging could be explained by the complete lack of provisions and shelter for the army. While Europe's elite partied in the city, a hundred thousand soldiers were forced to wait for new orders in the countryside. Dumonceau remembers his men being locked up inside a walled monastery garden, where:

> The rain was coming down in bucketsful, accompanied by a glacial cold which we felt the more keenly for its following immediately on the overwhelming heat. Soon the soil of the garden, churned up and drowning in waters, was nothing but a vast swamp of mud. We stood knee-deep in it, having neither straw to lie down on nor any shelter, and without wood to light a fire. And then, to cap it all, came a terrible hurricane. Finding it equally hard to stand up or lie down, we squatted dozing on our mantles in the mud; and awoke only to find the rain still pouring down and the hurricane growing steadily more furious. Chimneys and tiles were coming down all around us. ... Arms and equipment were lying in the mud. Our dismal fires had gone out. Our horses were shivering at least as violently as ourselves. Several succumbed during the night or else died the next day, destroyed by cold and misery.[41]

Vossler also found little enjoyment in Vilna. "I would have liked to spend some time in Vilna," remembered the German officer, "but with my wagons it was neither expedient nor safe to do so, nor would it have served any practical purpose, for no provisions were to be had from the frightened inhabitants, even for good money."[42]

In general, the forceful collection of provisions affected local Jews more than any other group. Eugene Labaume, captain of the Royal Geographical Engineers, had the misfortune to be stationed in Troki, the ancient capital of Lithuania. "This pleasant place formed a striking contrast to the road which we had just traversed, and every one admired its fine situation, and the charming effect which was produced by a large convent on a top of a mountain, which overlooked the towns. ... Those who had any idea of painting were never tired of admiring the beautiful spot. In the middle of the lake was an old ruined castle, the darkened walls of which projected on one side over the surface of the water, and on the other they seemed to touch gilded horizon." All the same, the pictorial ideal was a mirage:

> Troki appeared at first a delightful spot, but the illusion ceased the moment we entered it. We had scarcely approached the first houses when a number of Jews, followed by women, children and old men, who, throwing themselves at our feet, implored us to deliver them from the rapacity of the soldiers, who robbed and destroyed every thing in the houses. We could not grant them any thing but mere consolation. The borough where we're quartered had no magazines, and our soldiers having been long deprived of their rations, subsisted now only on pillage.

This caused the greatest confusion. And this fatal want of discipline is the most pernicious, as it is always a certain sign of the approaching ruin of an army.[43]

From Vilna, the Grande Armée pushed east aimlessly, pillaging and terrorising the local populations. The capture of Vitebsk at the end of July signified the nominal conquest of Lithuania, yet no one seemed to have a clear sense of the future direction of the campaign. In retrospect, Segur saw this as a threshold moment: "With the liberation of Lithuania the objective of the conflict had been attained, yet it seemed that the war had hardly begun. Places alone had been overcome, and not men. The Russian army was still intact, and its two flanks, separated by the ardour of an initial attack, had just been reunited. We were in the finest season of the year. Such was the situation when Napoleon decided to halt on the banks of the Dnieper and the Duna – a decision which he thought irrevocable. He was better able to deceive others concerning his intentions since he was deceiving himself."[44]

Unable to make a decision, Napoleon initially decided to winter in Lithuania, and commanded the cleanup of Vitebsk. This cleansing operation potentially threatened Vilna's status as the social and cultural epicentre of the campaign. Napoleon "ordered the guard to tear down some stone houses which spoiled the appearance of the palace square, and to clear away the rubbish. He gave thought to winter pleasures. Actors would be brought from Paris to Vitebsk, and since this city was empty of civilians, feminine spectators might be drawn to it from Warsaw and Vilna."[45] Thankfully, Vilna's society was saved from such social disgrace by Napoleon's restlessness. The "boredom of six long months of winter on the banks of those rivers had appeared to him then as the worst of enemies."[46] The emperor finally made a decision to move, and on August 10 he gave orders to cross the rivers.

The mood of the army was far less enthusiastic than before crossing the Niemen River less than two months earlier. Most soldiers were fearful of Russia. In his diary, Vossler expressed pride mixed with angst. "Now our move into enemy territory proper filled me with nothing but sombre forebodings. But we were an army hundreds of thousands strong, comrades in arms all in the flower of manhood, and many still rejoiced as they crossed the fateful river. On the far bank an ominous silence awaited them. Dense and menacing forests met the eye in every direction. The rare villages were deserted. Not a sign of human life anywhere. The fate of this huge army to which I belonged oppressed me profoundly."[47]

Vossler's gloomy picture of Russia was echoed by Henri Beyle, better known as the French writer Stendhal, who joined the campaign in the capacity of an imperial courier. "My own happiness at being here is not great," wrote the writer. "How a man changes! My old thirst for new sights has been entirely quenched. ... Would you believe it that, without any vexation that affects me more than anybody else, and without any personal sorrow, I am sometimes on the point of bursting with tears? In this ocean of barbarity there is not a sound that finds an echo in my soul! Everything is coarse, dirty, both physically and morally stinking." Stendhal joined the Russian campaign with fresh memories of Italy, where, during his administrative posting in Milan, he had become a passionate lover of Italian opera. The memorable tunes of divine arias steered him away from the harsh realities of war. Surrounded by the autumn-coloured landscape of the northern latitudes, he sang of southern pleasures: "Every time I saw Milan and Italy [on the map], everything I see repels me with its crudity. ... I imagine that my soul inhabits – that soul which composes, works, listens to Cimarosa and is in love with Angela [a singer at the La Scala Opera], amidst a beautiful climate – I imagine these heights as delicious hills." At the sight of the Russian frontier, however, the memory crescendo ends in a sudden fall. "Far from these hills, down in the plain, are fetid marshes – and here I am plunged, and nothing in the world except the sight of a map can remind me of my hills."[48]

On September 14, after the pitiless battle of Borodino (September 7), the Grande Armée entered the abandoned and smoldering environs of Moscow. The capture of the ancient Russian capital restored the spirit and passion of the army. "It was a beautiful summer's day," recalls Sergeant Bourgogne, "the sun was reflected on all the domes, spires, and gilded palaces. Many capitals I have seen – such as Paris, Berlin, Warsaw, Vienna, and Madrid – had only produced an ordinary impression on me. But this was quite different; the effect was to me – in fact, to everyone – magical. At that sight troubles, dangers, fatigues, privations were all forgotten, and the pleasure of entering Moscow absorbed all our minds. To take up good quarters for the winter, and to make conquest of another nature – such is the French soldier's character: from war to love, and from love to war!"[49] The burning of the city only increased the sense of magic, and even disheartened Stendhal came to admire this demonic scene from the intellectual heights of his private misery. "We emerged from the city, which was lit by the finest conflagration the world has ever seen: it formed a huge pyramid which, like prayers of the faithful, had its base on the earth and its peak in heaven. Above this atmosphere of flame and smoke there was bright moonlight. It was an imposing spectacle; but in order to enjoy it one would have had to be alone, or with intelligent people."[50]

After the all-consuming fire, on October 18, Napoleon decided to leave Moscow and retreat to more comfortable winter quarters back in Lithuania. The next morning the army of some hundred and ten thousand soldiers were ordered to march in the direction of the Russian town of Kaluga. Sergeant Bourgogne's Imperial Corps were the first to leave, wandering towards their unknown destiny and wondering about their future conquests:

> We set out in the afternoon, packing some liquor from our store on Mother Dubois's [cantinière] cart, as well as our large silver bowl; it was almost dark when we got outside the town. We found ourselves amongst a great number of carts and wagons, driven by men of every nationality, three or four in a line, and stretching for the length of a league. We heard all round us French, German, Spanish, Italian, Portuguese, and other languages, for there were Muscovite peasants among them, and a great number of Jews. This crowd of people, with their varied costumes and languages, the canteen masters with their wives and crying children, hurried forward in the most unheard of noise, tumult and disorder. Some had got their carts all smashed, and in consequence yelled and swore enough to drive one mad. This was the convoy of the whole army and we had a great deal of trouble in getting past it. We marched by the Kalonga [sic] road (we were then in Asia). ... Most of the carts were already shattered, and others could not move, the wheels sinking deep in the sandy road. We could hear screams in French, oaths in German, entreaties to the Almighty in Italian, and to the Holy Virgin in Spanish and Portuguese. After getting past this babel we were forced to wait for the left of the column.[51]

Vossler, who had not been in Moscow with the occupying troops, had very little sympathy for the demoralised yet still arrogant heroes of the conquest. He was shocked by their apparent lack of discipline and moral values:

> They had all been in Moscow where they had spent their time looting and from whence they brought with them whatever they could carry. We were amazed at their appearance. Many carried no weapons, others were armed after a fashion, but their muskets were either unserviceable or they had run out of ammunition. These men were no longer soldiers but marauders and camp-followers, utterly undisciplined, bedizened occasionally with odd pieces of equipment but mostly burdened with bales of wool, linen, silk of every colour and description, with men's and women's furs from sable to sheepskin, hats and caps of every shape and size, fashionable boots and shoes, kitchen ware of copper, brass and iron, cutlery of silver and tin, pewter plates and dishes, glasses, goblets, scissors, needles, thread, waxed twine, and so on and so forth; in short, with every kind of object which the well-equipped peacetime traveller, on horseback or on foot, whether gentleman, journeyman, merchant, artist or whatever, could possibly require. ... This was the spectacle which the first trickle of the retreating army presented. Their number

swelled rapidly from day to day. With this motley crew who had joined our detachment for their own and their booty's greater safety we continued on our way. All discipline had broken down.[52]

Within this horde of peoples, all national, linguistic and religious distinctions seemed to disappear, as if on the road to Vilna, Europe had liquefied into one giant nameless human stream rushing back to its sources. Then, suddenly but predictably, everything changed, and the panicky rush turned to a deadly freeze. "Until 7th November, the skies had remained clear and blue, and the winds no rougher than they are in Germany at this time of year. But on the 8th winter suddenly set in. A piercing northeasterly gale brought blizzards and a snap of frost which turned so bitter that by next day the cold had become all but unbearable."[53] The chill destroyed the last vestiges of martial order. "Now the bundles of looted clothing were unwrapped and our column began to resemble a masquerade."[54] At this point, there were still about eight hundred kilometres left to Vilna, the first proven outpost of Europe.

When he reached the historical outskirts of the Grand Duchy of Lithuania at the Dnieper River, Napoleon got lost again. In Segur's words, as "the Lithuanian forest into which he was about to plunge was unfamiliar to him, he called a council of the officers who had just crossed them on their way to join him." The emperor was advised to go to Borisov on the Berezina River, where the army could cross "the Lithuanian swamps over a series of wooden bridges" in order to be brought back safely to Vilna.[55] Three weeks later, exhausted by sickness, hunger, cold and constant Russian harassments, the demoralised army reached the river. The generals "were paying no attention to anyone but themselves, intent on saving either their poor possessions or their persons, marching among the soldiers who took no notice of them, to whom they gave no orders and from whom they could no longer expect anything, all ties between them being broken and all difference of rank effaced by a common misery."[56] Only a madman could still follow orders. On the bank of the Berezina, Bourgogne met a man "attired in *full uniform*! I asked him what that was for, and he only laughed at me. The poor fellow was ill; that laugh was the laugh of death, as he succumbed during the night."[57]

The crossing of the Berezina started on November 28th and was expected to last two days. The river was still not completely frozen and two bridges were thrown up by army engineers. The hastily constructed bridges were constantly collapsing under the heavy weight of the rushing crowds and heavily loaded wagons. At some point, the Russian battery on the left bank of the river opened fire. Chaos and panic overtook the retreating army as the disaster "had reached its outmost limit. An immense quantity of wagons, three heavy guns, several thousand men, and some women and a few children were abandoned on the enemy's side of the river. ... Some plunged into the water and tried to swim; others trusted themselves to the drifting cakes of ice. Still others rushed straight into the flames on the bridge which crumbled under their feet. Burned and frozen at the same time, they died from two opposite forms of torture, and their bodies soon piled up with the ice and beat against the trestles of the bridge."[58]

Half of the retreating army perished during the crossing, transforming, in the eyes of Bourgogne, the remaining divisions and battalions serving under the various flags of Napoleonic Europe into an undifferentiated "medley of Frenchmen, Italians, Spaniards, Portuguese, Croats, Germans, Poles, Romans, Italians, and even Prussians."[59] Those who crossed the Berezina "embraced and congratulated each other as if it were the Rhine they had crossed, still 400 leagues off."[60] It was an epic transformation, and, like the crossing of the Niemen or the conquest of Moscow, was worthy of a "clever painter ... who could have made a beautiful picture! He'd have painted *une nature morte*. Trees laden with hoar frost, snow and icicles. In the background, between white-powdered conifers, would be seen perfidious Bashkirs, waiting keenly for a favourable moment to throw themselves on their prey. The river itself would play the chief role and, at a pinch, could represent Acheron, the river of Hades in the fable. The damned on the left bank. The elect on the right."[61]

For the fortunate survivors of the crossing, including the innumerable deserters, Vilna became an unreachable destiny of hope. Cold and hunger were the main killers, but hot flames proved to be as hazardous as the glacial nights. Those who left the night fire "were usually found dead in the morning. Their corpses, frozen solid to the ground, were plundered by those that followed after, and used as seats at fires re-kindled with the chopped remains of their carts. Some, dragging themselves to a fire and craving for warmth, put their limbs right into the embers and perished, half-roasted and half-frozen to death."[62] The "roads were like battlefields, there were so many dead bodies; but as the snow fell all the time, the horror of the sight was softened. We had lost all sense of pity, besides; we were insensible even to our own sufferings, let alone those of others."[63] A sense of delusion and indifference settled in among the survivors. "All, without exception, had suffered some impairment, at least temporary, of their mental powers, which often manifested itself in a sort of dumb lethargy. The troops called it the 'Moscow Dumps.' "[64] According to Segur: "Sixty thousand men had crossed that river [the Berezina], and twenty thousand recruits had since joined them. Of these eighty thousand men, fully a half had perished—and the majority in the last four days, between Molodeczno and Vilna!"[65]

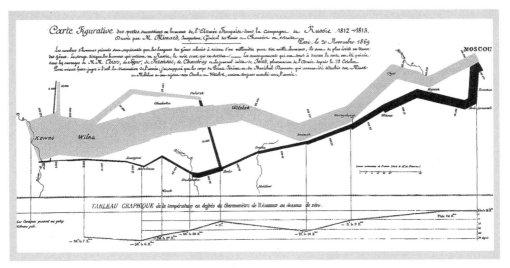

33. A graph representing the collapse of the Napoleonic army during the Russian campaign of 1812, designed by French engineer C. J. Minard in 1869. The graph displays the dramatic annihilation of the Grand Armée in parallel to the geographical direction of the campaign and the freezing temperatures during the retreat. Out of roughly 400,000 soldiers who passed through Vilna and its environs at the beginning of the campaign, only 8,000 left the city at the end of the retreat.

Sergeant Bourgogne reached the environs of Vilna on December 9 in a state of complete delirium. The next morning, sick and exhausted, he "plucked up a little courage" and with other ghostly figures moved towards the city:

> This terrible cold was more than I had ever felt before. I was almost fainting, and we seemed to walk through an atmosphere of ice. … I could hardly breathe: my nose felt frozen; my lips were glued together; my eyes streamed, dazzled by the snow. … In all the buildings we passed were unfortunate men not able to get any farther, and waiting there to die.
>
> Now we could see the spires and roofs of Wilna. I tried to hurry on to get there amongst the first, but the old Chasseurs of the Guard prevented me. They blocked up the road in such manner that no one could pass them without marching in order. These veterans, with ice hanging to their beards and moustaches, marched on, controlling their own sufferings to keep order in the ranks; but this order was impossible to maintain. Once in the outskirts of the town, everything was in confusion. At the door of a house I saw one of my old friends of the Grenadiers lying dead. They had arrived an hour before us.[66]

Most were oblivious of their whereabouts. "At 2.30 p.m.," remembers one of the survivors, with soaked and frost-bitten feet "we enter a big town full of unfortunates like ourselves. We are told it is Vilna."[67]

After Napoleon left Moscow, it was widely believed he was going to winter in Vilna. The emperor briefly described Vilna to his wife Marie Louise as a "fine city of 40,000 souls," able to accommodate the "vast stocks of food and other supplies assembled at Danzig and Königsberg [that could] be brought up by barge along the Vilia [River]."[68] All social, administrative and political communiqués between France (and Europe) and the Grande Armée went through the city. The constant flow of imperial communiqués, secret directives, bureaucratic instructions and military bulletins, in addition to numerous diplomatic, administrative and cultural visitations, made Vilna the gathering place of Napoleonic Europe. Stendhal, who was sent from Paris to Vilna to deliver mail to the emperor (including a letter from Empress Marie Louise), outlined the journey of a postman in a letter to his sister. "My itinerary to Vilna is as follows: I shall travel fast, with a courier in advance, as far as Königsberg. But at this point the sweet effects of pillage begin to make themselves evident, and are doubly so at Kovno: it is said that in the region of this town one can go fifty leagues without finding a living creature. ... In these ravaged wildernesses travel is very difficult, especially with a poor little Viennese calash that will be crushed beneath a thousand packages: every single person has had the idea of entrusting me with one."[69]

Occasional visitors from France were also able to reach the city. The young wife of the imperial marshal, Duke Oudinot, came to Vilna in October to nurse her wounded husband. She was impressed by its panoramic grandeur: "Nothing resembles the view as one surveys Vilna from the hills all around ... Although the Vilia vainly wends its way through a countryside it seems unable to fertilize, a multitude of domes and church towers rise brilliantly above the thirty-six convents."[70]

Already in November, the Polish officer Bangowski noted in his diary that "Vilna presents the most lamentable appearance. ... Streets encumbered with wounded, dead and dying, ravaged by the plague. No room in the churches, in the hospitals. No means even of removing horse carcasses. And ever more convoys of wounded turning up all the while from Moscow! Everyone's doing what he can to get by, without compassion from anyone else."[71] In spite of it, Vilna put up a festive spectacle on December 2, the eighth anniversary of the coronation of Napoleon. The celebration included "a 21-gun salute at 8 a.m.; as many shots again while the *Te Deum* was being sung in the cathedral, and again the salute at 4 p.m."[72] In the evening, there was a ball at the governor's palace. "As usual," noted a French participant, "it opened with a *polonaise*, which is nothing but a promenade. ... It's the custom for all officers to go to the ball booted and spurred and wearing stable trousers. The women present spoke French, as they all generally do at Vilna."[73]

Uneasiness finally settled in among the inhabitants on December 6, when it was discovered that Napoleon had circumvented Vilna on his flight to Paris. He ordered Murat and Berthier to stay "in that capital a full week, long enough to rally the army, and give it sufficient courage and strength to continue the retreat in a little less deplorable condition."[74] On the same day, Stendhal arrived in Vilna and was lucky enough to find a shelter at the Frank house, which had been turned into a comfortable military hostel. From there, he wrote of his ordeal to his sister. "I am in good health, my dearest. I often thought of you on the long march from Moscow, which took fifty days. I have lost everything, and have only the clothes I am wearing. What is much better is that I am thin. I have had much physical hardship, and no spiritual pleasure, but all that is done with, and I am ready to start again in the service of His Majesty."[75] The locals, however, were no longer eager to serve the interests of the empire. "Already on the first day" of their arrival, testified a French officer stationed in the city, "the shops, the inns and cafes, unable to accommodate the quantity of purchasers, were closed [and] the inhabitants, who feared our avidity would soon lead to a famine, took to hiding their provisions."[76] Dumonceau found the city to be "comparatively deserted; calm reigned, the dwellings were shut up from top to bottom, as in a town taken by assault."[77]

The French military administrators tried to impose some form of order and normalcy, which led to a bureaucratic massacre of survivors. In front of Segur's eyes, "for ten long hours, with the thermometer at sixteen or seventeen below zero [-27 or -28 degrees Centigrade], thousands of soldiers who fancied they had finally reached safety fell dead, either frozen or smothered in the crowd. ... These administrators, it must be said, were not aware of the desperate situation of the army; and for several hours they let our unfortunate companions die of hunger in sight of those great heaps of provisions, which the enemy was to seize on the morrow."[78] The crowd of desperate soldiers gathered outside the wall of the city. "Many fugitives reached Vilna as early as 6th December," noted Vossler, "and in the two days that followed the influx was such that it had needed only a river ahead and the Russians behind to reproduce at the gates of the city the scenes of the Berezina crossing. Indeed on the 9th they were re-enacted when the Russian spearhead reached the gates simultaneously with our rearguard and entered Vilna with them, pillaging and murdering as they went."[79] According to an eyewitness, a Frenchwoman who came to the city to nurse her son, the anxious horde at the Ostra Brama gate was plunging "forward, the crowd seemed to fancy they'd reached the Promised Land. It was there almost all the French from Moscow perished.

Fighting cold and hunger, they couldn't get into the town."[80] Dumonceau remembers clambering over this death-stricken mob: "pushing, shoving, hemmed in on all sides, horrified at having to get over it and at each step risking being overthrown by the quiverings, the convulsive spasms of the victims we were trampling underfoot."[81]

Inside the city, chaos ensued. In a matter of hours, recalls Baron Roch-Gotard, "Vilna become a real labyrinth, you simply didn't know where you were."[82] Duke Fezensac pushed into "a rich and populous city" in the crowd of "wandering ragged, starving soldiers."[83] Some, like Vossler, were lucky enough to find his comrades from Württemberg gathered "at the Lichtenstein café" where they spent all of their newly received advances paid from the Württemberg war chest on a three-day feast of wine and excellent food.[84] A few, in Segur's words, managed to survive because of "the pity of the Lithuanians, and the avarice of the Jews" who allowed them indoors. "Then it was a touching thing to witness the wonder of those poor fellows on finding themselves once again in an occupied house. A loaf of leavened bread seemed to them the most delicious of foods; and what unutterable pleasure did they take in eating it seated at a table. ... They seemed to have returned from the ends of the earth, so thoroughly had the violence and endless succession of hardship alienated them from their old ways of living, so terrible was the abyss from which they were emerging."[85] But most of the soldiers were reduced "to a kind of mob, more like a legion of convicts or hideous hobgoblins than troops," roaming in search of respite.[86] The sick, wounded and insane gathered around the churches and monasteries, which had been converted into barracks and hospitals. Alas, these were not places of comfort. Thousands "were turned away, though not by the living, for death reigned supreme here. A few of the doomed inmates were still breathing: they complained that for a long, long time they had been without beds, even without straw, and almost totally without attention. The yards, the corridors, and all the wards, filled with piles of corpses, were nothing more than charnel houses."[87]

At night, flames lighted up the winter sky. "The men," noted one of the local witnesses, "were lighting fires in the streets to keep themselves warm. A thousand men were to be seen spread out among the flames and leaping sparks. The Town Hall still bore some festive decoration. Looked at through the clouds of smoke rising to the sky, Napoleon's cipher seemed to be covered by a veil."[88] A huge bonfire in the courtyard of the governor's palace took the emperor's carriage as well as tents and bed camps. The mutinous soldiers also threw all the trophies Napoleon had taken from Moscow into the flames: icons, golden crosses, flags and old weapons.

34. French officers in Vilna rescued by a Samaritan monk from the hands of local assailants.

Sergeant Bourgogne spent this eventful night with his friend Colonel Picart in a Jewish inn on the outskirts of the city. He asked Picart "how it happened that he was on such friendly terms with the Jew, as [he] noticed they treated him as a member of the family. He said that he had passed himself off as the son of a Jewess, and that during the fortnight we had spent in town in July he had attended their synagogue with them, and in consequence of this he had always got some schnapps to drink and some nuts to crack." Bourgogne could not but respond with a sense of gratitude to the kindness he had received from his Jewish hosts. "I shall never forget the curious effect an inhabited house had on me. It seemed to me years since I had seen one. ... The Jew told me that the men who had arrived first in the morning had devoured everything. He advised us not to leave his house, even to sleep there, and that he would undertake to get us everything we wanted, also, to prevent others from coming in. Taking his advice, I settled to rest on a bench near the stove."[89]

Other French soldiers, too, discovered the Jews extremely helpful in moments of distress. "When no one could supply any more bread or sugar, or coffee, or tea, etc., they brought us spiced bread. Better still, they could even un-nest – God knows where from – means of transport, horse, sledges, when there were none to be had anywhere. Thanks to them some hundred of officers managed to escape from Russia's frozen plains. But 'le monsieur had to have money', even a lot of money, because they were robbers beyond all expression."[90] Bourgogne, however, took Picart's Jewish impersonation as a joke: "I had not laughed for long enough, but I burst out into a roar at this, until the blood poured down my lips. Picart went on with his funny stories, until suddenly we heard a rattle of artillery, and our host came hurriedly in. He looked dazed, and could not speak. At last he said that he had seen some Bavarian soldiers, followed by Cossacks, enter by the same gate at which we had come in."[91] With a sense of humility, the sergeant fled the city. "When I got outside the town, I could not help thinking of the state of our army: five months before it entered the Lithuanian capital, proud and rejoicing; now it went out, fugitive and miserable."[92]

As the Cossacks were encircling the city, the flight was easier to drum than to organize. Count Segur saw treachery at the highest levels of the French military commandant:

> At Vilna, as in Moscow, Napoleon had not had any official order given for retreat. He wanted our rout to be unannounced, wanted it to make itself known, to take our allies and their monarchs by surprise, so that we might avail ourselves of their confusion and get safely through the territory before the people were disposed to join with the Russians to overpower us. That is why everybody in Vilna – Lithuanians, foreigners, the prime minister himself – had been deceived. They did not believe in our defeat till they saw it, and the almost superstitious faith in Europe in the infallibility of Napoleon's genius gave him advantage over his enemies. But this same confidence had lulled his friends with false security, for in Vilna, as in Moscow, none of then had made any preparations for any actions whatever.[93]

Murat, the king of Naples and the chief commander of the army, cut off all talk about the defence of the city with a single phrase: "I'm not going to be taken here in this piss-pot."[94]

Many soldiers had neither the desire to fight, nor the ability to escape – so they ignored all orders. Like a siren's song, Vilna fooled those poor souls:

> If we had been able to hold twenty-four hours longer in Vilna, many lives would have been saved. That deadly city cost us nearly twenty thousand men, including three hundred officers and seven generals. The majority were stricken by winter rather than by the Russians, though the latter reaped the benefits. Others, physi-

35. The retreat of the Grand Armée through Vilna in 1812 (after the painting by J. Damel).

cally sound in appearance, were at the end of their resistance. After having had the courage to overcome so many hardships, they lost heart in sight of port, only four days' march away. They had reached a civilized city at last, and rather than set forth into the wilderness again, they chose to stay and trust to Fortune. In their case she was cruel![95]

Those who managed to move were no better off. The streets were filled with "thousands of corpses, completely naked, many of them bearing marks of dagger blows. But it certainly wasn't the Poles who'd committed these crimes," reasoned Captain François, for "they showed us great attachment. It was Platov's Cossacks who'd assassinated the sick and wounded whom the inhabitants, terrified of these brigands, had driven out of their houses."[96]

On the western outskirts of the city, on Ponary Hill, carnage ensued. Like death, the Cossacks seemed to be everywhere. During the confusion, the soldiers started to devour the last relics of the Napoleonic treasury. As collective madness took over, the two foes bonded into an unholy alliance ruled only by greed. For Segur, the empire expired on the frozen slopes of the hill.

In our conquering march eastwards this wooded knoll had seemed to our hussars little more than a slight irregularity in the earth's surface, from the top of which the entire plain of Vilna could be seen, and the strength of the enemy estimated. In truth, its steep but short slope had hardly been noticed. In a regular retreat it would have been an excellent position for turning around and checking the enemy; but in a chaotic flight, where everything that could be of use became a hindrance, when in blind haste we turned everything against ourselves, this hill and defile were an insurmountable obstacle, a wall of ice against which our best efforts were broken. It stripped us of everything – supplies, treasury, booty and wounded men. This misfortune was serious enough to stand above all our long succession of disasters; for it was here that the little money, honour, discipline, and strength remaining to us were irrevocably lost.

When, after fifteen hours of fruitless struggle, the drivers and soldiers forming the escort saw Murat and the column of fugitives go past them on the hillside; when they saw Ney himself withdrawing with the three thousand men remaining to De Wrede and Loison; when they turned around and saw the hill behind them littered with wagons and guns shattered and overturned, men and horses on the ground, dying on top of each other — then they no longer thought of saving anything, but only of forestalling the avidity of the foe by pillaging themselves.

The bursting of a wagon carrying loot from Moscow acted as a signal. Everybody fell upon the others' wagons, broke them open, and seized the most valuable objects. The soldiers of the rear-guard coming upon this confusion, threw down their arms and loaded themselves with the plunder. So furiously intent were they on this that they failed to heed the whistling bullets or shrieks of the Cossacks who were pursuing them. It is said that the Cossacks mingled with them without being noticed. For a few minutes Europeans and Tartars, friends and foes, were united in a common lust for gain. Frenchmen and Russians were seen side by side, all war forgotten, plundering the same wagon. Ten millions francs in gold and silver rapidly disappeared!

But along with these horrors, acts of noble devotion were noticed. There were men that day who forsook everything to carry off the wounded on their backs; others, unable to get their half-frozen companions out of the struggle, perished in defending them from the brutality of their fellow soldiers and the blows of the enemy.

... The catastrophe at Ponari was all the more shameful as it could have been easily foreseen, and even more easily avoided; for it was possible to pass around the hill on either side.[97]

On the top of the hill, Murat was greeted by an artillery battery freshly arrived from Germany. The commander of the battery asked him for orders. Murat gave a brusque answer: "Major, we are f----d. Get on your horse and run."[98] Galloping, Duke Fezensac took a last glance at Vilna. The rising smoke veiled the city, but beneath his feet he saw "a strange spectacle" of "men covered in gold and yet dying of hunger" and "scattered in the snow of Russia all the luxurious commodities of Paris."[99]

The first Russian sentry reached Vilna from the direction of the fleeing Napoleonic army. The Cossacks were led by the flamboyant poet Denis Davidov, who showed no pity for the dying enemy soldiers:

> From Novy Troki to the village of Ponari the road was clear and smooth. But from Ponari, where the road branches off to Kovno, mountains of dead men and horses, a host of carts, gun-carriages and caissons left barely enough room to get through; piles of enemy soldiers, barely alive, lay in the snow or sought shelter in the carts, awaiting a cold and hungry end. My path was lit up by blazing wooden huts and hovels whose wretched occupants were being burned alive. My sledge kept bumping against heads, legs and arms of men who had frozen to death, or were close to dying. My journey from Ponari to Vilna was accompanied by a strange chorus of moans and cries of human suffering which at times dissolved into something more akin to a joyous hymn of liberation.[100]

Patriotism aside, other officers of the Russian army were more reflective. For some time, Baron Boris Uxkull, a young Baltic-German supply officer, followed in the footsteps of the Cossack units, until he reached Vilna on December 1 (according to the Russian calendar). It was a nightmarish trek, marked by disbelief and self-incrimination. "We passed by all these phantoms, all these corpses, without a feeling or a shudder, we were so accustomed to the horrors of this destructive war. ... For eight days we watched all this, and for eight days I was surrounded by these terrors; for eight days I couldn't shut my eyes; these scenes will never be erased from my memory. How cruel man becomes the moment he loses his compassion and pity! The Cossacks continued playing tricks on these wretches."[101]

For Davidov, the re-conquered Vilna sparkled with sights of imperial glory. "I appeared before His Serene Highness on 1 December. What changes in the general headquarters! Whereas previously a ruined village and a smoky hut surrounded by sentries, or a log cabin with folding stools, served as a setting, I now saw a courtyard filled with fancy carriages and a crowd of Polish grandees in dress uniform, captured generals and our own generals and staff officers roaming all over the place!"[102] Uxkull saw a different picture. "We've finally arrived. What happiness! What joy! Our entry, which was supposed to represent a triumph, looked more like a masquerade. The costumes of the various regiments were really burlesque, and the Emperor, who arrived a day earlier and before whom we paraded, couldn't stop himself from laughing."[103]

36. Alexander I reviews the troops after the capture of Vilna by Russian forces in December of 1812 (from the diary of A. Chicherin).

The imperial review of troops signalled a pause in war manoeuvres. After chasing the remnants of the Napoleonic army beyond the frontier, the Russian forces were given a month of reprieve. The tsar took the same rooms in the general-governor's palace in Vilna where he had held court before the invasion in June. The Russian commanders and representatives of the allies followed suit and settled in the city in order to discuss further political strategies. With the occupation of Vilna came a hope for peace, and many Russian servicemen arrived in the town with a feeling of homecoming. In Vilna, Uxkull was reunited with his younger brother and took comfortable quarters at the elegant home of "Mme de Zidlerova," a young and "ravishingly pretty" widow. In the cosy and tender environment of the salon of the widow, who, after the death of her husband "had not abandoned the pleasures of this world," everything was "forgotten – danger, hunger, misery, cold and fever." The courtship between the young officer and the widow was brazenly swift. On the third day of his stay at her house, Uxkull calls her a deity who inflames his senses and imagination. A day later, she returns his adulation by calling him "her love and her lover." Days went by with "laughing and joking," remarked Uxkull in his diary. "My lovely hostess, after the fashion of her compatriots, sometimes sits on my knees and caresses me unscrupulously. I must confess to her my passion, in order to accelerate my victory and her defeat." In the darkness and coldness of a winter night, an "invisible light led me forward, and finally I touched the bed that contained so many charms, so many treasures. Two plump, rounded arms received me and pressed me against a breast softer than Persian silk, palpitating with pleasure and anticipation. A mouth burning with love sought my lips, which were already devouring the most secret of her charms. To slip beneath the cover, to press myself against her divine body, and swoon with lustfulness but a moment." As if mirroring the martial arts, the victory in amorous matters brought its own hazards: "Things will go on as before; but I'm afraid they will go on too quickly and too often for me, for I've been weakened, and my constitution may be ruined by all this 'too often' and 'too quickly.' "[104]

While love ruled supreme in some households, shivering cold shrouded the city. General Robert Wilson, a British military attaché to the Russian court, arrived in Vilna on December 17 and stayed there through Christmas and New Year. His diary paints the bewildering scene of death and triumph, united in the petrified landscape of a numbed mind:

December 17th, Wilna

I arrived at Wilna just as the Marshal [Kutuzov] was going to dine. From the plains of misery I passed to the banquet. After the dinner I found my quarters – a magnificent summer palace, but a winter ice-house; no fireplace, and only one stove, so that there are eighteen degrees of frost in the room in which I am obliged to sit and rest at night. Here I heard of Lord Tyrconnel's being sick in the house of an English professor at the University of Wilna. I immediately went to see him and found that he had been very ill, but was recovering. ... This evening I went to the play and was almost frozen. As it was a state occasion I was obliged to remain till the conclusion, but my teeth chattered again and when I rose to go I could scarcely use my limbs. There was not one lady in the house, which added to the wretchedness.

December 26th, Wilna

On the 20th died George, Earl of Tyrconnel, aged twenty-five years. ...Lord Tyrconnel had a vigour of mind which was polished with so much urbanity, that the exertion of it never alarmed the pride of others. ... On the 22nd the corpse was carried to the grave, escorted by two companies of the Imperial Guards, and interred with every honour that could be shown. I was, of course, chief mourner. The scene was solemn, and the tones of the music were irresistibly affecting. The human mind is strangely organized; existing misery is seldom participated in with deep sympathy, but fanciful woe melts the obduracy of habit and philosophy. ... "It is a strange world!" Adam is reported to have said when he entered into it; and so the last man will say. ... Yesterday was the Emperor's birthday. Parade, a confidential conference with the Emperor, mess, and twenty degrees of frost, were the incidents of the morning. The Marshal gave a great state dinner to the Emperor afterwards, on the occasion of his receiving the Order of St. George of the First Class.[105]

The unexpected Christmas thaw reminded Wilson of the impending mortal danger to the city. More than anything else, Vilna needed to purge itself of the dead. "Sickness had made very serious progress in the city. In fifteen days nine thousand prisoners have died, and in one eighteen hours seven hundred. The mortality has extended of course to the inhabitants. The physicians have ordered straw to be burnt before every house, but the pestilential atmosphere is not to be corrected by such lenitives; and as if fate resolved to spread the contagion to the utmost, there has been a thaw for the last twenty-four hours."[106] The gracious Baroque churches and monasteries turned into fetid urban cavities filled with rotting human flesh:

> The hospital of St. Basil presented the most awful and hideous sight: seven thousand five hundred bodies were piled like pigs of lead over one another in the corridors; carcasses were strewn about in every part; and all the broken windows and walls were stuffed with feet, hands, trunks and heads to fit the apertures, and keep out the air from the yet living. The putrefaction of the thawing flesh, where the parts touched and the process of decomposition was in action, emitted the most cadaverous smell.[107]

The dead patiently waited for the right moment to make their final lethal assault on the city: "In the spring Wilna must be a complete charnel-house. All the carcasses which were removed from the streets and hospitals are laid at a short distance from town in great masses; and then such parts as the wolves have not devoured during the winter will throw pestiferous miasmata back upon the city, which, from its position, is always shrouded in vapour."[108]

After travelling for a month through the horrible spectacle of death, Aleksandr Chicherin, a minor Russian officer and amateur painter, searched for normalcy in the reoccupied Vilna. He had been stationed in the city a few months earlier, and was simply expected "to rest for a while from life on the march, have a decent dinner, go to the theatre, stroll through boulevards, and amend his wardrobe."[109] More realistically, he just wanted to find a cup of good coffee and a piece of cake.

Chicherin was lodged in a house near the palace and could see the extensive preparations for the three-day spree of balls, parties, concerts and theatre performances marking the arrival of the Russian emperor. But because of his low rank, he ended up enjoying the festivities from a distance. Hence, he found Vilna to be no more than "a village: I did not attend the theatre; yesterday's ball proceeded without me; I did not go to the military parades, drills, and, in general, I do not go to any public gatherings. Yes, I almost forgot; yesterday I went to see the illuminations, but like a pondering philosopher, I meander through the streets of the city with the crowds trying to decipher the unfamiliar cryptograms" of the place.[110] In a different frame of mind, Uxkull, who, despite his private amorous adventures, was eager to explore the social life of the city, found the public spectacles to be much less esoteric: "This evening I visited the theatre; though I couldn't understand everything being said, I could easily see that the theatre wasn't worth much; as for the orchestra, it was terrible. There was a big audience, though most of the nobility have retired to their estates. The number of those women who carry their morals in their pockets and their virtues in their bonnets is quite large, but they repel me since I am paying court to my widow."[111]

Although Chicherin, not unlike Uxkull, thought he was "born to die for the fatherland," his belief in the war was shaken by the short stay in Vilna.[112] During his long walks through the city, his melancholy turns into existential angst – for the soul, victory could be as dangerous as defeat:

Everything I see around me makes me depressed. I am alone in the room, where I am tortured by melancholy and unfulfilled desires, and I do not have anybody to converse with; I stand up, dress up and go outside, where I hope to chase away my hopelessness by watching the life of the street. But what a strange mass of people I am encountering on my walks. Are these medical safe-guardians from epidemic diseases? Is this a destitute soul asking for help? Quickly, get rid of him, because he spreads diseases. Do you see this poor fellow, barely breathing near the bonfire that is supposed to eliminate the dangers of the epidemic? Run quickly – but if you are truly as compassionate as you think you are, you should have stabbed him with a sharp knife, because this is the only kind-hearted act he can hope to receive from you.

Now, please go with me to the busy thoroughfare of the city and you will see a different sort of revolting spectacle – the chaos of this world! Here everyone is running, waiting behind the doors, gathering around the windows. A general starts a conversation with a bureaucrat and tries to please him with sweet talk. A clerk rudely disperses the crowd – he is in a hurry – on his shoulders rests the fate of the fatherland.

It is simply impossible to describe what kind of things you can see if you live near the Imperial Headquarters, and what kind of melancholy all this turmoil induces! Is it feasible that this monstrosity that conceals a dagger under the mask of friendship – this poison in the air that comes from some corrupt breathing and infuses everything with a beautiful smell of flowers – always takes over people and incites their sinful desires? Is it possible that the love of the fatherland, truth, reason and justice – even in unison – will not be able to prevent this monstrous excitement from spreading around the city like a poisonous disease?![113]

In the end, for Chicherin, Vilna appeared to be a mirage, "a place so pleasant from a distance and so ornate with fantasies, but where it was impossible to find any enjoyment."[114] So when the order came to leave on Christmas Eve, he made a biting farewell: "goodbye Vilna, goodbye for ever."[115] Uxkull, who left the city on New Year's Day, was less morose. His affair with the widow ended in the style of a grand finale of *opéra bouffe*. To test the love of his "belle", Uxkull encouraged his comrade and roommate to court Mme de Zidlerova. The widow "taking the bait," Uxkull realised his friend "has triumphed. Is it possible? I never believed this woman was so loose ... but I'm consoling myself. For that matter, it's better to believe only half of what women say. Adieu, dear Vilna, charming city. When shall I ever see you again?"[116]

Josef and Christine Frank's "triumphal return to Vilna" had to wait until the end of the summer of 1813.[117] Apparently, everyone in town was impatient to see and greet the couple, as if their arrival truly trumpeted the end of the war. Symbolically, the Viennese expatriates moved into their damaged home on Castle Street on August 12, on the day when Austria officially declared war on Napoleon.

Frank formed his knowledge of the Napoleonic occupation of Vilna mostly through hearsay, but for his memoirist depiction of the retreat he chose the painting of a little-known artist (J. Damel) as the narrative basis of the story:

> Upon my return to Vilna, all inhabitants of the city were telling me about the most indescribable spectacle — the retreat of the Napoleonic army through the streets of Vilna. A young artist made a painting of this tragic masquerade. I call it a "masquerade" because it is difficult to recognize the army soldiers under their grotesque costumes and covering shrouds. One of the soldiers, instead of the helmet, sports a velvet lady's hat with a black satin ribbon. ... Everyone's face is marked by hopelessness. Professor Groddek [a German professor of antique philology] detected in this unprecedented collapse of the Napoleonic army some peculiar features of the French and Gallic national character. In his opinion, they celebrate victory with an outburst of vulgar jubilation, but defeat breaks them down completely. The grief over the loss drives them to insanity. Another local academic, professor Cappelli, noted that long ago, his compatriot Machiavelli had already made a similar observation by comparing the victorious French to lions and the defeated ones to hares.[118]

Less hypothetically, the doctor was also told that in the winter months,

37. A view of Vilna from the surrounding hills in the 1820s.

there were more than 40,000 unburied corpses in Vilna and its suburbs. Most of the dead still wore some sort of military uniform; they were solidly frozen and stayed in the same place and position of the moment of their death. Occasionally, young local pranksters rearranged them differently. Naturally, as soon as the weather became warmer, this heaping mass of corpses posed a hazardous danger of various infectious diseases. The authorities ordered a mass burial and once the corpses were collected from the city, they were buried in long ditches, previously dug up by the French for defensive reasons: *Inciderunt itaque in fossam quam sibi ipsi fecerunt.*[119]

The speedy burial of the corpses was supervised by Frank's colleagues, and by the summer, Vilna appeared to be thoroughly cleansed. Luckily, there were also no signs of an epidemic. Frank credited the efficiency and ingenuity of the newly appointed Russian authorities with preventing an outbreak. But it helped that the city was only partially inhabited, as many residents who fled were slow to return. Despite the war, there was plenty of food, and the good summer weather promised a great harvest, so the prices of produce quickly returned to their pre-war level. Of all the towns of Lithuania visited by the

Franks on their way home, Vilna seemed to be the least damaged. In fact, the professor found the city to be in better shape than before the war, thanks to the energetic new Russian governor, General Korsakov, who "ordered a clean-up of the suburbs from piled dung, created new promenades, planted trees and repainted the tarnished houses and bruised churches."[120]

In postwar Vilna, Frank's loyalty to the Russian empire compromised him in the eyes of many locals. While a general amnesty was given by the tsar to all of those who served in the Napoleonic army or the occupational regime, a deep mistrust and animosity between the pro-Russian and pro-French supporters was still ripping the town apart. The university became the epicentre of this hostility: many students had joined the Grande Armée and subsequently perished during the retreat. A vast majority of the professorship also welcomed Napoleon as the liberator of Lithuania. In spite of this wholehearted support, the university was not spared pillage. During the French occupation, its buildings were turned into barracks and hospitals, and practically all of its scientific equipment and academic inventory was looted and destroyed. (There were rumours about hungry soldiers drinking and eating all of the alcohol-soaked anatomical preparations stored at the university's clinic.) The Russian authorities blamed the collaborating faculty members for the damages. The old rector Śniadecki was forced to resign, and loyal Frank was suggested as his replacement. Frank declined the offer in the hope of preserving his academic neutrality and professional independence.

Amidst this academic turmoil, the Franks were trying to help many refugees and prisoners of war remaining in the city. The Franks were flooded with letters pleading for help:

> Not everyone knew that, during the war, I left Vilna. My father [in Vienna] had received countless letters from French, Dutch, German and, especially, Italian families pleading with me to find out about the fate of their relatives among the prisoners of war in Russia; in the case of death, I was asked to provide a death certificate necessary in order to resolve the issues of inheritance and other domestic concerns. In Vienna, I had too received such requests. With the help of Monsieur Horn [the head supervisor of POW in Lithuania], I tried to do my best. However, I could only find data on very few individuals. In general, people died unaccounted for: many froze to death on the road, were burned in military camps or drowned in the rivers; some died from hunger near their fatigued horses, because they did not have energy to feed them; and some were killed by Russian peasants and Polish Jews. 'Can you give me information about those who died in the hospitals of Vilna,' I asked monsieur Horn. 'Of course, but I can only provide information regarding the ones who died after the establishment of order. Before then, there was no opportunity to register the dead' was his answer.[121]

Among the survivors of the campaign, Frank found his sister's husband, Colonel Peternelli from Baden. In addition, the professor also met some of his colleagues, acquaintances and even former students from Austria, France, Savoy, Tyrol, Lombardy, Westphalia, Bohemia, Tuscany and Naples. His wife too discovered among the refugees her former colleague and friend, the famous Italian opera singer Tarquini, who was brought to Moscow to entertain Napoleon.

The war also greatly affected the well-being of the local population, and, in such cases, Frank could certainly be more useful and productive. Upon arrival in Vilna, he immediately started to investigate the geographical and social trajectories of various diseases. He pointed to the existence of a direct correlation between the spike in cardiovascular disorders and war-induced stress. And he also researched a psychological condition known today as post-traumatic stress disorder. Simultaneously, Frank instigated research on the spread of *plica Polonica*. To his disappointment, he found no evidence of the disease in Lithuania. After examining a few patients with the symptoms attributed to *plica Polonica*, he came to conclusion that the illness, if it ever existed, was neither hereditary, nor contagious, nor caused by the local climate. Based on his scientific observations, he determined that the syndrome was caused by nothing more than a misguided traditional remedy to fight various neurological disorders. *Plica Polonica* was an ailment caused by bad hygiene that was forced on mental patients by the traditions of medical inertia. Apparently, this unhealthy condition, like Sarmatia, was more invention than reality. Ignorant foreign observers, including some doctors, made a cultural mystery out of it by turning it into a medical sensation.

Frank also credited himself with dispersing some of the local social prejudice directed against the survivors of the Grande Armée's annihilation. Among the hundreds of civilian refugees of the retreat from Moscow who remained in Vilna, there was a certain Charlotte Kops née Devi, an intriguing young woman, whose national origins and social status were shrouded by the dramatic story of her survival. According to Frank, Madam Kops was an elegant and well-educated Englishwoman who, some years before 1812, married a Polish merchant in Moscow. Nobody knew why Madam Kops came to Russia, but possibly she worked there first as a governess. During the French occupation of Moscow, the merchant was appointed a city councillor and the couple was forced into flight with the Grande Armée. During the retreat, Madam Kops ambiguously claimed to have shielded herself and her husband from certain death. The couple safely reached Vilna, but on Ponary Hill they were attacked by the Cossacks and in the extreme cold, almost naked, they were forced to come back to the city. Despite the husband's collaboration with

38. Ostrabrama Street in Vilna in the first part of the nineteenth century.

the French, the Russian authorities allowed the couple to stay in Vilna, where they managed to set up a small smithy. Charlotte Kops, because of her beauty and intriguing life story, was immediately noticed by upper class onlookers and soon became the fixture of various disgraceful rumours and voyeuristic adventures. She was constantly harassed by amorous and sexually suggestive male comments, but local upper class women were especially mean to her, for, according to Frank, they repeatedly "went to look at her in hordes and through binoculars analyzed her features. 'She is very pretty,' one lady would say. 'Too bad that her manners are so English,' would answer the other."[122]

Frank was intrigued and probably even seduced by Madam Kops. He became her social patron and possibly a lover; but instead of secretly going to see her in the shop, he made the dramatic public statement of being often seen with her at various happenings. The professor even invited her to his family home, where he presented her to the members of the social elite of Vilna. For a moment, his public affair with Madam Kops scandalized the city, but this was possibly the reaction he was trying to provoke. After his return, Frank seemed to become more assertive in his criticism of the insular life of Vilna. Frank's open liaison with Mrs. Kops differed greatly from his earlier more secluded and perhaps more cherished relationship with Mrs. Simpson, the widow of the Jewish merchant.

Ten years after his return from Vienna, Frank began to contemplate leaving Vilna. He felt attached to the city and its people, but did not want to choose between his loyalty to the tsarist regime and the local resentment towards it. Frank's commitment to Vilna remained strong throughout the years and even after the death of his adopted son Victor, in 1819, he was still hoping to acquire a villa for his retirement in one of the picturesque corners of the city. He only decided to abandon Vilna in the summer of 1823, when the tsarist police uncovered an anti-Russian conspiracy at the university. The fear of revolution or a national (Polish-Lithuanian) revolt gripped the imperial administration: the rector of the university was detained and the mutinous students were sent to prison. Frank recognised that these arrests meant the end of the "Sarmatian concord." He knew that Vilna under the absolute rule of the Russian empire was going to be a hostile and oppressive place to live. Still, he recalls the family's decision to return to Vienna as one of the most painful moments of his life:

> I will always remember the people of Vilna fondly. The hardest was to say goodbye to my patients, friends and the city where I encountered so much good. I never regretted that I had spent the best years of my life in this generous country. I could have certainly gained more professional glory had I been teaching in one of the international centres of Europe, where foreign visitors are not a rarity. But in Vilna, like nowhere else in Europe, I had so many opportunities to practice my knowledge. It would make my heart bleed if the Lithuanians think that I only lived in Vilna for the sake of money I could spend later somewhere else. I would have happily retired in Lithuania had I not experienced a tremendous grief in the last year. I knew that sooner or later a storm would sweep through the university.[123]

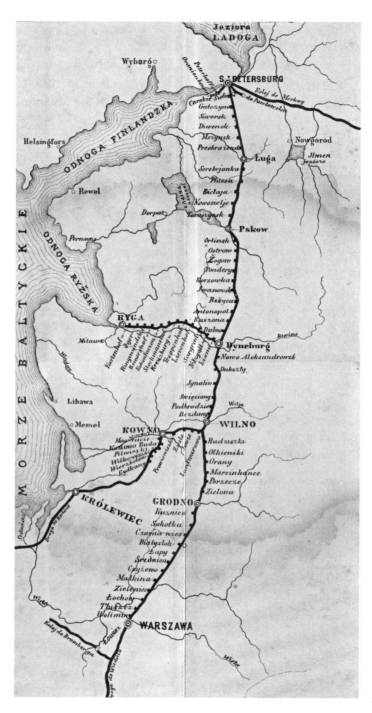

39. A plan of the Saint Petersburg to Warsaw railway, the main transportation artery connecting Russia with western Europe, 1863.

CHAPTER FIVE:

Russian Intrigue

> I want to travel in Europe, Alyosha, and I shall be going abroad from here. And yet I know very well that I'm only going to a graveyard, but it's most precious – yes, indeed! Precious are the dead that lie there. Every stone over them speaks of such ardent life in the past, of such a passionate faith in their achievements, their truth, their struggles, and their science, that I know beforehand that I shall fall on the ground and kiss those stones and weep over them and – and at the same time deeply convinced that it's long been a graveyard and nothing more. And I shall not weep of despair, but simply because I shall be happy in tears. I shall get drunk on my own emotions.

> *The Brothers Karamazov*, Feodor Dostoevsky

The Napoleonic wars changed Europe to benefit tsarist Russia. After the Russian army reached Paris, sweeping through the continent in pursuit of the relics of the Grande Armée, the country fully entered its imperial age. The Congress of Vienna, assembled by the victorious powers in 1814, sealed the fate of Vilna – the town, along with most of the territory of the former Grand Duchy, was to remain Russian. Although imperial Russia absorbed Lithuania in the dying years of the eighteenth century, it was only during the suffocating decades of the rule of Nicholas I (the unbending younger brother of Alexander I who came to power through the suppression of a liberal military mutiny in 1825) that the full scale of the obstructive imperial regime came to be felt. Inevitably, the War of 1812, christened in Russia as the Great Patriotic War, was turned into a key reference point of Russian authority over Vilna. Encouraged by its European neighbours, the tsarist family ruled over Vilna with a preconceived divine right believed to be the prerogative of any empire. Still, in the eyes of the wider Russian society, the Poles and Lithuanians, with their swinging loyalties and parochial stubbornness, were not to be trusted. The local nobility's dream of the resurrection of their failed Commonwealth was thought a major source of instability in Europe. In this geopolitical conception, Russia was supported by Prussia and Austria; France and England, on the other hand, were more sympathetic to the Polish-Lithuanian cause. Nonetheless, within the larger geopolitical map of Europe, Russian sway over Lithuania helped the continental balance of power last almost a century. Within Russia, Vilna guarded the imperial frontier to Western Europe. The city was considered a rightful Russian home, albeit plagued by disarray and an unruly spirit.

A half-century passed between the era of the Napoleonic wars and Leo Tolstoy's publication of *War and Peace*. Count Tolstoy (1828-1910), who spent more than a decade writing the novel, scrutinizes that historical period from the perspective of Russian society, and, among many other things, *War and Peace* is about Russia's place in Europe. In this intimately panoramic painting of life during war, Vilna becomes an important site of geopolitical transition. It is the place where Mother Russia turns into an empire, and thus barters the heroic idea of national self-sacrifice for the arrogance of an imperial conqueror. For Tolstoy, a crossing through Vilna was like a passage of honour: to the east of the city lay Russia – a familiar land offering spiritual comfort and self-respect; to the west – Europe – a foreign territory prompting national self-doubt and embarrassment.

Tolstoy made a brief stopover in Vilna in the spring of 1861 on his railway journey from Berlin to Saint Petersburg. The forty-one-year-old writer crossed the border between Prussia and Russia on April 12/24 (dated in both Julian and Gregorian calendars). He summarised the day in his diary: "Border. Healthy, happy, Russia is barely noticeable." The entry for April 13/25 – the most likely day of his Vilna visit – is more inscrutable. "Night with Jews. Lehman, cheerful mood. Chilly in the carriage, the vendor borrowed some money..."[1] Tolstoy created a more lengthy and memorable image of Vilna in his novel. In the first instance, the town appears briefly with the Grande Armée crossing into Russian territory. But a more detailed account emerges at the end of the novel, with the final portrait of the victorious Russian commander Kutuzov:

> On the 29th of November Kutuzov reached Vilna – his dear Vilna, as he used to call it. Twice during his military career Kutuzov had been governor of Vilna.
>
> In that wealthy town, which had escaped injury, Kutuzov found old friends and old associations, as well as comforts of which he had been so long deprived. And at once turning his back on all military and political cares, he plunged into the quiet routine of his accustomed life, so far as the passions raging all around him would permit. It was as though all that was being done, and had still to be done, in the world of history, was no concern of his now.
>
> ... The next day the commander-in-chief gave a dinner and ball, which the Tsar honoured with his presence.
>
> Kutuzov had received the Order of St. George of the first rank, and the Tsar had showed him the highest marks of respect, but every one was aware that the Tsar was displeased with the commander-in-chief.

... The Tsar's displeasure was increased in Vilna by Kutuzov's obvious unwillingness or incapacity to see the importance of the approaching campaign.

When the next morning the Tsar said to the officers gathered about him: "You have not only saved Russia, you have saved Europe," every one knew at once that the war was not over.

Kutuzov alone refused to see this, and frankly gave it as his opinion that no fresh war could improve the position of Russia, or add to her glory; that it could but weaken her position, and cast her down from that high pinnacle of glory at which, in his view, Russia was standing now. He tried to show the Tsar the impossibility of levying fresh troops, and talked of the hardship the people were suffering, the possibility of failure, and so on.

... The war of 1812, in addition to its national significance, dear to every Russian heart, was to take a new European character.

The movement of men from west to east was to be followed by a movement of peoples from east to west, and this new war needed a new representative, with other aims and qualities, and moved by impulses different from Kutuzov's.

For the movement from east to west, and the establishment of the position of peoples, Alexander was needed, just as Kutuzov was needed for the deliverance and the glory of Russia.

Kutuzov did not see what was meant by Europe, the balance of power, and Napoleon. He could not understand all that.

After the enemy had been annihilated, Russia had been delivered and raised to the highest pinnacle of her glory, the representative of the Russian people, a Russian of the Russians, had no more left to do. Nothing was left for the representative of the national war but to die. And he did die.[2]

While in Tolstoy's fiction, Vilna emerges as a comforting Russian town, in reality, tsarist rule over the city and Lithuania was not so placid. The hundred and twenty years of Russian domination (1795-1915) were punctuated by three insurrectionary wars – 1812, 1830-1831 and 1863-1864 – and the 1905 revolution. Each of these conflicts altered the political nature of the imperial regime as well as the local socio-cultural hierarchy.

The period before the 1830-31 insurrection was marked by a relative tolerance of Polish and, to a limited degree, Lithuanian cultural and religious activities. Overall, many traditional institutions and customs of Lithuania, such as its legal code, certain provincial privileges of the nobility, and the dominance of the Catholic church, were upheld. The political persecution and censorship in Vilna only increased after the discovery of a revolutionary plot among Polish students at the university in 1823. In general, the Imperial University had fostered a new generation of administrators and experts, such as doctors, geographers and geologists, for the entire Russian empire. Yet, especially after 1812, the university became the key centre of

Polish intellectual resistance to tsarist domination over the region. Its most famous students were the Polish Romantic poets Adam Mickiewicz and Juliusz Słowacki.

The university was closed in 1832 by a decree of Nicholas I after the suppression of the Polish-Lithuanian insurrection. In its place, the tsarist authorities opened the Medical Academy, which was also dissolved in 1842, and the Catholic Seminary, which was transferred to Saint Petersburg in 1844. Most of the institutional resources of the university – the professors, library materials and archives – were removed to other Russian academies. These and many other educational and cultural repressions diminished the intellectual status of Vilna: after more than two and a half centuries of active collegial life, Vilna ceased to be an important academic city.

Both sides – the Russians and Poles – understood Lithuania to be an occupied province. The Russians were attempting to suppress the cultural and linguistic Polonisation of the region, while the Poles were resisting its increased Russification. Following the scandalous eradication of the patriotic student organisations in Vilna, the Russian administration also introduced a new educational curriculum for the primary schools in Lithuania. In order to realign the region with the Russian imperial vision of the world, the teaching of history and geography was ordered to be conducted exclusively in the Russian language, instead of the customary Polish. This initiative attempted to counterbalance the cultural influence of the Catholic church and the Polish-speaking local nobility, but it did little to create a new generation of loyal Russian subjects.

At the core of the cultural struggle were the religious loyalties of the population. The Russian administration and intelligentsia often equated Polish patriotism with Jesuit conspiratorial fanaticism, thus creating a picture of the Russian-Polish conflict as a struggle between modern rationalism and medieval irrationality. After 1831, the tsarist regime initiated a far-reaching anti-Catholic campaign: the church's properties were requisitioned and monasteries closed down. However, the main victim of the tsarist religious oppressions in Lithuania was the Uniate church. In 1839, the practice of the Uniate faith was disallowed and its few million adherents were forcefully integrated into the Russian Orthodox church. In Vilna, this forced religious assimilation did little to challenge the Catholic demographic supremacy. In order to reduce Catholic visibility in the city, the tsarist authorities converted many churches into Orthodox shrines. Saint Casimir Church was turned into Saint Nicholas Basilica, adding distinctively Russian Orthodox features to its Roman Baroque facade.

40. Saint Casimir Catholic Church in Vilna as it appeared after the 1863-1864 Polish-Lithuanian insurrection against tsarist rule, when it was turned into the Saint Nicholas Russian Orthodox Cathedral.

Russification and the subsequent modernisation of Vilna affected local Jews in a different way. Before the annexation of Poland-Lithuania at the end of the eighteenth century, there were very few Jews in Russia. By the turn of the twentieth century, there were more than four and a half million Jews living in the Russian empire, almost two-thirds of European Jewry. With roughly seven hundred thousand Jews living in the Lithuanian provinces, the region held one of the highest Jewish population concentrations (roughly fifteen percent of the total) in Europe. The tsarist administration always treated this large Jewish population with great suspicion, and immediately after the incorporation of the annexed lands it placed restrictions on Jewish migration to other parts of the empire. The Pale of Jewish Settlement roughly coincided with the historical lands of the Polish-Lithuanian Commonwealth. On many occasions, the tsarist authorities also attempted to eliminate the communal autonomy and cultural distinctions of the Jews. In 1844, the Kahal, the oldest self-governing body of the Jewish community, was abolished. Russian-language schools for Jewish children were introduced throughout the Pale, and two state-run rabbinical seminaries, one of them in Vilna, were established.

41. The entrance to the courtyard of the Old Synagogue in Vilne, circa 1900.

In 1851, Jewish males were prohibited from wearing traditional garments and sidelocks (*peot*), and married Jewish women were ordered to stop shaving their heads. Most of these punitive initiatives were never enforced, and Jewish assimilation was limited. On the other hand, the large concentration of Jews in the Pale fostered an unparalleled flourishing of Jewish cultural, social and religious life. Subsequently, the Pale became the heartland of Ashkenazi Jewry, where important developments in modern Jewish history – Hassidism, Zionism, and Yiddish culture – came into maturity.

Among Jews, *Vilne* became known as the *Yerushalaim d'Lita* (Jerusalem of Lithuania). According to one legend, Napoleon was the first to give Vilne the name of Jerusalem. Reportedly, the numerical strength and piety of the city's Jewish community reminded the French Emperor of Jerusalem in the Holy Land, which he had visited during the failed Egyptian campaign of 1798-1799. But for most Jews, the title *Yerushalaim d'Lita* was not so much associated with Napoleon as with the flowering of Jewish culture which took place there. First and foremost, Vilne gained the title of Jerusalem of the North because of the scholarly reputation of Eliyahu ben Shlomo Zalman (1720-1797), more widely known as the Gaon of Vilne, whose life and work embodied the ideal of Jewish existence in exile. By the turn of the twentieth century, Vilne had became the place where, in the words of Benjamin Harshav, the modern Jewish revolution had occurred:

> [The] nickname "Jerusalem of Lithuania" was based on this fortress of Jewish learning and the printing of the whole Babylonian Talmud in Vilna. Yet apparently it was the secular movement, which in Vilna perceived itself as heir to the religious tradition, that invented and promoted this name. In 1859, a Hebrew book by the Maskil (enlightened writer) and scholar Rashi Fin (Samuel Joseph Fuenn) was published, describing the history of Vilna and its Jewish community. The book was called Kiryah Ne'emanah (Faithful City), describing Vilna in biblical terms used for Jerusalem. Had the name "Jerusalem of Lithuania" existed, Fin would have used it. It is, rather, the opposite: from the name of the book, the nickname was derived. The Vilna Yiddishist and secular movements, as well as modern Hebrew poetry, adopted the name, proud to continue the tradition of the Vilna Gaon.
>
> … Like Jena and Weimar, Cambridge and Oxford, Vilna was a small town, a cultural center serving an immense hinterland. The ties between Vilna and the network of small towns were very close, people travelled back and forth, the city served as a kind of 'shopping center' and cultural focus for the whole area, and many small towns fulfilled important roles as well: famous yeshivas were located in small towns such as Volozhin, Mir, Ponevezh; a major Hasidic sect, Chabad, that emerged in eastern Lithuania, had its capital in Lubavitch, a town of 1,667 Jews. Indeed, most Vilna writers and intellectuals were born elsewhere.… On the other hand, many young people from small towns came to the capital to study in its Rabbinical Seminary or in its Hebrew and Yiddish Teacher's Colleges, then to go back to a small town or emigrate to Palestine or the West.
>
> Hence, when a city of merely 60,000 Jews felt that it was a major center of a worldwide culture, it was because of its cultural institutions and the millions of Eastern European Jews they served and represented.[3]

For local Catholics, the name Jerusalem had a different meaning. In the 1660s, in gratitude for the deliverance of Lithuania from Russian occupation, the local Catholic bishop set up a pathway of Via Dolorosa on a hilly, forested bank of the Neris River, north of the city. This Baroque replica of Calvary became a major pilgrimage site in Lithuania, and had its imprint on local toponymy: a nearby brook was renamed Cedron and the neighbouring village acquired the name of Jerusalem, which is still used to this day.

The Russians, never more than a fifth of the total population, felt threatened by both the Catholic and the Jewish potency of the place. Throughout the imperial rule, Vilna's population was in permanent flux. While many people were moving in to the city from the surrounding provinces, great numbers were leaving it for more prosperous metropolitan centres around the world.

Its Russian population, consisting mostly of military and administrative officials and their families, was even more impermanent. The most transient were the Russian governors of Vilna: in the hundred and twenty years of tsarist administration, there were almost thirty of them.

But not all Russian, nor all Orthodox residents of the city were colonists. The cultural and religious links between Vilna and Byzantium (or, for that matter, Muscovy) had been in existence since the historical beginnings of the city. Many wives of pagan and Catholic Lithuanian grand dukes, for instance, came from Russian princely families. And the first local Christian martyrs were of the Byzantine Orthodox faith. This close and often intimate connection between Vilna and Eastern Christianity made the Russian imperial colonisation of the place a more imaginative, albeit no less brutal process. In essence, many Russians felt the city to be a rightful home, even if they experienced it only as a place of transit.

With increased political repressions and the closure of the university, Vilna's status as one of the largest and intellectually vibrant cities of the Russian empire gradually faded away. After 1812, Russian emperors and dignitaries rarely visited the city. By the end of the tsarist rule, Vilna was a medium-sized provincial town with little financial wealth or industrial potential. What saved the city from economic ruin and oblivion was the railway. The first train arrived from Dvinsk (Daugavpils in Latvia, or Dunaburg in German) from the direction of the imperial capital Saint Petersburg on September 4, 1860. The next year, the opening of a railway line to the Russian-Prussian frontier connected the city with Koenigsberg and Berlin.[4] Finally, with the completion of the Saint Petersburg – Warsaw railway in 1862, Vilna was securely bolted onto the map of the empire as an important transportation hub.

Travelling from Berlin to Saint Petersburg in the last decade of the nineteenth century, Danish ethnographer Age Meyer Benedictsen (1866-1927) described the trip through Lithuania in a series of random snapshots:

> Many people have passed through Lithuania without knowing it or giving it a thought. The big railway lines which connect the capitals of Russia and Germany cut right through Gediminas's heritage, right through the land where the Lithuanian peasants still reside. Seated in comfortable trains, men and women view indifferently the somewhat monotonous country with its wide acres of waving corn, with its undulating woodlands of birch and maple, oak and fir. One rushes past low wooden homesteads, and the train stops at stations with peculiar names, Schillen, Pilkallen, Gumbinnen, Eydtkuhnen, names which are meant to be German and yet sound so foreign; but it is only these names which interfere with the

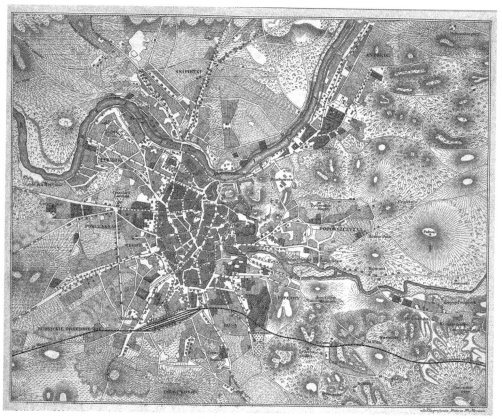

42. A plan of Vilna, 1882.

idea that one is travelling in Germany. Everything in the train is German, the passengers, the guards, the printed regulations; the railway stations look like those of Rhineland and Hanover, there is the same red capped "Vorstand", the same high-shouldered primness in the barmaids, the same waiters in the same "alldeutsche" dining room. Then one reaches the frontier, one sees for the last time the black, white and red flag, the spiked helmet and German order – across the line and you are in Russia. Passports must be shown, and one sees placards in those angular letters which rather annoy one because one does not understand them. Dark blue gendarmes with red braiding parade the deserted platform. Then the custom house officers arrive, carriages are changed, one gets Russian cows and hears the Russian tongue, as one might expect having arrived in Russia – and the train steams on its way. Again stations which for the uninitiated might pass for Russian, but which to the Russians themselves have a foreign ring: Gielgudiski, Vilkoviski, Pilviski and so on. In the carriages, Russian, German and perhaps Polish are to be heard. Gendarmes and black bloused soldiers with round caps, bells, long boots and grey mantles flung loosely over the shoulders are to be seen at each station and as a most peculiar type, novel to us Westerners, the celebrated Polish Jew, his loosely knit figure in his shabby clothes with his bent hands and unkempt beard, this aggregate of ugliness, who at first sight seems to explain everything – his character, his mode of living and his Pariah existence. Half a day and half a night has passed during which one has slept or lazily gazed at the flat country, listened to the wheels thundering across the river bridges, or rattling through pine forest. One may have noticed with some interest a group of long legged Cossacks with flat caps and thick necks who have pulled up on their small ugly horses near the railway line, they are so like what one has read about that one can't help feeling a little amused. Or one may have noticed clumsy wooden carriages harnessed to three fat horses which eagerly paw the ground and snort in answer to the driver's chatter; they have come from the neighboring manor house to meet the squire on his return from his trip abroad. Here and there gilded or green bulb-shaped domes are quickly passed and at last one pulls up at a big town, Dunaburg, and one has traversed Lithuania, of a truth without being any the wiser.[5]

While the railway made Lithuania more obscure, it also brought many accidental visitors to Vilna. In the initial stages of travel, all passengers travelling to or from Russia had to disembark and change trains in Vilna. The required stopover imprinted the name of the city on everyone's itinerary. But arrival by train put the city out of sight: the longest railway tunnel in the empire, launched in 1860 by Tsar Alexander II, cut straight through Paneriai (Ponary) Hill. For centuries, everyone arriving into the city could wonder at its panoramic exposition, but the dark tunnel with its steep ramparts – a marvel of nineteenth-century engineering – allowed no time or sight of it. After a few minutes of dimness, the train pulled into an ordinary train station built on the outskirts of the city. It was a poor introduction to Vilna.

From the middle of the nineteenth century, it became possible and fashionable for Russian intellectuals to travel to Europe. A leisure trip abroad was a seasonal affair: it usually coincided with the beginning of the summer season at the famous spas of western Europe or the winter holidays on the Mediterranean coast. Many of those who made the trip, like Tolstoy, wrote diaries or journals, where Vilna marked the beginning or end of the European adventure. In this context, the city became a gateway location, in both the experiential and narrative senses of the word.

The Russian playwright Aleksandr Ostrovsky (1823-1886) visited Vilna in the spring of 1862. Ostrovsky's plays exposed the degrading social conditions of the emerging Russian capitalist system, often from the perspective of women's plight. Nicholas I personally censored his writings and put him under police surveillance, but during the liberal years of Alexander II, he was allowed more personal and creative freedom. The social realism of his plays resonated with audiences: his works were so popular that even the English-language Murray's guide advised visitors to Moscow who "may not understand the dialogue" to attend his plays in order to "study the manners and customs of the country as depicted on the stage."[6]

Before his trip to Europe, the thirty-nine-year-old playwright resolved to write a journal. In contrast to Tolstoy (who was only able to return home on the newly-opened railway line), Ostrovsky was leaving Russia by train. His first entry was penned in Vilna:

April 2/April 14

We left Petersburg on April 2 (Monday) at 3 p.m. …We decided to stay in Vilna and see the local sights.

April 3/15 Lithuania

At 12:30 p.m. we arrived in Vilna. The weather is splendid, not a sight of snow; in Moscow, this sort of weather only occurs in late April. We stayed at the hotel of Zhmurkevich, behind the Ostra Brama gate. From the first sight, the city amazes you with its originality. All of it is built in stone, with narrow, unbelievably clean streets, tall houses with tiled roofs and majestic churches everywhere you look. We had lunch at Yodke's; it is a small tavern – just two rooms – and is serviced only by a young lad, the daughter of the owner and the owner himself (a comedian) who constantly reaches for a glass of Madeira. After lunch, we drove to view the town. Above the city looms a mountain with several peaks; on one of the cone-shaped peaks there is a tower. These hills and the city present an incredibly and uncommonly beautiful picture. We hired a coach, so we could drive up to the mountain; passed by the church of Saint John, the governor's house, the Cathedral (went inside), and reached the banks of the flooded Viliya River; at the nearby military barracks we left our coach and started to climb the steep slope of the hill. We very much wanted to look at the city from above and by four o'clock, well rested, we somehow reached the top of the mountain: apparently, the site was guarded by the military bastion and we were rudely commanded to get down without any delay. During our walk down the slope, a sweet student from local gymnasium gathered some early spring flowers (anemones). He gave them to us. Flowers here are already in bloom, while the fresh grass is just emerging. We went back to our coach and decided to drive to see the church of Saint Peter and Paul. On the left, there is the Viliya River, and on the right, there are hills covered with pine trees: a perfect place for a summer outing. The exterior of the church is nothing special, but the interior is splendid – all walls and domes are fully plastered. One can rarely encounter such an opulent spectacle.

April 4/16

The weather is overcast and cold: we trotted through the city, went to the Bernardine Church (architecturally the most significant in the city). In addition, we went to the Saint John Church, a huge and magnificent building and full of

43. The interior of the Church of Our Lord Jesus (Trinitarian) in Vilna, 1847.

people. In front of the church, a pretty Polish maiden assumes the duty of church superintendent. By thumping her delicate fingers on the plate, she tries to get the attention of the public. In general, there are plenty of beautiful Polish ladies in Vilna, and on some occasions, one can see even a few good-looking Jewish women. Here, for the first time, I saw the passion of the Catholic piety: men and women on their knees, with prayer books in their hands, in a complete seclusion of prayer; and this piety is seen not only in the churches, but also in the streets, especially in front of the Ostra Brama. This site is a local shrine – above the gate is the chapel with a miracle-working icon of the Mother of God, an icon of Greek [Orthodox] origins. (Initially, it belonged to the Orthodox, but later, somehow, the Poles acquired it.) At the Bernardine Church we saw a man in prostration, spread like a cross on cold stone floor. All churches are open all day long, and they are full with many praying people, mostly women, who during this Holy Week look extremely solemn. In contrast, the Jews celebrate their Passover finely dressed and clean (unlike on regular days), they stroll in the company of their overdressed wives and children. Most Jewish women decorate their headgear in the traditional way; we met very many Jewesses, all dressed in simple, grey blouses and on top of their wigs wearing (black) laced veils adorned with colourful ribbons and flowers. We breakfasted at Yodke's again, where I had a very good local fish. Honestly, Polish servants are very good, meticulous but without being too slavish; the same could be said about local coachmen.

April 5/17

Woke up – snow! We packed and went to the train station; we waited forever for the train; incidentally, delays are quite common with the French, and the criticism and scorn they receive are well deserved. In general, they are rude, and above all, they are scoundrels and charlatans.... Cold and snow. In Verzhblovo – a European style restaurant-buffet.

Prussia. Eydtkuhnen. Order and accuracy ... our train was late and we missed the train to Berlin.[7]

Ostrovsky's visit to Vilna was framed by two important events: the abolition of serfdom in the Russian empire and the second Polish-Lithuanian insurrection against tsarist rule. In Vilna, according to the official account, "the demonstrations had started as early as 1861 with revolutionary hymns sung inside the churches and in the open, public spaces – in front of the Mother of God of the Ostra Brama. On August 6, a grand procession of a huge singing crowd carrying revolutionary banners, nationals flags and symbols of Poland and Lithuania moved towards the outskirts of the city to the Pohulianka suburb to greet another procession that, according to the rumours, was coming to Vilna from the direction of Kovno." The local administration ordered the Cossacks to seal off the city. At this point, "the demonstrators, headed by fanatical young ladies, tried to squeeze through the rows of the soldiers guarding the city." These mutinous "mademoiselles turned their umbrellas into dangerous weapons: they pointed their sharp ends to the faces of the soldiers. The Cossacks lost patience, took up rifles and dispersed the crowd." There were some casualties: a nobleman and artisan "were injured, but quickly recovered." The tsarist authorities accused "the Polish newspapers abroad" of spreading a lie about "a great battle in the city with many people killed or drowned in the river." The Catholic bishop of Vilna was implicated for "declaring a three-week vigil for the (phantom) victims of this battle."[8] To prevent similar occurrences, the tsarist government declared martial law in the city. Yet the military rule failed to calm the rebellious population, and when Ostrovsky (with his spouse and a family friend) arrived in Vilna in the spring of 1862 during the Catholic Holy Week and Jewish Passover, Lithuania was on the verge of explosion. Within months, the countryside surrounding Vilna became a theatre of war, with the imperial forces battling armed units of local insurgents.

Once again Vilna re-entered the imperial map as a site of a decisive geopolitical battlefield. This time, however, the struggle was between the Polish and Russian character of the place. The annihilation of the "band of insurgents" in the spring of 1863 near the old Lithuanian capital, declared *Severnaya Pchela (Northern Bee)*, a liberal political and literary newspaper of Saint Petersburg, "extinguished the hope among the residents of Vilna" for the restoration of Polish national sovereignty. "At the sight of the victorious and joyful return of our [Russian] troops to Vilna, the Poles grieved openly" and put on black mourning clothes. [9]

In the same issue of *Severnaya Pchela,* a different article described everyday life in Vilna. The insurrection and the question of the city's national belonging was conspicuously absent from this portrait of the city aimed at visitors. The lack of modern urban amenities, such as street lighting, paved sidewalks and wide avenues, was identified as the greatest hazard for metropolitan visitors; and because all trains arrived in the city at night, Vilna, despite being situated in one of the most beautiful natural settings in Europe, gave an impression of a dark, unwelcoming, and potentially dangerous place. Another local nuisance noted by the reporter was the peculiar regime of the city's commercial life, which, to the great shock of Russian readers, followed the religious calendar of the Jewish faith, with Sundays and Christian holidays being the busiest shopping days of the month. Jewish merchants were also accused of making Vilna an obscenely expensive town, despite the visible poverty of its many residents. Overall, concluded the paper, Vilna was in desperate need of a strong ruling hand that could transform the medieval town into a modern city.

One aspect of Vilna's life, however, was praised as a noteworthy example of a model civic society. "Just by looking at the street life of Vilna," noted the reporter, "one can easily detect that women here are respected in the most admirable way. Unlike in Saint Petersburg, a young lady in Vilna can freely walk alone in the evening through the crowded streets without exposing herself to the insulting lewd comments of loitering sleazebags. In general, Don Juans, if they even exist here, are rare among the youth of Vilna. This should be viewed not only as a compliment to local men who show great respect to women, but also as a tribute to local women capable of earning such a reverence." The social roots of this gallantry were also easy to find, for "the education of women in the western regions of the empire is advancing rapidly, and, most importantly, learning here is not limited, as in the past, to superficial flirting, but shows some practical directions." In Vilna "young ladies are no longer salon dolls" and "many of them demonstrate a very sound and practical view on life."[10]

The Russian media interest in Vilna heralded dramatic political and cultural changes in Lithuania. In May of 1863, the imperial government sent the newly appointed general-governor Mikhail Muraviev to Vilna to crush the rebellion and make Lithuania a loyal and inseparable part of Russia. Muraviev, who was born in 1796, was familiar with political radicalism. In his youth, he was active in the liberal circles of Russia. (His brother was one of the Decembrists, a group of Russian officers who unsuccessfully tried to overthrow Nicholas I in 1825.) Despite his compromising family and social ties, Muraviev became a dependable servant of the Russian autocracy.

While the Russian army was chasing the rebels, Muraviev took the fight into the streets of Vilna. Just two weeks after his appointment, the new governor issued a law prohibiting local women from dressing in black or wearing any jewellery with macabre or funerary attributes: crosses, skulls, chains, black ribbons, etc. According to the order, any civil servant whose female family members wore black in public could immediately lose his job. A similar law forbade the use of the colour black in the painting or decorations of any building in the city – public or private. Funerals, too, were only allowed with special permits. In short, any signs of mourning, along with other Polish and Lithuanian patriotic symbols, were simply expelled from the city. Further, Muraviev brought the spectre of persecution straight into the city by ordering public hangings of the leaders of the rebellion. He became known as Muraviev the Hangman.

Next, Muraviev made an assault on language. The public use of Polish in the city was forbidden and the Latin alphabet of the Lithuanian language was outlawed and replaced with Cyrillic. In addition, the rights of the Polish-speaking nobility were severely restricted, and most Catholic monasteries and churches were closed. The historical name of Lithuania was also expunged from public usage. It was replaced with a more abstract spatial denominator, the *Severo-zapadnyi krai* (the North-Western region).

The repression made the city appear not so much Russian as tragic, and in 1867, three years after the revolt, British travellers on their way to Saint Petersburg were alerted by their travel guide to the contentious and melancholic qualities of the place:

> The repressive measures of Gen. Mouravieff [M.N. Muraviev] in 1863 and 1864 were dated from Wilna. Here the leaders of the hopeless insurrection in the provinces were confined, tried, hung and shot. The reduction in the N.W. provinces by deportation to distant parts of the empire is variously estimated at 50,000 to 100,000 souls. The political vicissitudes to which these provinces have been subjected and the mixed nature of their population afford a fertile and disastrous source of disagreement between the Russians and the Poles.

44. Vilna as the ancient gateway to the Russian Empire, 1872.

Wilna, 441 m. from St. Petersburg. Pop. 58,000. Chief town of the ancient independent Duchy of Lithuania ... lies in a hollow at the foot of several hills which rise to some height on the E.S., and W. The Viliya river runs out at the northern extremity of the hollow, and winding through deep and intricate ravines, clothed with foliage of the fir, the birch, and the lime, presents a most picturesque and smiling panorama, little in keeping with the stern deeds of retribution which have made Wilna so famous. ... The churches will repay a visit. They possess considerable architectural merit, and among their monuments will be found those of several families whose names are familiar to all readers of Polish history.[11]

In the same year, Russian writer Feodor Dostoevsky (1821-1881) passed through the city on his way to Germany. Dostoevsky conceived his trip as an escape. In the late fall of 1866, after a month-long courtship, the forty-six-year-old writer proposed to Anna Grigoryevna Snitkina, his twenty-one-year-old stenographer. At the time, Dostoevsky, according to Anna Grigoryevna, "'was standing at a crossroads and three paths lay open before him.' He could go to the East – Constantinople and Jerusalem – and remain there, 'perhaps forever'; he could go abroad to play roulette, and 'immolate himself in the game he found so utterly engrossing'; or he could 'marry again and seek joy and happiness in family life.' "[12] Anna Grigoryevna happily agreed to marry Dostoevsky and save him from wrongdoing. The wedding was celebrated in Saint Petersburg amidst the grandeur of the Izmailovsky Cathedral in the winter of 1867.

The happy life of the newlyweds was short-lived. At the time, Dostoevsky was supporting his extensive family, including a grown stepson, a sister-in-law and her several children. Besides his own huge debts, he had inherited enormous financial obligations from his late brother. Money was a constant problem and source of tension – daily quarrels, accusations, deceptions, intimidations and demands plagued the family. Anna Grigoryevna's "presence, moreover, was resented as that of an interloper who threatened to undermine the expectations of those accustomed to live off Dostoevsky's by no means secure or uninterrupted income."[13] As a result, the writer could only write and read at night and, as his young wife soon discovered, it was simply impossible for the newlyweds to spend any time alone.

The stress built up, and within days after the wedding, Anna Grigoryevna found out that Dostoevsky suffered from a severe form of epilepsy. The bride remembered it as a terrible sight. While talking to her, Feodor Mikhailovich became "extremely animated" and then "there was a horrible, inhuman scream, or more precisely, a howl – and he began to topple forward."[14] A few weeks later, Dostoevsky's family accused Anna Grigoryevna of provoking his seizure with her presence. Her position in the family had "become increasingly burdensome and frustrating; and it was largely because of her dissatisfaction, as well as her determination to save her marriage at all costs – even at the price of some personal financial sacrifice – that the Dostoevskys decided to go abroad in the spring of 1867."[15] The trip abroad was also encouraged by Anna's Swedish mother, whose "view of life," according to her daughter, "was more Western and more cultured; and she feared that the good habits inculcated by my upbringing would vanish thanks to our Russian style of living, with its disorderly hospitality."[16]

This was the first trip abroad for Anna Grigoryevna, and she was thrilled. But Dostoevsky had already been abroad a few times. The last time he had been in Europe was in 1864, after the death of his first wife. He lost all his money gambling in the casinos and hated it. This time, Dostoevsky pledged to make a more pleasant journey, and with that in mind, the couple said goodbye to the misery of Saint Petersburg. On a spring day, they were "accompanied to the railroad station by Anna Grigoryevna's relatives as well as by Emilya Feodorovna [sister-in-law], her daughter Katya, and Dostoevsky's old friend the Milyukovs (Milyukov had come to say good-bye to him in the Peter and Paul Fortress before he left for Siberia, and greeted him at the railroad on his return). Pasha, in a fit of pique, was not among the party; he refused to join in wishing Godspeed and a pleasant voyage to his stepfather and his new bride."[17] The Dostoevskys were planning to go first to Berlin and later to Dresden, where they intended to settle for several months. As usual, the journey to Germany required a night stopover in Vilna.

Before leaving, "Anna Grigoryevna had promised her mother to keep an account of the trip, and she purchased a notebook at the station just before the departure to fulfill that obligation. This diary, which she kept until the birth of her first child a little over a year later, provides a more extensive and detailed account of the day-to-day events in Dostoevsky's life than we possess for any other period of his existence."[18] In general, her diary details the "immediate and quite straitened circumstances in which they lived, the problem of adjusting to Dostoevsky's continually changing mood, and the difficulties of living in a foreign environment where they did not know a soul and were constantly thrown back on themselves for companionship."[19] Anna Grigoryevna opens her daily account of life with Dostoevsky in Vilna:

> 2 o'clock in the afternoon of April 15 we arrived at Vilna. Very soon, the lackey from Han, the hotel on Bolshaya [Great] Street, picked us up and drove us to the hotel. At the gate of the hotel, we were stopped by an acquaintance of Feodor Mikhailovich, Mister Barsov. He told us that he lives in Vilna, and he will pick us up at six and then show us around the city. In the hotel we had to climb many stairs, because we were showed one room after the other – but all of them were terribly dirty. Fedya wanted to leave until we finally found a good room where we could peacefully settle for the night. The hotel servants were very strange – no matter how long you rang for their service, they never responded. There was something else uncanny about them: two of them were missing the left eye, and Fedya thought that in this town, the one-eyed servants might not be out of ordinary, because those with a missing eye were probably less expensive to hire.
>
> We had lunch and went to see the city. It looks quite big but with narrow streets, wooden walkways and tiled red roofs. Today is Easter Saturday, and because of it,

the streets are very busy. In particular, there are many Yids with their wives, all covered in yellow and red shawls and laced scarves. The coachmen here are very cheap. We got tired of touring on foot and hired a coach; he drove us around the town almost for nothing. Everybody is in a holiday mood; the streets are full of people carrying various pastry and Easter cakes. The Catholic churches are full of parishioners. We went to say a prayer at the Russian church of Saint Nicolas the Miracle-Worker on Bolshaya Street. After that we briefly went to the Catholic church on Ivanovo Street. Later we saw a cross on the hill and the Viliya River. This is a very rapid river, but not wide; the view from the river bank to the distant mountains, the cross and the cemetery is very beautiful. It must be very nice here in the summer when everything is in bloom. We visited the [Nevsky]

45. "Greetings from Vilna: Bolshaya (Great) Street." The Dostoevskys stayed in the hotel located on this street.

chapel on Georgevsky square that was recently erected to commemorate the pacification of the Poles; I liked it very much, it is such a beautiful, simple, and elegant chapel. At seven p.m. we came back to the hotel, had some tea and went to sleep. All the hotel staff left for church, but before they went out, one of the servants instructed us to lock ourselves in from the inside. Feodor Mikhailovich thought this was a perfect scheme to rob us while everybody was away. He started to block all the doors with tables and our luggage. At night, at a quarter to two o'clock, Fedya had a seizure, a very strong one; it lasted for fifteen minutes. ... [The next morning], when we were ready to leave, some Yid came to our room and asked us to buy something from him. We had forgotten to bring along soap, so I bought a piece of egg soap for 15 kopecks. A friend of his offered us some kind of Polish icon, which, according to his words, cost him 15 roubles, but he was willing to sell to us for much cheaper; all the same, we declined to buy it. Before long, our entire room swarmed with Yids who wanted to help us; everyone was saying farewell and rushed to move our luggage, and, in the end, all of them of course asked for a tip. We were already sitting on the coach and had started to move when suddenly we were besieged by another Yid; he wanted us to sell two amber cigarette holders –

we told him to get lost. At the station we waited for a very long time. We bought tickets for the direct train to Berlin and paid 26 roubles and 35 kopeks each. We were the only passengers in the second-class carriage, so we had plenty of sleep. ... Around eight o'clock in the morning we arrived at Verzhblovo, where we had our last meal in Russia. ... When we came back to our seats, some official, probably a German, came to our carriage and very rudely asked: "Name?" Fedya got angry and asked if he was a German and wanted to say: "What is your name?" After this incident, we got back our passports and moved on to Eydtkuhnen. The two stations (Verzhblovo and Eydtkuhnen) are separated by a rivulet, which separates Russia from the Prussian domain.[20]

Dostoevsky's uneasy encounter with Vilna is a reflection of the writer's own version of the Russian official xenophobia. A small circle of liberal Russian intellectuals was sympathetic to the political goals of the Polish-Lithuanian insurgents, but Dostoevsky was not within this group. Despite being a convicted political offender, the writer was firmly on the side of the autocracy. He supported the repressive measures of the imperial administration and shed no tears for the perished, exiled and dispossessed inhabitants of Lithuania. It was, he believed, the only way to purge the region of the insidious influence of Polish Catholicism. The festive Catholic tone and Jewish character of the city only inflamed his chauvinism. For Dostoevsky, " 'Jew' and 'usurer' were synonymous, an established fact that required no substantiation."[21] And in typical anti-Semitic fashion, the Dostoevskys regarded the Jews as local non-entities: "[the Jew] has even lost the title to his name; he is the "Yid" – the *zhid, zhidok, zhidishka, zhidyonok.*"[22] In contrast, the Catholic Poles proved to be much more secretive and, therefore, a more dangerous enemy to the Russian spirit. The traditional animosity between the Russian and Polish intelligentsia had existed since at least the eighteenth century, but it became particularly visible during and after the Polish-Lithuanian insurrection. Dostoevsky was obsessed with the idea of a Polish conspiracy to annihilate the Russian empire and the Russian Orthodox church. He was especially traumatised by the recent attempt to assassinate Alexander II, which paradoxically had nothing to do with the Polish-Lithuanian insurrection.

On April 4, 1866, the Russian emperor was shot at in Saint Petersburg by a student named Dimitry Karakozov. The emperor was not hurt, but Karakozov was immediately "dragged to Alexander II, who personally took his pistol from him and asked if he were a Pole. It seemed inconceivable to the Tsar that an attempt on his life should be made by anyone but a foreigner; yet Karakozov, who came from a family of small, impoverished landowners and who had been expelled from the university (like Raskolnikov) for failing to pay his fees, replied: 'Pure Russian.' "[23] Subsequently, "Count N.M. Muraviev, who had suppressed the Polish rebellion of 1863 with bloody ferocity ... was appointed head of the commission to investigate the background of the assassination attempt and given virtually the powers of a dictator."[24] Dostoevsky, willingly or out of fear – as a political ex-convict, he was still under police surveillance – applauded the dictatorial censorship instituted by Muraviev. The writer also praised the editorial policy of the archconservative and Slavophile newspaper, *Moskovskii Vedomosti* (*Moscow Gazette*), which insisted that "the assassination attempt could only have originated in a Polish plot," even though Karakozov was proved to be Russian with no connection to Poland or Poles.[25]

Dostoevsky's public delusion about the Polish conspiracy was intertwined with personal anxieties about the origins of his family. Dostoevsky was born in Moscow into an impoverished Russian noble family: his father was a doctor and his mother was from a family of wealthy Moscow merchants. However, the Dostoevsky family's roots were in the old Polish-Lithuanian Commonwealth.[26] The writer's grandfather was a Uniate archpriest in Polish-ruled Podolia (now western Ukraine) and the family claimed descent from seventeenth-century Lithuanian nobility. The family's patrimonial home was in Dostoevo, northeast of Pinsk (modern-day southern Belarus); this region saw a "continual strife between conflicting nationalities and creeds (Russian Orthodoxy and Polish Catholicism), and branches of the Dostoevsky family fought on both sides."[27] The Orthodox Dostoevskys had belonged to the poor and disadvantaged noble class (the Orthodox nobility in Lithuania had fewer civil rights than the Catholics), and "sank into the lowly class of the non-monastic clergy."[28] The acceptance of the Uniate priesthood by Dostoevsky's great-grandfather was an ideological compromise that aimed to preserve certain social (noble) privileges for the family. "Dostoevsky's horrified fascination with the Jesuits, whom he believed capable of any villainy to win power over men's souls, may perhaps have been stimulated by some remark about the creed of his forebears."[29] Once the region was incorporated into the tsarist empire, the Uniates were socially marginalised, and the Dostoevsky family lost its noble status. Later, Dostoevsky's father accepted Russian Orthodoxy and reacquired the status of a noble through service in the army. The children of the doctor nonetheless "thought of themselves as belonging to the old gentry-aristocracy rather than the new service created by Peter the Great – the class to which, in fact, their father had just acceded. But their actual place in society was in flagrant contradiction with this flattering self-image."[30]

In summary, from his father's side Dostoevsky belonged to the disenfranchised chapter of the Lithuanian *szlachta*, whose members in a sense betrayed local traditions (and, hence, lost family homes) for the imperial privileges of a newly acquired Russian identity. Vilna defensively stood against such cultural and political transgressions, reminding everyone, including Russians, of the resistant nature of local traditions. Whether Dostoevsky's hectic, indeed paranoid, reaction to Vilna's religious and national peculiarities are evidence of his "schizophrenic" identity is a matter of debate. One thing is clear: the barricade of furniture at the door of his room in the inn was the act of a threatened, insecure person.

Dostoevsky was hoping to stay in Vilna incognito – not because he was fearful of being recognised as a famous Russian writer, but because he was fleeing his creditors in Saint Petersburg. Barsov, who was a minor local literati and barely known to Dostoevsky, made his secret a mockery. Once he was greeted at the gate of the hotel, it became obvious to Dostoevsky that his trip abroad was public knowledge. (Later, the irritated Dostoevsky deliberately avoided meeting Barsov at the agreed hour.) Perhaps the angst that took the form of xenophobia had a more immediate source of aggravation. Dostoevsky was in flight, but was caught out by his own fame.

Dostoevsky reputedly stated that Russians in Asia were Europeans, but in Europe they were Asians. In Vilna, the tsarist regime assumed a more nuanced role: it took up the challenge of modernising the city by turning it into a locus of Russian heritage. Official guidebooks to the city made their best effort to reframe the city's past in the light of Russian history. Vilna was declared to be rightfully a Russian city because "from the earliest times, the Lithuanian tribe lived in close proximity to the neighbouring Russian tribes, and since the time of its foundation, Vilna has always been a half-Russian town. The name of the city is probably also of Russian origin. Clearly, the city got its name from the little river called Vilna – now known as *Vileyka* – which flows into the river of *Viliya*, in old times known as *Veliya*. As early as the fourteenth century, a German chronicler (Vygand of Magdeburg), who described the expedition of the German knights into Samogitia and Lithuania, called Vilna a Russian city (*Civitas Ruthenica*)."[31]

In the Russian view, Muraviev deserved credit for making Vilna's soil nurturing for the Russian soul. In 1898, local authorities unveiled a statue to Muraviev with a thankful speech:

> After the suppression of the rebellion, Muraviev stayed in his appointed post, but this time, his goal was a total transformation of the internal, domestic life of the

region. A thick layer of Polish dictum, like a deep and heavy snow-blanket, was covering the ancestral, familiar and dear Russian soil of the region. This foreign mantle was swept away and the land was finally cleansed; the mutinous fire was also extinguished. However, there was still a pressing matter of ensuing the blossoming of the still weak saplings of Russian life, language, education, morals, customs and the Orthodox church that finally had taken their roots in this motherly Russian soil. Under the care of the administration, these Russian features, like nature in early spring, instantly sprouted, grew stronger, flourished and, later, fully matured. Finally, with their colossal abundance, they covered this entire precious ancestral Russian land. In those days, it was extremely important to utilise every resource so a Russian individual, the master of his own land, could rightfully assume his patriarchal throne. ... Thanks to Muraviev, local Russian life has been enlivened and empowered. Today, the Russian language is heard everywhere and Russian bureaucracy is evident in all corners of the region; the spiritual Russian life is whirling; shining Orthodox churches delight everyone. A resolute hope for a bright Russian future has been born.[32]

Soon, two more monuments were erected to reinforce the Russian spirit of Vilna: a simple bust of poet Aleksandr Pushkin and a colossal sculpture of Empress Catherine II. And in the spirit of a "bright Russian future," Vilna belatedly was also given a modern shape:

Since 1903, Vilna has been illuminated by electric energy generated in the local power plant which was built near the [Green] bridge on the right bank of the River Vilya just across from the centre of the city. The plant supplies energy for public institutions and private houses. Under direct supervision of the former governor, general V.V. von Wahl, who today serves in the Imperial State Council, a correct system of house numbering was finally implemented. This system is based on the example of Saint Petersburg. In addition, issues related to the development of a sewage system, electric power grid, etc., are being discussed in the city.

In terms of elegance and the quality of modern buildings, the best street is the recently constructed Georgievskij Prospect that runs from the Cathedral Square towards the Viliya River. Across the river, the prospect heads straight to the newly incorporated dacha suburb of Zverinec, which has been renamed to Aleksandria. ... In the old times, this vast property was owned by the family of Witgenstein, whose last member to live in the Russian Empire was the duchess Hohenlohe, the wife of the current German chancellor. Today, Zverinec, the former hunting ground of local [Lithuanian] dukes, belongs to a private proprietor, V.V. Martinson, who has divided this extensive tract of land with newly laid out straight streets. The parcelled-out property is being rapidly developed into residential blocks. However, two Russian Orthodox shrines – the Church of the Mother of God and the Church of St. Catherine built near the former villa of the general-governor – were also built here. Today, Vilna remains a historical curiosity, despite the fact that during its 600 years of existence many of its historical monuments have been

46. Swimming in the Viliya River across from Cathedral Square, near the site of the first power plant in Vilna, circa 1900. Despite the modernisation of the city's infrastructure, provincial Vilna retained a nonchalant, almost rural, way of life.

ravaged by wars, fires and social upheavals. But with every passing year, the old Vilna is being outshined by the emerging modern Vilna.[33]

Benedictsen, who visited Vilna at the turn of the twentieth century, put the city's cultural divisions in this modern context of imperial rule:

This country and these peoples are now ruled by the Russians, not exactly by the Russian people, not by a long way in fact, but by the Russian Government officers with their helpers, the police, the gendarmes, and the Cossacks. Nor was it likely that the few thousand Polish noblemen could reign here forever, they were but pioneers, and when the main force was done for, the defiant ones were shot individually, and the new power, which was more hard-fisted, took the reins.

Vilna illustrates to this very day in a striking manner this fourfold divided country. In the old castle where in former times the Grand Duke of Lithuania reigned, the Russian central administration, the Governor General of the whole

Lithuanian land, now holds his sway. On all the clumsy yellow stucco buildings, on barracks, on the main post-office, on the police stations and on the colleges of the town, shines the black-gilded spread-eagle, the Muscovite coat-of-arms. Russian police and gendarmes patrol the streets, every signboard and every placard are in Russian, every street bears a Russian name, everything Polish has been carefully scraped off. But if one looks beyond the uniform in the upper classes it is not difficult to discover that they are not all Russians.

There was a time when it was prohibited, simply prohibited, to speak Polish in Vilna; now it is permitted, except at all gatherings, and in fact much Polish is spoken. All these grave straight men and women with the bright eyes are Polish; they posses that 'wzdiek' (charm and grace) which does not belong to the Russian women. Polish is the language of the drawing rooms in the town, over the sofa may be seen the portrait of the Polish poet-king Adam Mickiewicz, in the bookcase are to be found all the great names in Polish literature, and in marble or plaster Kosciuszko looks down from his appointed place. In almost every house one could find the same sentiments and hope.

It was the fortress of the Polish spirit in the East, now it has been levelled to the ground, but the Poles still cling to the place, hoping for the renewal of former days.

And holiest of the holy, the image of God's own Mother shines from the exalted station over 'the pointed gate' [Ostra Brama] in Vilna. This wonderworking image is the pride and the comfort of Vilna and all its Roman Catholic people. Surrounded by a halo of burning wax candles, this exquisite image from its rich frame looks down upon countless devotees. Whenever one passes the narrow street which ends in 'the pointed gate' above which the chapel of the image has been built, one sees cripples and beggars on their knees praying and making the sign of the cross, and everyone must uncover their head when passing through this holy place.

But the busy crowds in Vilna who trade and throng the streets, who hurry and slave are the Jews, for Vilna more than anything is the town of the Jews. One meets them at once at the railway station, as servants from small dirty hotels, as flat-catchers to pounce upon the runway; they act as cabdrivers, and nearly all the street urchins seem to be Jewish. Here one sees the unadulterated type of the Polish Jew, from the boy with his half keen half impudent expression, and the girl with a much too big nose, the sparkling eyes, and the challenging mouth, to the stooping toiler, whose appearance seems but to indicate the one thing: 'Geschaft machen'! irrespective of his being a porter, a driver or a hawker; and winds up with the grand old man of which no people in the world can boast a finer and more handsome type than can the Jews, the patriarchal old man with his flowing white hair and beard, his gentle serious eyes and his serene gait. It is strange that these nervous hawkers can end thus. It is a living repudiation of the ugly verdict pronounced by the enemies of the Jews that the souls of the Jews have been transformed into grasping hands.

The fourth people in Vilna, the Lithuanians themselves, are not only met as the peasants en route, as the vadmal garbed silent one at the market, and not often even there, for the White Russian peasants have made their way right into Vilna, and have long ago ousted the Lithuanians from the land. Things Lithuanian in Vilna are like the water mark in a gay coloured postage stamp. The name of the town is Lithuanian, the suburbs still have Lithuanian names, Antokoln and Boksta, 'On the Mountain' and 'The Tower". The ruins of the stronghold of Gediminas and the Temple of Fire rise high above the roofs of the town, desolate and neglected, a symbol of the condition of his people.[34]

In 1904, the tsarist regime liberalised the language laws of the region, and the 1905 revolution brought the political demands of the suppressed nationalities into the streets. Vilna became an openly polyglot city of contested identities, with a growing population of over 200,000 inhabitants. Before 1905, the city had 15 periodical publications, all Russian; by 1911, there were already 69 periodicals, among them 35 Polish, 20 Lithuanian, 7 Russian, 5 Jewish and 2 Byelorussian.[35]

For some Russians, this sudden burst of local polyphony offered an opportunity to experience and remember the city, the home of liberating multiplicities, where one was allowed to enjoy the imperial contradictions of a cosmopolitan identity. The seminal Russian philosopher and literary critic Mikhail Bakhtin (1895-1975) was born in Orel, but spent his childhood and young adolescence in Vilna, living there from 1904 to 1910. Bakhtin's family belonged to the privileged upper layer of Russian state administrators. (After leaving Vilna, the family moved to Odessa on the Black Sea coast.) His father was director of the local branch of the Russian Imperial Bank. As a result, Bakhtin shared the advantages and inconveniences of the resented but dominant Russian minority, and there is little indication of him being directly involved with the subaltern cultures or linguistic milieus of the city.

Bakhtin left no description of his life in Vilna. However, according to the recollections of his brother Nikolai, the city left a defining imprint on Bakhtin's comprehension of the world. And some of Bakhtin's biographers suggest a direct link between the scholar's literary formulation of linguistic dialogue and narrative polyphony to his adolescence spent in imperial Vilna.

The Vilnius of Bakhtin's youth was thus a realized example of heteroglossia, the phenomenon that was to become a cornerstone of his theories. Heteroglossia, or the mingling of different language groups, cultures, and classes, was for Bakhtin the ideal condition, guaranteeing a perpetual linguistic and intellectual revolution which guards against the hegemony of any "single language of truth" or "official language" in a given society, against ossification and stagnation in thought. Indeed, in one of his essays of the 1930s, "The Prehistory of Novelist Discourse," which maintains that the linguistic pluralism of Hellenic Greece fostered the development of the Greek novel, Bakhtin describes Samosata, the home town of Lucian, in terms that apply equally to Vilnius as he knew it. The local inhabitants of Samosata were Syrians who spoke Aramaic, while the educated elite spoke and wrote in Greek. But Samosata was ruled by the Romans, who had a legion stationed there, and hence Latin was the official language. And since the town was situated on a trade route, many other languages were heard there as well. [36]

The Bakhtin brothers went to the First Gymnasium of Vilna, located in the Baroque buildings of the defunct university next to the palace of the Russian governor. At school, the older brother became a leader of nonconformist students who, in his own words, were "in a continuous state of intellectual tension, knowing that they had thousands of books to read and an infinity of things to learn, but believing that when they absorbed the centuries of human thought, they would evolve a line of their own and in turn become creators." They read everything, from Marx to Nietzsche, worshiped Leonardo de Vinci and Wagner, and imitated Baudelaire. "A former member of the Vilnius group recalled that 'occasionally they spent the night feasting and carousing, or hoping to induce visions in smoking hashish, but more often they walked until dawn around Vilnius reciting poetry and philosophizing.' "[37]

The provincial decadence of Vilna's life followed the revolutionary spirit of the time, best captured and promoted by the Russian cultural movement broadly known as Symbolism. The key advocate of Russian Symbolism, which fused the national with the cosmopolitan, was the journal *Mir Iskusstva* ("The World of Art"), published in Saint Petersburg between 1898 and 1905. Sergei Diaghilev, the mastermind behind the sensational *Ballets Russes* seasons in Paris in the 1910s, led the journal. One of the closest artistic allies of Diaghilev was painter Mstislav Dobuzhinsky (1875-1957), who had strong biographical ties to Vilna.

Dobuzhinsky's parents were not a conventional couple: his mother was an opera singer who, after parting with her husband, left the son to his care. On his paternal side, Dobuzhinsky came from a family of old Lithuanian nobility. However, his grandfather and father were high-ranking officers in the tsarist army. In spite of it, neither showed any shame over their non-Russian roots. (In his home in Saint Petersburg, Dobuzhinsky's grandfather proudly displayed portraits of Polish national heroes.) Dobuzhinsky's family led the typical nomadic life of imperial servants, moving from one city and region of the empire to another, following the various military postings of the father. At one point, his father was stationed in Vilna, where he retired.

On Easter in 1884, nine-year-old Dobuzhinsky came for the first time to Vilna to visit his uncle. The city made a lasting impression:

> Spring with its gently blue skies was already in Vilna. After the geometrical and austere Saint Petersburg, I suddenly encountered narrow crooked lanes with multicoloured houses with slanting red-shingled roofs surrounded by soaring church towers and spires. Everything around me was festive, fully warmed by the sun, and the air reverberated with a remarkable and celebratory Easter resonance. Here, for the first time I heard the sound of Catholic bells. This was not a hum or everlasting bell-echo of the immeasurable orthodox piety that I came to know during my visits to Novgorod. Here, the sound of bells arrived in a triumphal and dignified way, in waves.[38]

Four years later, Dobuzhinsky moved from Saint Petersburg to Vilna with his father, where he graduated from the local Russian gymnasium. He left Vilna in 1895 for the imperial capital to study law.

In Vilna, the Dobuzhinskys carried the marks of their helical national identity. They were Russian colonists with traces of local, Lithuanian loyalties. In his memoirs, Dobuzhinsky describes the ways in which Russianness had been stamped on the city. "Our suburban neighbourhood was called *Peski* and it was just being developed. Most streets were already laid out, but there were no houses, only fences, painted in white, yellow or an odd pink – the most popular colours in Vilna. At the intersections of the empty streets signs were already posted with [Russian] place-names: Tombov, Yaroslavl, Voronezh and Kostroma Streets. These geographical names had the goal of imprinting Russia on the city and even then, this process of intense Russification troubled me greatly."[39] Russia itself remained a mystery to Dobuzhinsky: "after growing up in the 'European' Saint Petersburg and Baroque and Catholic Vilna, I looked at Russian towns with the eyes of a stranger."[40]

Dobuzhinsky's father had dreamed of making his son a European man. The son wanted to become a painter. The two wishes came true when, in 1899, Dobuzhinsky, after an unsatisfying bureaucratic carreer in Saint Petersburg, went to study painting in fin de siècle Munich. There, he met Jawlensky and Kandinsky, the high priests of decadent art. In later years, Dobuzhinsky studied and lived in other social centres of modern art: Berlin, Dresden, Paris, and Venice. Yet he credited his early exposure to Vilna to be aesthetically as informative as his later knowledge of those cities:

> The most elegant churches of Vilna were built in the eighteenth century, and there I learned the spirit of that age. In addition, Vilna accumulated a whole spectrum of architectural layers from Gothic, ornate Baroque and Classicism (the Governor's palace where Napoleon had stayed). There was also a delightful late Gothic brick

47. A street in Vilna; postcard from a drawing by M. Dobuzhinsky, circa 1914.

church of Saint Anna – in winter, surrounded by snow, this small church looked like a perfect theatre decoration. It was said that Napoleon, seeing it, felt extreme grief for the fact that he could not take this little Gothic toy with him to Paris. After beloved Saint Petersburg, my eye and taste organically continued to evolve by being surrounded with the true masterpieces of Vilna. Here, I became attuned to the importance of architectural proportions, the elegance of flat surfaces interrupted with a cartouche or decorative shield (for instance, the Cathedral or Saint John's Church), the beauty of rocaille – and most importantly, I started to feel the poetry of architecture.[41]

Consequently, when the budding artist went to western Europe for the first time during his student years – in this case, Dresden – he "felt completely surrounded by the familiar decorations of his native Vilna, with the same Rococo and the same flat facades of eighteenth century buildings around the Old Market Square."[42] Years later, on his way from Munich to Russia, Dobuzhinsky made a brief visit to Vilna. The artist's reaction to the city was the same – pure enchantment: "as always, my beloved city delighted me. And every time, when after each trip abroad – usually on my way to Saint

Petersburg – I made a customary stopover, Vilna, with its exquisite Baroque, never failed a test of comparison."[43] It was also, for him, a place of painting:

> In the summer of 1903 ... I returned to my beloved Vilna with my wife and little daughter, Verochka. Here I made a few novel paintings in the mixed technique of watercolours and graphic design. They were novel because I became much bolder in my techniques: I started to sharpen my point of view and strengthen my sense of composition.
>
> In Vilna, for the first time, if one can discount 2 or 3 paintings of my student years, I started to draw in chalk – a courtyard, fully filled with boxes and a protruding Baroque belfry; a long empty wall of the Peter and Paul Church with a tree in front of it, and other small architectural motifs. I also tried to draw forest, but mostly unsuccessfully.
>
> In the following years, I mostly painted in Vilna, where I would often return from Saint Petersburg. Then I was not ashamed to paint openly in streets. Painting Vilna was a cosy, domestic affair, since nobody troubled me there, except for the occasional foul smell of the picturesque Vilna "ghetto" – my favourite spot – with its narrow and crooked alleys, arched gateways and colourful little houses. When I had finished my painting session, old Jewish merchant-women, who were usually sitting with their baskets near the "rinshtok" [gutter], told me: "Come back to us again." Once I noticed somebody's finger pointing from behind at my painting: "The proportions are incorrect," I was reprimanded by an art school student. I thanked him for his suggestions. Another time, when I was painting a pictorial vacant lot I heard a voice: "A third artist paints this place – it must be a lucky corner." I turned around and saw a passing policeman giving me his honours.[44]

For Dobuzhinsky, not unlike Bakhtin, this intimate and aestheticised relationship with Vilna informed his cosmopolitan outlook. Yet for most Russians, the city still provoked strictly nationalistic feelings. In 1870, conservative and religious poet Feodor Tyutchev (1803-1873) – an early oracle of Russian Symbolism – pronounced the city a holy grail of the Russian spirit: "Above the ancient Russian Vilna/ Shine crosses of the homeland/And Orthodox sounds of copper-bells/ Resound in the heavens."[45] However, in Vilna, after the post-1905 revolution, when other nationalities – Poles, Lithuanians, Jews and Byelorussians – came to claim the city as their own, such atavistic and xenophobic views sought fortification. In 1912, the hundredth anniversary of the failed Napoleonic attack on Russia was marked by a series of celebratory and educational events, including patriotic excursions to the hill where the Grande Armée had collapsed.[46] The next year, a new Russian Orthodox shrine was consecrated in commemoration of three centuries of the Romanov dynasty rule. Designed in traditional Byzantine-Muscovite style and built on the highest elevation point possible in the modern quarters of the city, it was meant to silently dominate over the Catholic Baroque domes of the old town.

A year later, at the beginning of a new war, Vilna was honoured by the visitation of Nicholas II, the last emperor of Russia, on his obligatory tour of the frontline. Bernard Pares (1867-1949), the official British observer with the Russian armies in the field, followed the emperor's military entourage to Vilna. Pares arrived in the city on October 8, 1914 – six weeks after the start of the military campaign – and was surprised to find the city displaying extreme signs of loyalty to the Russian monarchy:

> The Emperor's visit to the Vilna was a great success. He rode through the town unguarded. The streets were crowded, the reception most cordial. … There are not many Russians except officials. At the beginning of war the nearness of the enemy was felt with much anxiety. Now there is an atmosphere of work and assurance. The Grand Hotel and several public buildings are converted into hospitals, where the Polish language is largely used. The Emperor visited all the chief hospitals, and spoke with many wounded, distributing medals in such numbers that the supply ran short. He received a Jewish deputation and spoke with thanks of the sympathetic attitude of the Jews in this hour so solemn for Russia. The general feeling may be described like a new page of history. Among Poles, educated and uneducated, enthusiasm is general. This is all the more striking because in no circumstances could Vilna be considered as politically Polish.[47]

Pares's description of patriotic Vilna was perhaps a fantasy of British war propaganda, which portrayed Russia as a reliable ally in the war against Germany. On the exact same day, Stanley Washburn, an American-born military correspondent for *The Times* of London, who was closely familiar with Russia, also passed through Vilna on his way to the front. His impressions of the city were less enthusiastic. "We reached Vilna the following morning [October 8]. I had been through there a half dozen times before but never stopped. This town is one of the largest Jewish towns in Russia and is very old. As there was nothing of interest there I contented myself with strolling around for an hour or two and then returned to the train."[48]

By the winter of 1914, hundreds of thousands of Russian troops were pouring through the city into the zigzaging front line running deep into German territory. Among them was a war reporter, Valery Bryusov (1873-1924), who made his literary fame as one of the most daring advocates of the Russian decadent art and bohemian lifestyle. Bryusov's poetry scandalised the public with literary imagery of overt sexuality and sadism. In his youth, however, the poet was a great admirer of Tyutchev, whose sentimental and patriotic verses were rediscovered by the new generation of Russian Symbolists. The Russian army was blessed with victories, but facing wartime Vilna, Bryusov (who was fully aware of Tyutchev's chauvinism) established a more sinister

VILNIUS.   Šv. Kazimiero koplyčia.

48. Saint Casimir Chapel in Vilna; postcard from a photograph by J. Bułhak

tone in picturing the Russian sway over the city. The war awakens a realisation of the foreignness of the imperial rule:

More often the streets of Vilna
Are draped in mourning.
The war harvest is great
The open crypts loom large.

More than often, usually in a corner
Of the darkened churches,
Sits helplessly in her absentminded tragedy
A mother, sister or a daughter.

The war like a heavenly thunder,
Shudders the frightening world...
Yet dreams still lull the miracle child,
The patron of Vilna – Casimir.

The undeclared dream, the same as always,
Like a dream of bygone time,
Elevates the shrine of Saint Anna,
With the crowning beauty of its masonry.

And the sea of local sorrows,
Full of pity and misfortunes,
Roars in the Jewish quarter
Under the shrieks of Russian victories.

"More often"[49]

Within the year, Russian victories in East Prussia had turned into defeats, and once the German army crossed the border of the empire, Vilna became a front-line town. In the summer of 1915, with the Russian army losing battles against Germany in the provinces of Poland, the Russian government suddenly found a propaganda asset in the Polish (and Lithuanian) cause. Grand Duke Nicholas, the supreme commander of the Russian forces and a cousin once removed of Tsar Nicholas II, issued a proclamation promising a restoration of the Polish state in alliance with Russia at the end of the war. Still, the Poles, so many times betrayed by the imperial powers of Europe, were not keen to trust Russian autocracy. Nonetheless, the tsarist courting of Poles exonerated the Russian regime in the eyes of its key military allies, France and Britain, who were eager to counteract the German and Austrian geopolitical goal to absorb all of the Polish lands into their sphere of control.

Stephen Graham (1884-1975), another British journalist and, in his own words, a great admirer of Russians, spent the summer of 1915 in Vilna. He was spellbound by the affection and respect he reportedly witnessed between the two rival (Polish and Russian) nations and opposing (Catholic and Orthodox) religions in the midst of the feverishly militarised daily routine:

I have just been staying in the fine old city of Vilna, a city of courtly Poles, the home of many of the old noble families of Poland. It is now thronged with Russian officers and soldiers. Along the main street is an incessant procession of troops, and as you look down you see vistas of bayonet spikes waving like reeds in a wind. As you lie in bed at night you listen to the tramp, tramp, tramp of soldiers. Or you look out at the window and see wagons and guns passing for twenty minutes on end, or you see prancing over the cobbles and the mud the Cossacks of the Don,

49. Russian Vilna, circa 1900.

of Volga, of Seven Rivers. In the days of the revolutionary outburst, the Poles bit their lips in hate at the sight of the Russian soldiers, they cursed under their breath, darted out with revolvers and shot, aimed bombs. Today they smile, tears run down their cheeks; they even cheer. Whoever would have thought to see the day when the Poles would cheer the Russian troops marching through the streets of their own cities!

The Russians are forgiven. They come now to deliver the Slavs, not, as formerly, to trample on them. Go into a restaurant and order your dinner in Russian, and you are smiled at and treated specially. To be a Russian is to be a *friend*. The Russians also, with that complete turn-round of feeling of which the Slavonic peoples are so capable, are quite affectionate towards the Poles. It is said that since the proclamation of the Grand Duke Nicholas there has been quite a demand for Polish grammars and dictionaries on the part of Russians wishing to learn Polish. I, for my part, directly read that proclamation, [and] decided to learn some Polish, for I understood that Poland had suddenly begun to count.

A very touching spectacle may be seen every day just now at the Sacred Gate of Vilna [Ostra Brama]. Above the gateway is a chapel with wide-open doors showing a richly gilded and flower-decked image of the Virgin. At one side stands a row of leaden organ pipes, at the other stands a priest. Music is wafted through the air with incense and the sound of prayers. Down below in the narrow, muddy roadway kneel many poor men and women with prayer books in their hands. They are Poles.

But through the gateway come incessantly, all day and all night, Russian troops going to the front. And as he approaches, every soldier, be he officer or private, lifts his hat and passes through the praying throng uncovered. This is beautiful. Let Russia always be so in the presence of the Mother of Poland.[50]

This mirage of national harmony did not include the Jews, who were blamed for all the ills of Russia and Poland as well. The saddest sight in Vilna, noted Graham, was "the clusters of poor, homeless Jews" who had been forced to flee their homes by the encroaching front, and crowded "into the city with all that remains to them in their hand."[51] The defeat of the Russian army reactivated populist anti-Semitism. "All Russians seemed to know a Jew at once by his face and his manners, so intense is the dislike of the type. I think," alleged the British journalist, "it is due to the fundamental opposition of the Jewish character to that which is most precious in the Slav, [such as] the gay carelessness, the despising of material possessions, the love of the neighbour, the mystical." So in spite of their tragic plight and marginal status, the Jews, determined Graham, "with their grasp of trade, their sympathy with Westernism and contempt of Easternism, endanger the Russian ideal."[52]

Graham saw the solution to the Jewish alienation in the Zionist dream of a political nationhood. "The Jewish difficulty is that the Poles have been promised something as Poles, but the Jews have been promised nothing." In the long run, "one of the possibilities of the war is the fall of the Turkish Empire and the liberation of Syria from the Mohammedan yoke." In such an outcome, mused the reporter, "Palestine becomes vacant, or at least eligible for a new Government. It seems to me that something might be done for the establishment of the Jews in Palestine." This radical geopolitical scheme could be secured by the newly re-framed post-war imperial world order, and "once a [Jewish] Government has been formed, it could be made optional for the Jews to give up their various European national papers and become Jewish subjects." The Jews "would have the financial and moral protection of their own Government. They could in time form a democracy in Palestine if they wished it; they could have their own army and navy if necessary. This would be a great blessing to the world." In its turn, the Jewish state would save the tsarist empire, with its Russian and Orthodox soul, from national humiliation, for "the chief reason that the Russian peasant has for calling the Jew accursed is that he has no land of his own. For instance, when the Russians were retreating in Poland I asked a common soldier the reason. His answer was – 'The Jews betray us ... they dog our steps and sell us at every corner.' "[53]

Geopolitics aside, the proximity of the German forces to Vilna infused Graham's mind with Mephistophelian powers of macabre creativity.

Bewildered by the future prospects of the war-torn world, Graham nonetheless grasped the epochal significance of the moment by tagging the city with its German name. The textual conversion of Vilna to Wilna signalled the near end of the Russian rule:

> What days I had at Wilna tramping in the rain! I found myself so much nearer to the war than I had been before. The war became more intimate, it created and released a musical flood of thoughts and impressions, so that all the time I walked I was like Abt Vogler at the organ. The tramp of thousands to conflict and death, the battle music, the passion of war and the dance of the orgy, the colours and the flags, the emblems and signs, the victories and the terrible slaughters, the conquests of kingdoms, the abasing of old gods, and the building of new States, blends in the soul in one great passionate and appalling music.[54]

Lyrical Bryusov was emotionally touched by war in Vilna, too, but from a different vantage point. The Russian Symbolist viewed the inevitable surge in violence with the eyes of a wandering soul whose decadent aloofness was perhaps no more than a mask to cover patriotic grief over the potential loss of Vilna. Under the thundering march of the encroaching battlefield, the poet roamed the streets of "the ancient Russian Vilna" with a nostalgic feeling of no return:

> Again I am alone – a homeless drifter,
> Yet it is so easy to breathe.
> Where now, my troubled spirit,
> What wanderings will be next?
>
> "In Vilna"[55]

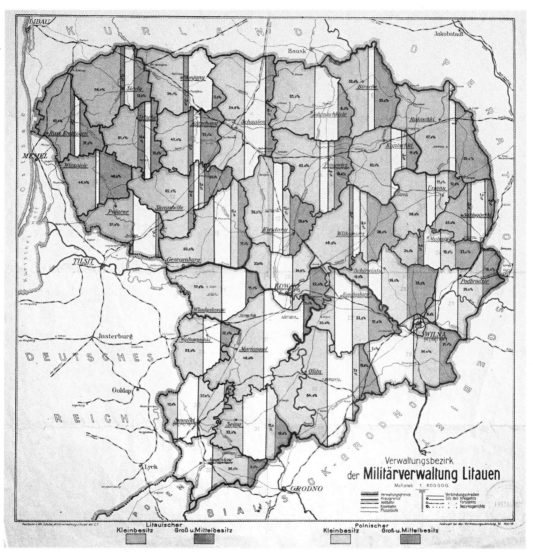

50. A statistical map of Lithuania, designed by the German occupational forces to highlight the ethnic divisions of the country, 1918.

CHAPTER SIX:

German Intrusion

> The war, despite its destruction, or, indeed, owing to its pervasive horror, had become an evocative force, a stimulus not to social change but to personal imagination and inwardness, an avenue to a new and vital realm of activity.
>
> Modris Eksteins

The first German sentry reached the vicinity of Wilna on *Tishri* 10, 5676, according to the Jewish calendar; it was September 4, 1915, following the (Russian) Julian tradition, and September 17 on the Gregorian (western European) calendar. The date marked one of the holiest Jewish days, Yom Kippur. On this Day of Atonement, which marks the end of the Days of Awe and launches a new year, human sins are pardoned and reconciliation with God is reaffirmed. This is not a joyous festival, but a sober rite of fasting and self-denial, which starts with visits to cemeteries and ends with the prayer of *N'iloh*. The Hebrew word *N'iloh* means closing, and it originally referred to the locking of the gates of the Temple. Later, after the destruction of the Temple, it acquired a more celestial meaning as the shutting of the entrance to Heaven. It is a threshold moment of the year that seals human fate.[1]

On the eve of Yom Kippur, an Eastern European Jewish town becomes silent, as all worldly things are postponed in expectation of a new beginning. Joseph Roth, a writer with Viennese credentials, compared the scene of the Yom Kippur ritual to that of the Jewish funeral. "The streets suddenly go dark as candlelight breaks from windows, and the shutters are closed in fearful haste – and so tightly closed that one has the impression they won't be opened again until Judgment Day. ... Candles burn for all the dead. Other candles are lit for the living. The dead are only one step away from the world as the living are from the next. The great praying begins. ... From a thousand windows there breaks a wailing prayer, interspersed by soft, mild, otherworldly melodies copied from those of the heavens."[2]

In 1915, the silence and flickering lights of Yom Kippur were extinguished by the chaos of the Russian flight and the imminent German arrival. The chief of staff of the Vilna military district was Paul von Rennenkampf, a Russian general of Baltic-German aristocratic origins, who had, alongside German and other international forces, led the tsarist troops in the suppression of the Boxer Rebellion in China at the turn of the twentieth century. In the early days of the war, Protestant Rennenkampf prayed at the only Lutheran church in Vilna for the health of the tsar and the victory of Russian guns. This time around, tsarist high command could only hope to delay the inevitable: the Russian Tenth Army, scrambling to defend Lithuania, was no match for its better equipped military cousin, the German Tenth Army, which made a push towards Vilna in the summer of 1915.

Russian despair was evident in the counterproductive military orders which attempted to make the city disappear from the advancing German horizon. In August, Vilna was plunged into darkness and enforced lethargy: street lighting was banned and a total blackout was put on all house windows facing west. The Russian authorities also prohibited all social gatherings and cultural activities, and put severe restrictions on civilian movement in the streets. No matter; once the Germans broke through the poorly defended front line, a panic-stricken hustle ensued.

> After Kowno's fall [at the end of August], Wilna prepared for evacuation. Streets had long been crowded with carts of refugees fleeing east. Now the government departed, officials and agencies cramming the train station to bursting with packages and freight. With them they took their monuments and statues, symbols of tsarist rule. Parishioners surrounded churches to prevent bells from being taken away. The city shut down, mail and telephone service was severed. As the Germans neared, cannon were soon heard from three sides. Zeppelins floated over the city to drop bombs on darkened streets. The retreating Russians were determined to leave as little as possible to the advancing Germans. In the evenings, the city's fringes were lit by flames, as fire 'evacuated' what railroads could not. The government sought to mobilize all local reservists, so that their manpower would not fall to the enemy. Soon planned measures turned to panic. Arson teams set fire to homesteads, farms, and manors, pillaging, looting and driving people east by force. On September 9, 1915, the army chief ordered that all men from 18 to 45 were to retreat with the army. A crazy manhunt began, as natives and deserters hid or fled to the woods. Those caught by police were sent to collection centers to be moved out. Intensifying Zeppelin bombardments, shattering the train station and dropping explosives at random, announced the end. The last Russian regiments and Cossacks marched out of a city that seemed dead. In the dreamlike interval before the arrival of German soldiers, life slowly began to stir again, as locals organized civic committees, police militia, and newspapers. The last farewell of the Tsar's forces was the sound of explosions, as bridges were blown up.[3]

Beſetzung von Wilna
ruſſiſche Gouvernementſtadt
Auguſt 1915.

51. "The capture of Wilna, a Russian city of government, August, 1915." On this commemorative postcard both the date of the German capture of the city and its representational viewpoint are incorrect: Wilna was taken by the Germans in September and the river embankment, in reality, runs in the opposite direction from the one depicted in the picture.

In the early hours of September 19, as the last Russian soldiers fled the city, one hundred twenty years of tsarist rule came to an end. In a brief moment, local residents took over the city, until the German army came to claim the spoils.

The German high commanders, like Napoleon in 1812, envisioned the capture of Wilna as a strategic victory. It opened, according to general Erich von Ludendorff, the possibility of the ending the war with "a decisive defeat of the Russian armies."[4] Despite the high hopes in Berlin, the German advance on the Eastern Front brought no prospect of peace. At the end of 1915, the German-Russian front stabilised along the northern and eastern edges of Lithuania, making Wilna a frontier town.

From the occupied territories of the *Severo-zapadnyi* (North-Western) region of the Russian empire, the Germans formed the *Ober-Ost* (Upper-Eastern) territory. Within its boundaries, the failed military strategist Ludendorff – by then appointed the chief of staff in the East – concentrated on the great German "work for civilisation." "The monotony of trench warfare," wrote the general, "was greatly relieved for the men by their industrial employment. I sympathized with this feeling, and was glad to find a fresh field in which to serve the Fatherland. A very stimulating piece of work had fallen to me, and it absorbed my whole attention. We felt that we were working for Germany's future, even in a strange land." [5]

In Lithuania, Ludendorff saw the future of the *Vaterland* in the heroic light of German national tribulations. Under such illumination, the view of Kowno, where he established the military headquarters of the *Ober-Ost* region, turned into a historical panorama of the works of German civilisation:

> On the farther bank of the Niemen there stands the tower of an old German castle of the Teutonic Knights, a symbol of German civilization in the East, and not far from it there is a memorial of French schemes for the conquest of the world – that hill upon which Napoleon stood in 1812 as he watched the great army crossing the river.
>
> My mind was flooded with overwhelming historical memories; I determined to resume in the occupied territory that work of civilization at which the Germans had labored in those lands for many centuries. The population, made up as it is of such a mixture of races, would never accomplish anything of its own accord, and, left to itself, would succumb to Polish domination. ... A happy future of assured prosperity seemed to be opening out for the Fatherland.[6]

Tying the future prosperity of Germany to the history of the conquered territory was more successful than making it serve the present needs of the empire. Despite its historical and geographical proximity, the *Ober-Ost*, in the eyes of the German officials, was *terra incognito*:

> The country was in a devastated condition owing to the war, and only where we had been in occupation for some time was there any approach to order. ... The population, apart from the German portion, held aloof from us. The German districts, especially the Balts, had welcomed our troops. The Letts were opportunists, and awaited events. The Lithuanians believed the hour of deliverance was at hand, and when the good times they anticipated did not materialize, owing to the cruel exigencies of war, they become suspicious once more, and turned against us. The

Wilna: Gesammtansicht vom Schlossberg aus gesehen.

52. Wilna: the view from Castle Hill.

Poles were hostile, as they feared, quite justifiably, a pro-Lithuanian policy on our part. The White Ruthenians were of no account, as the Poles had robbed them of their nationality and given nothing in return. In the autumn of 1915, I thought I would like to obtain some idea of the distribution of this race. At first they were, literally, not to be found. Subsequently we discovered they were a widely scattered people, apparently of Polish origin, but with such a low standard of civilization that much time would be required before we could do anything for them. The Jew did not know what attitude to adopt, but gave us no trouble, and we were at least able to converse with him, which was hardly ever possible with the Poles, Lithuanians, and Letts. The language difficulties weighed heavily against us and cannot be overestimated. Owing to the dearth of German works of reference on the subject, we knew very little about the country or the people, and found ourselves in a strange world. In a region as large as East and West Prussia, Pomerania, and Posen together we were faced with an appalling task. We had to construct and organize everything afresh.[7]

As in the past, the re-organisation of the conquered territories started with pillaging, which, in the words of Ludendorff, "was done in as orderly a manner as possible, but a certain amount of confusion was inevitable."[8] The confusion, however, was not to be blamed on the inappropriateness or inefficiency of German order, but on "the regrettable conditions imposed by the exigencies of war."

Yet, "to the individual who suffers it is a matter of indifference *how* he loses his property. He understands nothing of the necessities of war, and therefore is ready enough to talk about the enemy's barbaric methods of warfare."[9]

While Kowno brought on dreams of glory, Wilna challenged them, in that "extraordinary difficulties had still to be overcome."[10] These difficulties arose not so much from the German inability to control the exigencies of war as much as from the puzzling geographical location of the city. Somewhere between Kowno and Wilna, noticed writer Alfred Brust (1896-1934), who arrived in Lithuania in the ranks of the occupying army, "the dogmatic division between West and East turns senseless, for everything—religions, languages, cultures, peoples, histories, and architectural styles – intertwines here."[11] Kowno, remarked Richard Dehmel, German press censor for the *Ober-Ost* territories, "differs little from East Prussian provincial towns … and the city's panorama reminds one of Venice with its lagoons rather than Moscow or Petersburg. True Russia begins only in Wilna, the city of a hundred churches and a thousand bordellos. But, even there, Lithuanian and Polish spirits reign."[12]

According to the Russian statistics, Vilna had close to 200,000 inhabitants just before the war, roughly forty percent of whom were Jewish, more than thirty percent Polish, about twenty percent Russian and the rest consisting of small Lithuanian, Byelorussian, German and Tartar minorities. The demographic situation changed dramatically once the German counter-offensive began in the spring of 1915. Although a majority of Russians evacuated the city, it was swarmed by several thousand refugees from the Lithuanian countryside. Many of the refugees were Jews who were forced to leave their homes under the orders of the Russian administration, as potential "enemy sympathisers."

The German occupation of Wilna was initially announced in three languages: German, Russian and Polish. General Pfeil, the commander of the occupying army, trumpeted the end of tsarist tyranny: "The German military forces pushed the Russian army out of the territory of the Polish city of Wilna. Several German army divisions entered into the notable and legendary city of Wilna. The city has always been a pearl of the Polish realm … and, Germany is a friend of this realm."[13] The very next day, Pfeil was visited by representatives of the Lithuanian and Jewish communities, who objected to the German placement of the city within the Polish realm. Wilna, explained the delegates, was a polyglot city, a capital of Lithuania with a predominantly Jewish population. Afterwards, the general institutionalised a semi-official multilingualism. As the German language replaced

Russian as the official *lingua franca*, the new administration also recognised the public usage of additional languages: Polish, Yiddish, Lithuanian and Byelorussian.

In order to clarify the national diffusion and the future prospects of the place, the Germans started their rule with a census. They counted a total of 140,840 inhabitants, divided into several linguistic groups based on the mother-tongue principle, with Polish (fifty percent) and Yiddish (forty-four percent) claiming the largest share. Together, Lithuanian-, Russian-, and Byelorussian-speaking inhabitants comprised less than ten percent of the population, with Russians having the greatest drop in numbers. There were also about one thousand Germans (less than one percent) found among the city's civilian population. The city's religious affiliation mirrored its ethnic segregation, with more than half of its inhabitants being Catholics and forty-three percent belonging to the Judaic faith. In addition, there were tiny Greek Orthodox and Protestant minorities.[14]

The statistics revealed a demographical landscape that was not received favourably in Berlin. Among the peoples of the occupied region, the Germans clearly favoured the Lithuanians, whom they assumed to be less politically and culturally active and hence more compliant with the German dictum. While the imperial administration schemed about the establishment of a tributary Lithuanian principality, Ludendorff raised his concern that "any prince at Vilna would have had the Polish nobility at his court, the officers of the army would have been Poles, and so would the majority of the civil officials." As a result, only "Prussian Germans could keep Lithuania for the Lithuanians, and provide officials and officers, which they could not do in anything like sufficient numbers. States capable of an independent existence are not produced by political catchwords, nor are small nations kept alive thereby. I was, therefore, by no means pleased with vague solutions, which seemed so very dangerous for Germany's future."[15]

This intense preoccupation with the political future of the city brought no relief to its current inhabitants. The German administration placed Lithuania under food requisition orders and instituted heavy labour requirements for city residents. As food supplies dwindled, waves of epidemics swept through the city. In order to prevent the spread of diseases, the military routinely banned markets and ordered disinfection of shops. It also proscribed funerary processions and "forced everyone to get vaccinations against cholera, measles, etc., prohibited the population from changing residences, and finally registered and examined prostitutes."[16] Notwithstanding, these measures failed to save the city:

The Russians had left a legacy of cholera, which was stamped out by November 1915; but the physical privation of those sixteen months led to an epidemic of typhoid, which raged from the beginning of 1917 for nine months and was accompanied for a time by dysentery. In the summer of that year there was hardly a house in Vilna which did not display a red ticket warning the public that the plague had entered there. Urgent cases usually had to wait two or three days before the ambulance could call to remove them to the isolation hospital, and in many instances it arrived too late. People had to queue up for coffins. The hearses were unable to cope with the demand, so that coffins were ranged along the pavement to await the wagons upon which they were piled. Vilna became a city of the dead, and those who still moved about felt that they were mere ghosts.[17]

The German administration was more successful in sanitising the city's Russian cartographic and topographic relics. Most street names were translated from Russian into German; but, oddly, Muraviev Square was changed to Napoleon Platz. The Russian Orthodox church of Saint Nicholas (the former Catholic church of Saint Casimir) was converted into a Protestant shrine in order to accommodate the spiritual needs of the German Tenth Army. Tsar Nicholas II had prayed there for heavenly blessing during the early days of the war – Kaiser Wilhelm II did the same while touring the Russian Front in the summer of 1916.

Despite its proximity to the front line, its multinational population and its undetermined future, the Germans were quick to claim the city as their own. To the linguistic plurality of the local press, the German military command added its own newspaper *Wilnaer Zeitung*. The first issue of the newspaper came out on January 20, 1916, with a headline on the capitulation of Montenegro. However, the leading article of the issue was simply entitled "Das deutsche Wilna" ("The German Wilna").

Wilnaer Zeitung was a creature of the occupation, published by the Tenth Army to a targeted audience of German soldiers stationed in and around the city. On its pages, military news easily blended with mundane civic stories, and local German, Yiddish, Polish and Lithuanian theatre reviews took up as much space as reports about the strategic advances of the German army. Every week, the newspaper published the train schedule of Wilna's railway station – an indication of the city's role as an important transit hub, connecting the German *Vaterland* with the Eastern Front. In March of 1916, the paper initiated a series of feuilleton-style articles – vignettes of everyday urban life – with a heading of "Wanderstunden in Wilna" ("Wanderings through Wilna"). These vignettes, explained the editor, are written for those

Germans soldiers on leave who possess a desire to find out more about the city. They appeared once a week and initially took the form of short tour guides, leading the wandering soldiers to local tourist destinations: the Cathedral, the churches, the Jewish Quarter, or the more interesting suburban districts of the city. Within a few weeks, the tone and format of these unsigned articles had changed – from being instructive and descriptive newspaper pieces, they turned into examples of belletristic writing.

Wilnaer Zeitung was co-edited by Paul Otto Heinrich Fechter, a cultural and literary critic, who, in 1914, wrote one of the first books on Expressionism as an art movement. Fechter was born in 1880, in the West Prussian town of Elbing (near Forster's hometown), into a family of lumber merchants with close commercial connections to Lithuania. Like so many talented people at the time, he was drawn to Berlin, the bustling capital of the German Empire, where he studied architecture, mathematics and physics. At twenty-six, he completed his philosophical doctoral thesis on dialectics. An academic profession, however, was not on Fechter's mind, and he turned to creative journalism, becoming a feuilleton editor, first in Dresden and later in Berlin. Fechter wrote extensively on modern theatre and literature, and, as an early advocate of Expressionism, he became fully absorbed by the fast-moving spectacle and experience of metropolitan urbanity.[18]

During the war, Fechter avoided active military service, but not without having a close understanding of modern warfare. (His younger brother, Hans Fechter, was one of the first submarine pilots of the German imperial fleet.) Posted as a feuilleton writer of *Wilnaer Zeitung*, Fechter tried as much as possible to utilise his creative hand. The propagandistic demands and severe censorship of the military newspaper offered little space to manoeuvre: his knowledge of expressionist art, modern theatre and refined literature was better kept to himself. Imaginative Fechter, however, found a tiny literary niche in the narratives of "Wanderstunden in Wilna," where he could combine the artistic sensibilities of a metropolitan *flaneur* with the restrictive subject matter of military affairs. These urban vignettes were collected in a guide-book and published under the same title by the newspaper. The book was authored by Paul Monty, an English-sounding pseudonym used by Fechter. It went to three subsequent editions – the last was published in 1918, at the end of the German occupation – and was officially endorsed by the military commanders of the *Ober-Ost* territories.

Monty/Fechter sets his journey through Wilna as an escape from military responsibilities, which, ironically, opens up the possibility of a more thorough conquest:

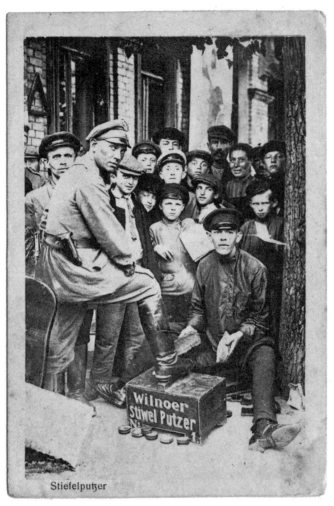

Stiefelputzer

53. German soldier-flaneur in Wilna, 1916.

In this world, the right to conquer foreign cities is a privilege reserved only to a few mighty rulers and military leaders, but every traveller can successfully master unknown cities if he perfects the art of wandering. If the traveller is a clever strategist, he will certainly consult various maps and chronicles before he ventures into a strange town. If the traveller is an artist – and wandering is the freest form of art – he will approach the city from a completely different perspective. Without any hesitation, the urban wanderer will let fresh air guide him through the unfamiliar streets of the far-flung city. This form of travelling has the potential of breaking every kind of fortification. Fortunately for the traveller, our good old Wilna is blessed with a perpetual breeze, creating perfect conditions for endless roaming through its streets and squares.[19]

This experience of Wilna tells an unrealised story of modernity and youthfulness, the outward attributes of the German soldier. "The history of the city," announces the guidebook, "can not be summarised by chronicles and books. The age of the place is most obviously reflected by the self-expression of the place. The modern functions of the city are defined by its historical ordeals and contemporary energy. If a human face mirrors the life and fate of an individual, then the city's character is visible in the general layout of the place." "The map of Wilna," continues the author of the guide, "looks like the face of an old person who might have lived a long life but never truly experienced the most important, threshold moments in life." [20] According to the author, the aging cartography revealed a pattern of historical regression:

> Wilna, like many other ancient towns, experienced many devastating fires. Both hard times and a lack of gifted leaders always infringed on a full recovery of the city. This is how the old, wrinkly face of the city matured: since there was no general plan, each house was built with no consideration to other buildings, Hence, a straight line became a curve, and with time, and because of the hilly terrain, these curves evolved into an web. Looking at Wilna, the entwined puzzling network of the ancient streets of Rome appears coherent and rational. [21]

This twisted urban skeleton, continues Monty, "with its crooked streets and knotted lanes has no clearly demarcated street hierarchy," and, hence, it has no "heart that could regulate its everyday life." In summary, "the city map summons an incision," a radical cartographical surgery delivering the energy of modern Europe into the clogged urban arteries of aged Wilna.

The regeneration of the city must begin by eliminating the meandering narrow lanes of the old town and by widening its main thoroughfares. New boulevards ought to be laid out and comatose urban squares need to be redeveloped; unruly local rivers should be embanked and the engulfing nature must be tamed. Most importantly, the city should openly embrace the railway station – the essential link in the German war machine. For this purpose, "the crooked ancient streets should be straightened up and broadened so the centre of the town has direct access to the train station. This clear-cut slit will create a main urban axis that will immediately harmonise the map with the function of the city." In a satirical tone, Monty suggests that the legendary practitioner of urban modernity "Baron Haussmann, the creator of Parisian boulevards, would find plenty of inspiring work." But until this magic time of modern transformation comes, visitors to Wilna "will have to tolerate the barely existing local street logic, because a navigation through this incomprehensible urban maze is only possible by accepting its outmoded rationale." [22]

By Monty's own admission, following this logic, a traveller will inevitably find himself wandering aimlessly through the labyrinth of unidentifiable locations. "In many cities, one can orient himself by remembering the names of the streets and by noting their geographical relationship. Not so in Wilna, where a visitor has to cross the same street several times before he can even distinguish it from other streets."[23] In addition, while the town possesses many "big and small squares that look very charming in spring, there is no main square that could unify the city's life. All the squares, like the city's crooked streets, had emerged capriciously, without any clear public function in mind." There is nothing in Wilna, for example, comparable to "the Marktplatz in Hildesheim, the Altmarkt in Dresden or the Piazza in Florence." The huge Cathedral Square of Wilna is "a seemingly limitless expanse that on one side is bounded by the city, but on the other side is freed by wilderness." It is "not even a square but an untamed park, a green tunnel that shoots up to Castle Hill and merges the city with the surrounding home gardens."[24] The intrusion of nature checks all modern activities; as a result, "the progressive contemporary urban rhythm has yet to invade Wilna's squares, which are still governed by the pervasive lethargy of the past."[25]

Monty points to the difference between what a passing observer finds and what is revealed to those who enter the puzzle. "Any person who looks down at the town from the surrounding hills or some tall buildings, such as the lofty military barracks near the train station," states the guide, "can see that Wilna is a big city. Many travellers, who only stop here for a couple hours on their way to more important destinations, witness only the uninviting spectacle of an impoverished provincial town with inadequately paved streets. This first gloomy impression extinguishes any desire to explore the city. But only by immersing ourselves into its winding terrain is it possible to discover the town's colourfully intertwined life."[26] Accordingly, Monty invites travellers to become flaneurs, and use his text as a diagram of potentially intriguing urban encounters. In other words, in the absence of a good map or modern topographical features, it is only through an act of aimless strolling that Wilna can attain the progressive spirit of modern life.

The writer's target audience, and hence, the potential "field practitioners" of the suggested urban itineraries, were front-line soldiers stationed in and around Wilna. The guide contains no practical tourist information, such as specific details concerning accommodations, food and transportation, for the soldier does not need such knowledge. His lodgings and food are provided by the military. There were some other German-language publications published by the same press of the Tenth Army that specifically concentrated on

54. A plan of Wilna and its environs with highlighted main thoroughfares cutting through the city, 1917.

the architectural and historical landscape of the city, stressing its affiliation to Teutonic culture.[27] In contrast, Monty attempted to familiarise his readers with Wilna through a set of random and expressionistic excursions, allowing a greater degree of personal freedom and imagination.

As the war became more brutal and moved beyond the immediate environs of the civilised, peaceful and familiar world, the German soldier, in the words of historian Eksteins, would gradually lose his affiliation with the cultural milieu of his native land and become a borderline figure. "As an agent of both destruction and regeneration, of death and rebirth, the soldier was inclined to see himself as a 'frontier' personality, as a paladin of change and new life. He was a traveller who had journeyed, on order, to the limits of existence, and there on the periphery he 'lived' in a unique way, on the edge of no man's land, on the margin of normal categories."[28] On the Eastern front, this "frontier personality" of the soldier was strengthened by the simple fact that he was the conqueror of a strange, unfamiliar land. Not only had the soldier voyaged to the extremes of human existence, but he had also travelled to the borderlines of the German world. Here, in the occupied territories, he was asked to be a pioneer, a bearer of German *Kultur*. Lacking in rational spatial order and metropolitan experience, Wilna, in Monty's words, only "speaks to our emotions,"[29] which, ironically, makes the city a perfect place to test the limits of German *Vaterland* and *Kultur*.

Monty reveals both a genuine interest in and detailed acquaintance with the place; presumably he spent a reasonable amount of time in the city becoming fully accustomed to its "outmoded spatial rationality." And arguably his awareness, and more importantly, personal respect for local cultural, religious and historical complexities, turned Monty into a passionate partisan of the city. Throughout the guided narrative of Wilna, Monty often refers to the city as "our city." The possessive term can simultaneously be interpreted as a hint of familiarity and as a signal of domination. The Tenth Army was a combative force, and its long trench-line of defence spanned the northern part of the Russian-German front that had frozen some hundred kilometres east of the city in the late fall of 1915. Yet in contrast to the German fighting armies on the Western Front, the Tenth Army was also an occupying army, with full administrative responsibilities. As Ludendorff suggested, the soldiers of the Tenth Army, but especially its high-ranking officers, had a dual patriotic duty: to fight the enemy and to colonise, that is, to Germanise, the occupied region. So in a way, Monty, through his unorthodox guidebook, attempts to acclimatise German soldiers to the idea and practices of colonial domination. His tours of Wilna bond the military responsibilities of battling front-line soldiers to the artful pleasures of urban wandering. Monty teaches the touring soldiers how to infiltrate the unknown spaces of the city without losing a strong sense of German identity.

The introduction to the city is the train station, a heavily regulated place of cyclical but anonymous arrivals and departures. Here, at the point where, in Monty's words, "war and peace come together," neither the city nor those "who come here from abroad" have yet to acquire an identity marked by a recognisable insignia of their belonging.[30] The train station is a fluid place, "a giant waiting room where everyone is a traveler released from his dependent relationship with fatherland and family home."[31] The German soldier, how-

55. The waiting hall of Wilna train station, 1916.

ever, is not a free traveler, since his mobility is determined and constrained by the shifting trajectories of war. "The wartime traveler is not an individual," reminds the author of the guide, "but an object, a living cargo, who is forced to conceal all his domestic ties with everyday life."[32] The front line, rather than urban life, regulates the routine of the train station:

> Wilna's train station is like any train station during wartime – everything here serves the needs of war. There is not the slightest indication of confusion or disorder: military and civilian trains always arrive and depart on time. And the trains move in both directions: westwards towards home and eastwards towards new battlefields. The train station does not fully belong to the city, because it conforms to the rules and regulations of the colossal war-machine that runs the entire world.[33]

In the eyes of the transient and subordinate soldier, the clockwork rhythm of the station still manages to camouflage the immediacy of war. The waiting room, train schedules, ticket-sellers, buffets, baggage claim rooms and everything else that makes a train journey possible, offer comfort to military and civilian passengers alike. At the station, women and men of all ages share the same act of coming or going, and German officers and soldiers appear to mingle freely with local peasants and civilian employees. The station is a no man's land but, in contrast to the front line, it seemingly belongs to everyone. Conclusively, in Monty's view, in this spatial intersection of war and peace, "individual destinies intertwine," but only for a brief moment in order to be immediately untangled.[34]

Initially, the impact of the city on the voyager's destiny and destination is minimal, and only "outside the station, where the city truly begins," does the soldier become fully enveloped by its domesticity. "In the train station," observes Monty, "a traveller is homeless; outside it, he is immediately confronted with the advertisement of his new residence. The city swiftly entraps him and takes him away. From now on, the traveller does not have to search for anything – he only needs to follow. And until the waiting hall of the station takes the departing soldier back to the war, the city fully controls his fate."[35]

Outside the train station, Wilna opens up as a nameless and faceless city, a place with no clear connections to Germany or direct associations for the soldier. But with each new encounter, the soldier adds a new feature to the city's anonymous face. Gradually, Wilna begins to resemble home.

Monty arrives in unfamiliar Wilna with the map of a continental divide in his mind. Everywhere he finds signs of being spirited away from Europe. Peculiar local traditions, customs and architectural details are quickly spotted within the anticipated geography of Russian expanses, Asian spaces and Oriental quarters. And even the native imprints of modernity take a distinctively un-western turn. The newly laid-out Lukischkiplatz on the boulevard-like Georgsstrasse is a "typical Russian wasteland, without any clear relation to the surrounding buildings." And the Georgsplatz, situated in the middle of the city's modern shopping area, "lacks architectural coherence and a European sense of spatial order."[36]

Only under closer scrutiny does the city reveal its affinities with the homeland. The Gothic church of St. Anna, for instance, pleases the German visitor with its architectural "energy that could only be found among the cathedrals of Southern Germany."[37] The descending picturesque views from Castle Hill evoke the lyrical words of the unidentified but presumably recognised "famous German poet."[38] And the narrow winding cobbled streets of Wilna's old town recapitulate youthful street adventures in "small university towns" of Germany that could be summarised by a familiar student tune.[39] Through these predominantly middle-class German spatial and biographical references,

56. Wilna Labour House Exhibition, 1916. As the poster shows, the German authorities in Wilna recognised the public usage of five languages – German, Lithuanian, Byelorussian, Polish and Yiddish.

the incomprehensible spatiality of Wilna is fraternised, courted and finally becomes domesticated. These unveiled scraps of familiar terrain reassure the displaced German soldiers of the geographical proximity of the homeland, but under this scenario, the occupied city stands as an imperfect reminder of the idyllic German life. Hence, Monty finds Wilna to be located "between the homeland and a foreign land" (*"zwischen Heimat und Fremde"*).[40]

For the front-line soldier, the discovery of the in-between condition of Wilna is first and foremost a learning experience:

> When a soldier returns to the city from the war zone, his relationships with the world and people go through enormous changes. If the soldier came back directly from the front line, where he had led a primitive life of forest existence, a rapid acclimatisation into urban life is impossible. At the front, the soldier's feet get used to swampy and muddy terrain, but in the city, he faces a solid street pavement. The soldier needs to master anew the unhurried pace and rhythm of various street movements. In these circumstances, an ordinary event, such as walking, becomes an extraordinary act.
>
> But if fate brings this front-line creature to Wilna, he needs to learn something else: he must master navigation through its narrow passages. The main streets of Wilna are like the streets everywhere in Europe: people promenade on broad sidewalks that clearly separate the street from the buildings. In Germany, we call this part of the street the Bürgersteig, since we almost forgot another [French] name for it, the Trottoir, which, among the people, came to be known as Trittoir. But how to describe, in German, or any other foreign tongue, the uncivilised sidewalks of our city? What term could explain this narrow plank along the gutter that constantly squeaks and moves under your feet: it suddenly goes up and then disappears completely in the mud. Of course, rarely does this seesawing plank belong entirely to one person – all the pedestrians are very keen to use it. So, a fascinating dance with constantly new movements evolves around it: first, you leap on it, then, you raise up, twist and bounce again, trying to keep a balance. It is not a walk, but a quadrille dance.[41]

Mastering the streets is essential in finding a way to the city's heart, because in Wilna "there are some secret lanes and pathways that are familiar only to

57. Wilna: a wartime scene at a busy flea market.

local residents. These intimate passageways connect countless houses and courtyards, but you cannot find them on any map. Their romantic spirit is an anomaly in our society ruled by extensive railway travelling, but our modern idea of commercial passages originated from these intimately ancestral places."[42] The alleys of Wilna are like modern shopping arcades, where the action never stops.

> Every city in Europe has some secret passages, but they are usually very quiet, deserted places. But not in Wilna! Here, to this day, the mysterious alleyways of Wilna are full of life. Still, the most intriguing aspect of Wilna is not that these passages are always alive, but that every inhabitant of the city intimately knows them. Along these privatised public lanes, the entire commercial life of the city is organised. You can buy anything you want: furniture, sausages, shoes, iron beds, furs, etc. In Wilna, these alleys are as important to the general well-being of the city as grand boulevards in a modern metropolis. In these secret alleys, life has yet to become history.[43]

Through the narrow alleyways of the old town, Monty inevitably leads his readers to the Jewish Quarter, where history is the most alive. In contrast to the former imperial masters of Lithuania – the Russians – the Germans were fascinated by the Jewish life of the city. The linguistic affinity between the

German and Yiddish languages made fraternisation easier. (*Wilnaer Zeitung* even printed the Hebrew alphabet, so German soldiers could read Yiddish shop signs.) Yet to the Germans, the Jews remained a mysterious nation – a cultural puzzlement of biblical proportions. "At the heart of the big city of Wilna," announces Monty, "there is an ocean island where the people of Israel lead an isolated life. In the past, the gates of the ghetto kept the Jews together, but today, traditions and piety keep them apart from the rest of the people." A journey into this urban atoll is not without certain physical risks, because "regardless of weather conditions, the sky in the Jewish quarter is always dark. A westerner who accidentally comes to the shores of this island is immediately assaulted by the sea of dirt and poverty. His hearing is offended by perpetual dissonance; and the nose – well, the nose is unmercifully attacked by all kinds of foul smells. To the wandering European, a stroll through the Jewish neighbourhood is an extremely challenging affair, because only local residents can endure its stifling rancid air."[44]

In this unapproachable, displeasing, threatening and physically offensive, but at the same time mysterious and mirage-like urban environment, the German soldier-aesthete suddenly becomes a colonial ethnographer whose patience is soon to be rewarded with the hectic spectacle of an Oriental bazaar:

> In winter, the residents stay tucked away from cold and wind in their homes. But on a warm summer day, the crooked, cramped street with its narrow sidewalks and impassable pavement turns into a stage. This local scenography is familiar to everyone who has travelled to the Orient. Yet, in contrast to Tangier or Algiers, where the bustling mass of people is dispersed by the interconnected street pattern, here, the street assembles people into a crowd. On this street, where domestic life flows out into the open from every corner, the private secluded life of a single individual melts into a communal episode. Various trades commence within the endless gateways, courtyards and hallways of the buildings: every corner, alcove and opening in the wall bursts with action. The entire Ghetto is a giant market place, and commerce, an ancient disposition of this nation, regulates every gesture of the local residents. Most stores, however, look like caves without any light or fresh air. ... You leave the Jewish Quarter with two memorable images: the abundance of shopping baskets and children.[45]

Monty's ethnographic evaluation of the commercial bustle of the Jewish Quarter dismisses the official German policies that attempted to regulate every market transaction. Food was rationed and the majority of the urban population was on the brink of starvation, but according to numerous administrative decrees, most commercial dealings, especially those that involved selling farm produce, were prohibited. Monty witnessed, described or imagined the illegal and semi-illegal market life of the city, which served the basic needs of its impoverished and hungry residents. In general, this was not a large-scale trade, since it relied on the unpredictable flow of smuggled agricultural goods from the Lithuanian countryside. Even the German military authorities had to admit that the wartime "spectacle" of local Jewish commercial life had little to do with the traditional business practices and norms of "Oriental" Jewry. In fact, impoverished Wilna's Jewish Quarter served the ethnographical desires of the German officialdom poorly. "On one occasion," remembers Hirsch Abramowicz, who was a resident of the city during the Great War, "the Germans devised a rather original way to exploit the passion for fish among the inhabitants of Vilna. Notices in Yiddish were pasted up in every Jewish neighbourhood stating that on Friday, fish would be sold in the marketplace at ten pfennings per pound and in unlimited quantities. On Friday, people streamed into the marketplace by the thousands, but there was no fish for sale. The Germans needed to shoot film footage of Vilna's Jewish population, and this was the only way it was possible to assemble a large crowd in those days."[46]

Nonetheless, in Monty's Wilna, the busy life of the Jewish Quarter "keeps boiling here all the time, until, suddenly, all shopping baskets, weights and children disappear. The Sabbath call closes all the commercial caverns and the customary street racket quickly calms down. The drama of everyday life is finally over."[47] But even this religious act of the Jewish weekly cycle was dramatically altered by the German occupation. The German administrative regulations did not only significantly modify the commercial spaces and habits of the city's residents, but also forced the breaking of the traditional sanctity of the Sabbath call. Periodically, throughout the occupied territories, "Jewish stores were ordered to be open for business for several hours on Saturday. This put an end to the small-town fear of desecrating the Sabbath. The Germans had no regard for these religious feelings and frequently forced Jews to clean the streets, repair the pavement, and so on, on the Sabbath."[48] Despite these enforced modes of modernising Jewish traditions, or perhaps because of them, Monty continued to explore the Jewish Quarter by following the secretive paths of the religious and pious Jews.

Once the first commercial act of the everyday drama of the Jewish Quarter is over, a second act of the Jewish religious spectacle begins. In order to witness this act, the soldier-ethnographer has to break the social and physical walls that separate him from the inhabitants of the Jewish district. He must become a participant in the communal event and, rather than simply observ-

Ein malerischer Winkel

Weihnachtsgrüsse aus Wilna

58. "Christmas greetings from Wilna: a picturesque corner," 1916.

ing and recording the Jewish religious customs, he has to re-enact this cyclical episode of ancient traditions. Accordingly, on the Sabbath evening, Monty invites the soldier to join the enigmatic ceremony of the "ancient Jewish tribe." But first, the modern hero has to find the spiritual heart of the Jewish religious life of Wilna: the Great Synagogue, which usually remains unapproachable to foreign invaders.

> All significant religious [Christian] buildings of Wilna are clearly visible and are easy to find; in contrast, the famous Great Synagogue is concealed from the peering eyes of the traveller. It is simply impossible to find it, because it is hidden

behind the ordinary-looking and unexceptional houses of the Jewish Quarter. The traveller might pass by this House of God a hundred times without ever suspecting its existence. A single opening, one of those mysterious Wilna gates, reveals its unadvertised location: the gate of the building marked as Deutsche Strasse [German Street] 12 is the magic entrance point into the elusive world of the Great Synagogue.

The best time to enter this mysterious universe is around six o'clock on a Friday evening. Only a few steps away, the busy and noisy Deutsche Strasse is full of shops with modern window displays, but once the traveller crosses the threshold of the gate, he is immediately transported back into ancient history. The narrow, winding lane greets him with the stuffy air of the ghetto: the walls of the buildings are adorned with unrecognisable Hebrew letters. Enormous crowds of pious Jewish men rush by the traveller, but not a single building around him indicates the sacred presence of the House of God summoning this commotion. Is it possible that this insignificant house in front of him, which swallows this procession of people, is the final destination of his exploration? The traveller, without being fully aware of where it will take him, must follow the stream of faithful men. He must be patient and follow the footsteps of those who had just disappeared inside the building. A dark stairway leads downstairs and then, unexpectedly, it becomes clear what hides behind this narrow walkway. Finally, the Great Temple is found! The building, like a symbol of the time when the religion forced its followers to bow their heads, is submerged deep into the ground. Centuries have darkened its walls, but the synagogue has preserved its incredible sense of reverence and piety. Near the synagogue there is a bathhouse and a library, which makes this entire building complex the nexus of the Jewish universe. A religious man can live his entire life without leaving the courtyard of the Great Synagogue. His life, guarded by traditions and customs that came here from distant countries and centuries, exists only a few steps away from the wartime turmoil of contemporary Wilna.[49]

At the end of this urban expedition into the religious epicentre of Wilna Jewry, Monty comes to a realisation that the two worlds – the city and the "Jewish island" – not only live two separate lives, but also orient themselves to different temporal and geographical orders. Hence, for the modern traveller, it becomes extremely difficult to frame this compact Jewish world, which seems to burst with the religious piety and mysticism of ancient times. The encountered Jews – young and old men who come to the synagogue courtyard for religious and social reasons – simply ignore him, and the incidental flaneur leaves the Jewish Quarter with a bewildering feeling of being out of place, as if he had been chased away from Wilna by some cultural force that refuses to acknowledge his presence.

He tries his artistic and ethnographic luck in a remote corner of Wilna, the old Jewish cemetery on the other side of the river. As a rule, Monty does not

59. A holy day in the Old Synagogue of Wilna, 1916.

try to place the living Jewish world within the European or German worlds, yet, faced with the Jewish dead in the final act of his "Jewish drama," he feels obliged to force at least the Jewish past into German cultural chronology. The trip to the Jewish cemetery starts with crossing the waters: the cemetery is reached from the centre of the city by a ferry ride. In this old and relatively remote graveyard, surrounded by "strange, foreign and indecipherable" tombs, the traveller attempts to encircle the Jewish universe with the biographical marks of notable Germans. "It is obvious that not a single corpse has crossed the gates of the cemetery for several decades," observes the guide. "Everything here is marked by decay, oblivion and an expired past. The first graves appeared when Martin Luther was still a child—the last burials here took place at the time of Goethe's death."[50]

After visiting the local Jewish world, Monty moves further away from the old town into one of the most exotic suburbs of Wilna, Lukischki (Lukiškės). In this semi-rural corner of the city, framed by a "typically Russian urban space," the Lukischkiplatz, the unfinished closure of a modern boulevard, the Georgstrasse, the imposing structure of the tsarist prison and the Wilja River, the modern hero finds another impenetrable site of Wilna, the so-called Turkish Quarter. It "should be pointed out from the beginning," warns Monty, "that the so-called Turkish Quarter does not mean that there is an entire neighbourhood in Wilna inhabited by our trustworthy allies, the Ottomans. This name is given to one of the city's districts occupied by the followers of the Muslim faith."[51] But, given its association with Islam, the small neighbourhood becomes an imprint of the Orient on northern Wilna's soil. "We cross the Lukischkiplatz, a vast urban expanse," continues the guide, "and enter into the contrasting world of an Oriental urban maze."[52]

Closer inspection of this Oriental labyrinth reveals the existence of a less mysterious but no less exotic local spectacle. Surprisingly, only the newly built but unassuming mosque and the old Muslim cemetery are left as residues of the former "Oriental maze." The so-called Turkish corner is nothing more than a picturesque village only a few blocks away from the city centre: "If stone pavements and brick houses indicate urban place, then we know that here we are in a true village. We are surrounded exclusively by wooden houses and long fences and the street facades of the buildings are outlined by the most fantastic wooden carvings." In contrast to the Jewish neighbourhood, which conspicuously exists outside the perimeters of war, this neighbourhood, which had been housing local Muslim Tartars since the fifteenth century, is fully rearranged by the spectre of war. Monty's curiosity about the city's Muslim population stems from a geopolitical awareness of the role of the Ottoman Empire as a key ally of Germany in the current conflict. He walks into the village looking for some visible reassurances of this alliance. Alas, he is greeted by silent indifference. The needs of war nonetheless dictate his every gaze, and, ironically, the wooden houses with their graciously carved details do not stimulate aesthetic appreciation, but provoke a strictly utilitarian response. "In wartime," concludes Monty, "you can not resist thinking about all these wooden constructions as being extremely usefully turned into firewood. But it seems that the locals will fervently protect every single wooden detail of their houses."[53]

In the end, this rural enclave does not deliver the expected Oriental experience, and Monty quickly withdraws to a more promising and enigmatic site, the small Muslim cemetery located next to the neighbourhood. Here, he makes a brief sympathetic commentary about the sad historic fate of the displaced Tartar soldiers who were brought from their Crimean homeland some centuries ago:

> A strange feeling engulfs one while looking at rows of these foreign graves overshadowed by the high dome of the nearby Christian church of the prison. High above the graves perches a shiny cross, an imperial symbol that dominates over the homeless half-moon of the mosque. The forefathers of the local residents were prisoners of war whose graveyard dreams are the last vestiges of the Islamic faith. Sorrow and grief linger over the mosque and the entire Turkish district.[54]

60. The wooden mosque of Wilna, 1916.

Confronted with the historically distant dead, Monty leaves this "melancholic neighbourhood" and concludes the tour of the city with the two following entries: "On the other side of the river" and "Over the roofs" are literally concerned with the joys and dangers of losing oneself in the sights of the foreign city. In the end, his geographically imprecise and lyric wanderings through the city produce a contradictory effect. While they familiarised the German soldiers with the most private and secluded features of the city, they also re-established an emotional distance between the conqueror-artist and the inhabitants of the place. Apparently, the "new home" is not only populated by unfamiliar people, but is also haunted by various ghostly memories of home.

Initially, Monty's wanderings implied a purely physical activity – a free rambling through the city without any burden of personal memories or pre-existing knowledge of the place. Simultaneously, it was meant to open up the mysteries of the city. In contrast to military conquest, which is usually a collective act and involves a certain degree of planning, wandering is supposed to be an individual act of spatial conquest. Eksteins, however, reminds us that during the middle years of the Great War, the "war became increasingly a matter of individual interpretative power," and Monty's proposed itinerary through Wilna seems to conform to this idea.[55] With each new journey, new adventure and new formation, the relationship between the soldier and the city becomes less anonymous, and the boundary between the two loses its initial sharpness and precision. The protagonist of Wilna's excursions finds it progressively more difficult to separate the occupied city from his melancholically remembered anonymous German hometown. The corporeal and unreal merge into a seductive, dangerously hypnotic surreal, and the travelling soldier starts to nervously experience, rather than just see the city. The unmediated closeness of and prolonged exposure to the city provokes an emotional outburst that leads to a dangerous excavation of the soldier's inner world.

In one of the most autobiographical entries of the guidebook, Monty maps out a short journey through his living room. "I can not identify the itinerary of this journey," declares the writer, "because this road is very short, and besides, it is not for public use. I only need to stand up from my table and come closer to the window of my room, and I can see all the landmarks of Wilna. The entire city is situated in a valley that spreads between our private little hill and Castle Hill. My window simultaneously frames and reflects this endless space of Russian proportions. From here, my eye can easily glide over the roofs, frontons and towers of the city."[56] But instead of examining the panoramic wonders of this "Russian expanse," Monty gazes over intimate scenes that fill the courtyards and apartments of the exposed city. Slowly but surely, his voyeuristic escape leads to a painful self-discovery. Once the private sights of the city are conquered, the author-traveller finds himself surrounded by the glaring spectre of home. This is not the glorious and ecstatic apparition of the *Vaterland* encountered by Marshal Ludendorff in Kowno, but a tormenting and disorienting vision, a delirium that can only lead to personal crisis. As it becomes more familiar, the town inflames emotions. The triumphant voyeur becomes a fugitive, a victim of his own curiosity, which unexpectedly turns into a fatal attraction. Under scrutiny, Wilna becomes a siren, and its mesmerising effects on the soldier could be compared to the final stage of typhus fever – the disease that ravaged so many lives at the end of the Great War – described by Thomas Mann as "debilitation ... at its worst" when "no one can say whether the patient's mind has sunk into the void of night or if it has become a stranger to his body and has turned away to wander in distant, deep, silent dreams, unmarked by visible signs or audible sounds. The body lies in total apathy. This is the moment of crisis."[57] An escape – a dose of reality – is the only solution to this sickly relationship between the city and soldier:

> An unusual sensation captures the soldier who gazes at the city from above. After spending months deep in the forest, the city lights and shadows stir up memories. As if he were hallucinating, the soldier sees the streets and squares of his native town. The war has created something phenomenal, something that moves between the fatherland and a foreign land.
>
> After surviving all seasons of the year in the wilderness – after a year at the front line – we acquire an uncontrollable desire for the city. At least, we want to see undamaged houses with intact roofs and unbroken windows. We sit in the window and gaze at this town – the name of which we never wanted to know – and feel its sway over our life. The mystery of the city unfolds: unknown but so dear, foreign but so intimate, this city lies bare in front of our eyes. Strange yet familiar, the town below speaks to our feelings. Its stony body becomes less enigmatic; but its soul, its inner voice, illuminated by the bright midday light, remains mute. Only after dark does it slowly start to open up. In the dark, when the glow of the Sabbath candles reaches us from the unveiled windows, and when on a warm summer night a gentle murmur from the homes of its inhabitants (who, because of the war, are forbidden to go outside into the streets) starts to drift about, our feelings, seduced by such secrets, calm down. Yet it would be much better if our emotions would have been left untouched, so we could leave all these whispers and rustles, and go back into the darkness of night unscathed.[58]

Such a torturously foreign sentimental bond to Wilna – a rarity at the time – must be contrasted to the more prosaic relationship between the city and its German occupiers, which, on some occasions, were as physically intense and emotionally charged as Monty's dreamy urban invasions. Wilna, like any town near the front, had its share of public houses, and for many German soldiers their brief encounters had obvious sexual aspects. In this case, the re-lationship between the two "partners" was kept in private, personal memories, since the German military and social censorship did not allow discussion of such topics to reach the public in the *Vaterland*. The extent of these socially asymmetrical relationships is difficult to gauge, but some of the interaction between local women and German soldiers was based on more equal social and material co-dependency. For instance, Lucien Finance, an Alsatian serv-ing the German army in Wilna, married a local woman. His reminiscences of

61. Wilna in the fourth year of world war, 1917.

the city (recorded in 1995!) indicate a reasonable degree of reciprocity between local Polish residents and German soldiers. Incidentally, the German military commanders did not trust the Latinised "men from Alsace-Lorraine ... they were, therefore, generally sent to the East."[59] Hence, many "unreliable" Alsatians were stationed in and around Wilna, and perhaps this factor alone, as Finance suggested, might help to explain the higher degree of sociability of the German soldiers with the local population. After all, the Alsatians, like most residents of Wilna, possessed a frontier identity: most of them were bilingual and their national loyalties depended on the imperial and dynastic fortunes of the opposing European forces.

Travelling via Berlin and Königsberg, private Finance, a native of the small Alsatian town of Seleste, was involuntarily brought to Wilna. Here he experienced his first fierce battle, during which, he remembered decades later, he had "probably done many terrible things." "Somebody had to die," recounts Finance, "and it was either them [the Russians] or I." After the "heroic defence" of the Green Bridge in Wilna, Finance's commander wanted to nominate him for the Iron Cross. But he cared less about military vanity than his personal survival: "I told him I did not need the Iron Cross. Instead,

I asked him to help me stay away from the front. The commander promised to employ me at his office, because, as he explained, 'such a brave man deserves our respect!' Consequently, the captain placed me in the accounting bureau of the military headquarters."[60] As a result of his bravery being noticed, from the first day of the German occupation of Wilna until the final withdrawal of the German troops in November of 1918, Lucien Finance lived in the city.

Soon he fell in love with Maria, a Polish woman who worked in the local bank, and at the end of his stay in Wilna he married her. (After the war, Maria moved with him to France.) Consequently, in Finance's recollections, Wilna emerges as a place where the rather ordinary if unconventional events of his family life intertwine with everyday front-line experiences: battles, injuries, sudden death, illness, hunger, looting, discipline, hierarchical subordination, desertion and so on. Therefore, in his distant memories, trivial personal details and intimate experiences of the city outweigh the panoramic or heroic experiences of the place. In short, for Lucien Finance, as perhaps for many other German soldiers, Wilna possessed no direct ideological or clear geopolitical meaning. It was simply, as he put it, a familiar place on the "other side of Europe" where he was lodged by the unpredictable forces of the imperialist war.[61]

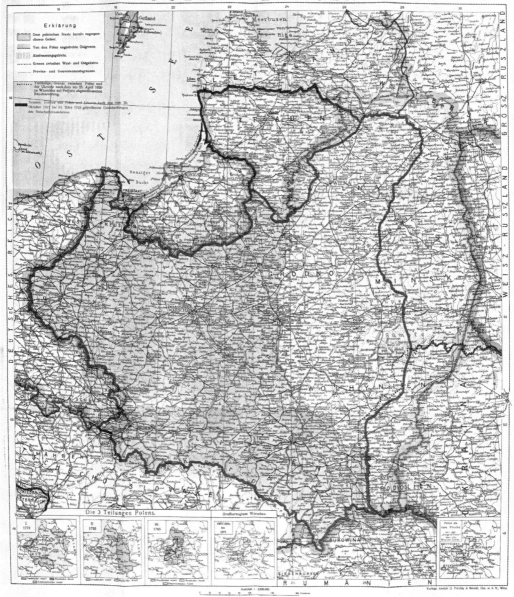

62. A German map of Poland and Lithuania delineating the shifting borders of the new states, circa 1923.

CHAPTER SEVEN:

The Absent Nation

> It is not without some difficulty that a foreigner learns to understand the conflict which occured in recent times between Poland and Lithuania concerning the beautiful city of Wilno. If he is a reader of history he may remember that Wilno was once the capital of the Grand Duchy of Lithuania and that in bygone times the Grand Dukes of Lithuania were at the same time Kings of Poland. ... In a word there seems to be some mystery about this city of Wilno, where sometimes everybody is Lithuanian and sometimes nobody is.
>
> "Some puzzling appearances" in *The Story of Wilno*, 1942

In the eastern part of Europe peace was slow to come. The signing of the armistice on the Western Front in November 1918, which demanded German withdrawal from all occupied territories, only furthered the frontier-like condition of Vilnius. In the vast territory left by the German forces – from the Baltic to the Black Sea – a string of fledgling states were attempting to carve out their political existence from the spoils of imperial Europe. Russia, now radically transformed through the twofold revolution of 1917 into a Soviet state and plagued by civil strife, terror and hunger, was eager but unable to re-establish its pre-war dominance over the region. Imperial Germany, now the Weimar Republic, was also politically weak, militarily restrained and too socially deflated to make a great difference in the geopolitical rearrangement of the region, and the winning powers – Great Britain, France and USA – were too distant, divided and non-committal towards solving local problems of national and ideological fragmentation. On the ground, political pragmatism became the rule of engagement: the enemy of the enemy was a friend, regardless of national colour, ideological foundation or future prospects of alliance. Nevertheless, most governments, supported by the western powers, were fighting back the advancing Red Army, but the warfare between and within the new states was as vicious as the one based on the global struggle between communism and capitalism. In the end, as various peoples were solidified into states, theories of internationalism and class struggle were replaced by the concept of national self-determination. Modern Europe was becoming a continent of nation-states – a patchwork of various countries plastered together by external animosities and internal mistrusts. In large part, this new Europe was overlaid on the same geographical terrain as the long-forgotten region of Sarmatia, a part of the continent marked by spatial fluidity and historical contradictions.

Empires were built as royal family affairs; republics, at least in theory, were matters of popular assemblies. As the future of the nation-state in Europe was discussed by the winners, masses of people displaced by the war and ensuing revolutions, and exhausted by years of deprivation and disease (1918 was the year of the flu pandemic that took millions of lives), were trying to find home. For countless Europeans, geographical mobility was not a matter of choice. Searching for home and, in many cases, lost family, was an arduous task without any end in sight. For some, the constant changes made in the political cartography of Europe brought a different misplacement: as new states emerged, one could easily end up in a strange country without changing residence.

So in these years of geographical turmoil, home was something more than what could be pinned down by a house address (which, incidentally, might have changed overnight by the ideological obsession of any new regime to rename places and streets). Multiple displacements fired up a desire to live an identity independent from war and social upheavals. Home became a place rooted in people, in a feeling of communal solidarity and social camaraderie. The idea of nationhood and new forms of statehood offered some kind of comfort. A nation-state was an answer to the inherited problems of the old world, but it did not serve everyone equally or identically. On a collectivised journey of a self-discovery, New Europe demanded the surrender of a significant part of one's past, discarding personal memory and private experience as attributes of a bygone age.

Some nations, like Poland, had emerged from the swirling process of modern statecraft as battered victors, establishing lessened replicas of the old imperial order with a large, diverse territory and a heterogeneous, multicultural population. Others, like Lithuania, which had been less successful in achieving its national goals, were left with wounded pride, territorial retrenchment, political insignificance and cultural marginalisation. In this realm of unequal opportunities, Vilnius had tried unsuccessfully to find a niche by becoming a leverage site, a place where the life of nationhood did not have to be re-allied with the practice of statehood. This idea of Vilnius's exceptionality within the new map of Europe was an intellectual phantasm, advocated by some local activists who searched for answers for modern dilemmas within the expired realm of the Grand Duchy of Lithuania. Their philosophical explorations never came to fruition, because, according to one of the advocates of the idea, the chaos in the postwar city, augmented by yet another wave of refugees and external military and ideological pressures, was so immense that there was neither social aptitude nor political will to change anything.[1] In essence, the governing political principles of military occupation never abandoned the city, for even after the last German troops left in the early days of 1919, Vilnius was treated by all the conflicting sides – the Polish, Lithuanian and Soviet governments – as conquered territory.

The national question of Vilnius, that is, the issue of its political belonging, threatened the ambassadorial sanctum of the Paris Peace Conference assembled by the winning parties in 1919 to map the future of postwar Europe. Yet the issue was too complicated, and, at the same time, too mundane for the leaders of the great powers to make it a diplomatic lesson of national reconciliation. The Lithuanians claimed Vilnius as the rightful historical capital of independent Lithuania; the Poles rejected such claims on the basis of the cultural and linguistic affinities of Wilno to Poland. The Soviet regime, in diplomatic isolation, voiced its opinion that although Vilna had been part of Russia, the Bolsheviks were ready to share it with the oppressed peoples (mostly peasants) of Lithuanian and Byelorussian origins. Nobody asked or wanted to hear what Vilne meant to the Jews.

But the diplomatic wrangling over the city was left unsettled, in part because no side truly controlled the region. In a brief period of two years (1918-1920), the city had experienced a stream of occupying armies, everything from the Red Army to Polish legionaries and Lithuanian volunteers. Local residents became accustomed to life in a battlefield, and those brave enough to venture outside their homes made a spectacle out of it by watching fights between different warring factions from the safety of a distant rise. Violence was random, but predictable – the Bolsheviks targeted representatives of the "national bourgeoisie"; the Poles targeted mostly communists and Jews, with the spectre of a pogrom hanging over every new occupation. Having no clear military advantage, Lithuanian authorities tried to impose linguistic supremacy by attempting to govern the city in Lithuanian, a language unknown to the vast majority of its residents.

In 1920 the city became the capital of a renegade military principality, awkwardly called Middle Lithuania, and presided over by a legion of insubordinate Polish officers. Finally, in 1922, after a flawed referendum (many non-Polish parties boycotted it), Wilno was incorporated into the Republic of Poland as the centre of a newly created Polish province. But the issue of the

63. Wilno: St. George Avenue, circa 1920.

city's national status refused to go away because of the Lithuanian demand to return it to their country. Indeed, despite being a provincial town in Poland, Vilnius had been the constitutional capital of Lithuania. Such legal framing put both countries in a permanent state of war: the border – in reality, the line of a ceasefire – between Poland and Lithuania was never ratified, and no established postal or transport network was allowed to cross this frontier. The Polish adoption of the city was never an all-embracing affair, and even two decades after the end of the Great War, its contested status was noted in *The National Geographic Magazine*. In 1938, the magazine ran a photo spread with the telling heading: "Wilno, Stepchild of the Polish Frontier."

The German writer Alfred Döblin greatly disliked travelling. His unease in leaving home even for a short trip was, no doubt, amplified by the isolating experience of war in the trenches of the Western Front; but he also thought of travelling as a frivolous pursuit, suitable only to the idle bourgeois or bored simpletons. He was interested, however, in city life, especially in its modern, metropolitan expression. Berlin, or more accurately, the bustling working-class district surrounding the chaotic square of Alexanderplatz, was the centre of his universe. He lived in the neighbourhood with his wife and three children, worked as a medical doctor at the local public health office and, through his literary imagination – and his most famous novel, *Berlin Alexanderplatz* – made the square synonymous with the modernist zeitgeist. Urban exploration, with all its unpredictable eventualities and commonplace melodrama, was made into a representational code of every metropolitan experience, but Döblin also transformed it into a form of political artistry, a social critique of the modern age without a hint of nostalgia, sentimentality or ideological banality.

City life runs through Döblin's bloodlines, delineating modern patterns of urban migration. The writer was a true Berliner and knew the city as his home, although, like so many of its residents at the time, he was not a native. He was born in 1878 in the Baltic Sea port city of Stettin, where his father, Max Döblin, owned a small business. At forty, the father left the family and fled with his mistress to Hamburg. Some years later, he was reportedly seen in America. Meanwhile, Döblin's abandoned and impoverished mother and her five children moved to Berlin. This move, in the writer's words, determined his "entire way of being." The abrupt change from the relative comfort of provincial Stettin to abysmal poverty in metropolitan Berlin made him realise that he had become a permanent member of "the nation that was poor." Years later, Döblin joined the ranks of the professional class, but he never shed his allegiance to the poor of the world.[2]

The writer grew up German, even if, as he recalls in his post-WWII autobiography, he "had been told at home in Stettin that [his] parents were of Jewish origin." His grandparents still spoke Yiddish – but his parents already spoke German, with some Polish thrown in. Döblin perceived some of this cultural confusion in his estranged father, whom he simultaneously "loudly cursed and silently admired."[3] Max Döblin was a person without a homeland. He was, in the words of his son, ethnologically "the victim of resettlement. All his values were reevaluated and devaluated."[4] Döblin was eager to reverse this cultural nomadism by trying to reconcile himself with the lost world of his ancestors: "Only in my generation has the memory, including the joyous memory of our background, and the old respect, been heavily and gradually revived." He claimed a success: "I – survived the great resettlement."[5]

This was a substantial leap, because in Döblin's childhood, his family's religion and ethnicity went mostly unobserved. His assimilated parents celebrated merely two Jewish holidays – the New Year and Yom Kippur – and that "was about the only thing concerning Judaism that I noticed about our family." At school too, "instruction in Judaism was equivocal and more voluntary. ... As for teaching, the actual religious teaching – I read it and listened to it. It was, and remained, superficial to me. It did not affect me emotionally. I felt no connection to it."[6]

During the Great War, Döblin served as a physician in the German army, helping to ease the unfolding human tragedies in the overcrowded field hospitals of the Western front. He returned from the trenches a committed pacifist, an anti-nationalist and a relentless critic of the new political regimes of Europe. He also wrote a biographical novel about Wallenstein, one of the most ruthless and treacherous generals of the Thirty Years War. The novelist became more interested in Jewish politics only after when, in "the first half of the nineteen-twenties, something resembling pogroms were taking place in Berlin, in the city's eastern section, on Gollnow Street and its surroundings." He joined a discussion group investigating the issues of anti-Semitism, and was asked by some prominent German Zionist intellectuals to take a trip to Palestine. The suggestion had an atypical effect on Döblin: "I did not, to be sure, agree to go to Palestine, but I found that I wanted to know more about the Jews. I discovered that I didn't know them. I could not call Jews those of my acquaintances who called themselves Jews. They weren't Jews in their beliefs, in their language, they were perhaps the vestige of an extinct people who had long ago assimilated into their environment. So I asked myself and others: where are the Jews? I was told: in Poland."[7]

The writer-doctor went to Poland in the fall of 1924 on behalf of *Die Neue Rundschau,* the magazine that published most of his literary works. Döblin was asked to write a series of reports about various social, cultural and political aspects of the modern Polish nation-state, still an alien territorial and national body in the eyes of most Germans. While the magazine paid for the three-week trip, the actual travel itinerary was determined by Döblin's personal interests and creative sensibilities. Döblin knew very little about Poland, and was not terribly interested in reading volumes of academic books, which he suspected to be biased, tedious and outdated. In his narrative explorations of Berlin, he relied on the representational technique of what he called the factual imagination (*Tatsachenphantasie*), creating an expressionistic form of reality based on the principle of montage. He explored and narrated Poland in a similar fashion. Two years after the trip, Döblin published a book with a simple title – *Reise in Polen* (*Journey to Poland*). The book worked against the growing stream of anti-Polish and anti-Jewish publications – and it had the rare quality of introspective analysis.

Throughout the nineteenth century, the acculturated western European Jews often viewed their eastern European brethren with a mixture of resentment and fascination. Ethnographer Age Meyer Benedictsen, whose father was a wealthy Danish Jew, visited Lithuania in the last decade of the century. He belonged to the generation of Döblin's parents – "the victims of the resettlement." His detailed description of Lithuanian Jewry reveals a contradictory sense of superiority and shame mixed with pity and amazement, often exhibited by western Jews at the moment of their encounter with the unassimilated Jewish masses of the European east:

> The Jews have been in Lithuania from the earliest time of which we have any reliable record, but they have neither been willing nor able to assimilate with the natives of the country. Their great numbers, their prejudices, their religious fanaticism, and their ancient exceptional legislation have tended to consolidate their position as an altogether alien element in the country. The many centuries have rather estranged them from the native race than united them with the latter, they do not speak the language of the country among themselves, but use their own Hebrew-German dialect, they do not dress like the rest of the people; although they have been forbidden to use their old peculiar dress, they manage by their dress to look different from other people. They have neither friends nor enemies nor interests in common with the people. The policy of the Jews has in the main been opportunistic, and it has been so of necessity; they have never been willing to make real friends for fear thereby of making enemies. They have carefully scented from which quarter they for the time being might expect to meet with the greatest protection, and they have never dared to rely on living in security; they have probably not taken the interest in living there that they would have done had they felt they were living in a country of their own. Lithuania has been the place where the Jews have had the simplest and most sincere belief in the Messiah. Nowhere have they been more prepared to receive the Redeemer than in this out-of-the-way corner, where the surroundings have allowed them to preserve all the memories, their traditions and customs in all their mystic dimness. To this very day the Lithuanian Jews say with the same confidence as centuries ago: 'He comes assuredly and He comes soon.'
>
> One should view the Lithuanian Jew in the light of this firm belief, or in any case the hereditary propensities which bottom in this belief, in order to attempt to understand him, for only then can one forgive his whole mode of life; something great can even be discerned in this people, who otherwise involuntarily impress one unfavourably.
>
> The Lithuanian Jews feel themselves as strangers, half homeless amongst a people who shun them, their whole existence is one continuous endeavour to keep a position of balance in the easiest way, to find the necessary bread, striving in their own shifty way to attain as much power as possible, and it does not concern the Jewish conception much whether this power be for the good or evil of the country in which they live. Humble and wretched as the Jew often appears to be, the pride of race still dwells within him. What does he care for the roughness and contempt of the infidels, he only gives away when he is obliged to, his mental pride does not

suffer under it. ... Dirty, mean, and greedy from a superficial point of view, the Jew still possesses the gold of the soul which can glitter at the proper time, and if one approaches him without any stupid prejudice one can see what is good in him, then the best human qualities, sympathy and helpfulness become apparent.

This two-sided state of affairs is the cause of that false position under which the Jews sigh in Lithuania, and there are many amongst them who have lost sight of the goal, being engrossed by the means of how to attain it.[8]

At the turn of the twentieth century, an increasing number of German-Jewish intellectuals started to search for their ancestral cultural roots in the numerous *shtetlakh* of Eastern Europe. These ethnographical, literary and sometimes genealogical discoveries were promoted by an influential magazine with a suggestive title, *Ost und West*. The magazine initiated a theme of reconciliation between the two branches of Ashkenazi Jewry: the emancipated western European – the *Westjuden* – and the more traditional eastern European – the *Ostjuden*. Its editorial policy "repeatedly spoke of a 'harmonious' Jewish identity, an identity poised between tradition and modernity and between East and West."[9] Social contacts between the two communities increased during the war years, when the German army took control over a vast Russian territory inhabited by the *Ostjuden*. The war and the magazine, whose last issue came out a year before Döblin's trip to Poland, enabled the "Jews between twenty and forty to break with their parents' assimilative outlook while also distancing themselves from the negative side of *Ostjudentum*."[10]

Döblin's initial reaction to the archetypical "Polish Jew" was marked by an exaggerated feeling of disbelief. In Warsaw, on the first day of his journey, he came across his own perceptual powerlessness to place Jewish identity within the fast-moving urban terrain of modern Europe:

I stand at a trolley stop, perusing the very obliging streetcar signs, which indicate every passing line and its route. All at once, a lone man with a bearded face comes toward me through the crowd: he wears a black, ragged gabardine, a black visored cap on his head, and top boots on his legs. And right behind him, talking loudly, in words that I can recognize as German, another one, likewise in a black gaberdine, a big man, with a broad red face, red fuzz on his cheeks, over his lips. ... I feel a jolt in my head. They vanish in the throng. People pay them no heed. They are Jews. I am stunned, no, frightened.[11]

Within hours of his first Jewish sighting, Döblin's ethnographical angst turned into cultural fascination, and he quickly learned to see Polish Jews in the context of their own universe. He followed them everywhere, until, in Krakow – at the end of the journey – he found the cultural arrogance and social practices of assimilated western Jews unbearable and indefensible.

"I know what the enlightened gentlemen, the Jewish Enlighteners, will say. They laugh at the 'stupid backward' members of their own nation, they're ashamed of them. ... I am neither an Enlightener nor a member of these national masses, a Western European passerby – I view those 'Enlightened' ones like Africans who flaunt the glass beads they've gotten from sailors, the dirty cuffs on their dangling arms, the brand-new dented top hats on their heads. How poor, how shabby, how unworthy and soullesslly devastated the Western World is, giving them those cuffs; how are they supposed to know."[12] Still, characteristically for his solitary frame of mind, and without challenging his own cultural loyalties, Döblin isolated himself from both types of Jewish identity. He chose the role of an independent observer, an impartial eyewitness to both worlds.

On paper, Döblin's trip to Poland was a socio-political, journalistic investigation of independent Poland on behalf of the left-leaning German media. The writer had strong personal affiliations with various streams of the socialist movement, but he never became a rigid ideologue or party functionary. His political views were influenced by Russian anarchist thought and he was very critical of the restrictive political function and coercive social practices of the state. He also objected to the idea of the modern nation-state, and went to Poland to see what "the delusion of the unique significance of the state and the recognition of its power live on."[13]

Poland did not change his negative view of the modern state or nationalist politics, although he never argued against national self-determination. The European nation-state, thought Döblin, automatically became an oppressive structure because its national character was incapable of encompassing local heterogeneity and diversity. The resurrected Poland was far from a linguistically and territorially monolithic country. The state statistics, as Döblin noted, could not conceal its post-imperial, multinational character: "I have the official Polish Almanac for 1924; I will not allow myself to be intimidated by the statistics. According to the census of 1921, this Poland has four hundred thousand square kilometres of surface area, inhabited by twenty-seven million people. Eleven million of these people were supplied by the old Congress of Poland, eight by Austria, four by Prussia. Four million are missing: they occupy the 'Eastern territory,' the districts of Grodno, Wilno, Minsk, Volhynia."[14] Roughly two-thirds of the population was Polish, fourteen percent Ukrainian, almost ten percent was Jewish, more than five percent was Byelorussian, about two and a half percent was German, and less than half a percent was Lithuanian. Döblin wanted to explore this newly reconstituted

Photographs by Maynard Owen Williams

WILNO READS IN MANY LANGUAGES

64. Wilno reads in many languages.

Polish state through the prism of its polymorphous society. He quickly became overwhelmed by the task. "I soon throw in the towel," announced the
writer, "because I don't speak the language, or rather the languages of the
country: Polish, Ukrainian, Byelorussian, Yiddish, Lithuanian."[15]

Discouraged by his own linguistic shortcomings, the writer became an
attentive reader of the landscape. The birth of the Polish nation-state came
under the sign of war, and throughout the journey he repeatedly came across
various topographical imprints of the past conflict: ruins, depopulated cities,
veteran parades, war cemeteries, etc. But his investigation was also guided by
the spectre of future wars: the hatred found among various ethnic groups of
Poland, political mistrust of neighbouring countries, the ideological manipu-
lation of the masses, cultural isolationism, and above all, the international

worship of militarism. In the middle of the trip, he coined his political motto: "Today's states are the graves of nations."[16]

Distressed by his social findings, Döblin – at the time a self-proclaimed atheist – escaped into the religious worlds of multicultural Poland. He was mesmerised by every holy site and spiritual sight: exuberant Catholic spectacles, secluded Russian Orthodox ceremonies, and intimate Hassidic worship. Within this kaleidoscopic and often antagonistic spiritual plurality, Döblin mapped out the direction of his journey: "Is it a dead world and or a new world? I don't know which is dead. The old one isn't dead. I feel intimately and violently attracted to it. And I know that my compass is reliable. It never points to anything aesthetic, it always points to living, urgent things."[17] Steadily but surely, the trip took on the shape of a personal pilgrimage.

Döblin leaves bustling Warsaw at the beginning of the eight-day festival of Sukkoth, the Feast of Tabernacles. This ancient (but, for the writer, unfamiliar) Jewish holiday transfers the nomadic traditions of a desert people onto the busy topography of a modern city. The living fusion of East and West, old and new, and secular and spiritual exhilarates him – and reveals the compatibility of the two worlds:

> The Feast of Tabernacles is right around the corner. Planks are already carried to the courtyards of Jewish streets, ordinary boxboards, raw, to be hammered and trimmed into shape. A door is inserted; the roof is covered with verdure. Hut by hut grows in the courtyards. Every family has a table and benches, they push them inside. In many courtyards, they shunt wire from the electric system, over to the roof of the tabernacle, to light the interior. ... They are now going to celebrate a feast of nature in the dark courtyards of the metropolis, next to garbage cans, on roof-high balconies. It looks like a gesture of the indestructible masses: despite everything![18]

After a night's journey in a shared sleeper, Döblin reaches the scenic outskirts of Wilno. He has no prior knowledge of the city, and, muted by his inability to converse in any of local languages, is unable to gain a clear sense of it from his travelling companions. But the passing scenery puts the city on the map. From a discomforting proximity of the slumbering train, Wilno unexpectedly emerges as a captivating place:

> Starting at dawn, I gazed out the train window. I was interrupted only once, when my fellow dozer above me lowered his fat legs in white woollen stockings full of holes and, moaning, pulled on his muddy jackboot right in front of my face. At seven a.m., the landscape changes. It becomes hilly, undulating. Earlier, it stretched along evenly, like a steppe, sometimes with meadows and farmland. Now it becomes undulating, hilly. Woods, firs, and deciduous forest recur frequently. A castlelike

building shoots past on the left, a ruin. The entrances and outlets of tunnels are guarded by sentries with rifles; the country is in a state of unrest. The newspapers report attacks by Bolshevists and anonymous gangs; I suddenly feel that these are more than attacks by gangs, these are war movements. We lumber very slowly across a high narrow bridge. How wonderfully lively is the landscape. The hills turn into mountains. The red and yellow of the withering trees; in between, the hushed dark green of the tall firs. Long rows of railroad cars on the tracks, movement inside the train. Outside, small houses, individuals, groups, on streets. Wilno Station.[19]

With fresh memories of the hectic street life of metropolitan Warsaw, Döblin goes for a walk. Around the provincial, sleepy train station, Wilno appears trivial. The seemingly directionless streets lead nowhere until, after a few turns, drifting Döblin stumbles upon an ancient gate:

In the frosty morning, I stroll along an avenue. It is flanked by low houses, most of them old and wretched. Then, from the left, a street runs into an avenue, a rather narrow street without a real sidewalk. I keep looking about for the main thoroughfare, I assume there has to be one. Then the arch of a tall, sizable gateway looms over the street; I hear singing, I pass, seeking, through the old structure. A crowd of people is lying on the right: peasants, townsfolk, male and women, on the ground, kneeling, bowing their heads all the way down. But these are not singers, the singing comes from somewhere else, from above. And when I turn around, I see a chapel up on the arch. And, open to the street, an altar stands there, with many burning candles and a tangle of things that I cannot distinguish. The people coming up the street are holding their hats or caps. I too doffed my hat under the archway. A miracle-working effigy of God's mother is up there. The Madonna looks lively. She appears over a tremendous half-moon, which resembles the huge curling horn of an animal. She is visible from the chest up. Her sacerdotal clothes are richly ornamental. Her crowned head leans to the right. Her two hands lie crossed on her chest. Her narrow throat emerges from splendid and very colourful garments and cloaks. Then comes a high narrow face, her eyes are open only a crack, her lips are shut. Sharp golden rays surround her entire head. She prays, or is entranced, or listens, mild and melancholy, or is absorbed in her sorrow, trying to transcend it: I cannot pinpoint her expression. The image looks suggestive, touched. The seekers here tend to fuse their pain with that of the celestial being and to withdraw more calmly. It is a great achievement of art that it can make such an image and that a painted image can serve as an example.[20]

While Döblin's magical encounter with the Ostra Brama was incidental, his introduction to the Christian faith was a long process culminating in 1941 with his conversion to Catholicism. At the time, Döblin was in exile in California with his family; the conversion finalised a break, not only with the writer's communist and atheist affiliations, but also with his Jewish heritage.

65. Ostra Brama gate; a photograph by J. Bułhak.

Döblin cites his meandering but resolute path towards Catholicism as a sequence of unrelated revelations: "There are two types of encounters one must be grateful for. One is the encounter with persons who fulfill our wishes and answer our questions. The other is the encounter with those people, or books, or events or images, that create wishes in us and cause us to ask questions."[21] The perceptual effects of such encounters are invisible, that is, they occur in an unpremeditated and untraceable manner, just like a person comes "to his own home in its own way: unnoticed, simply."[22]

Wilno's role in Döblin's conversion can only be a speculative one. But perhaps one can parallel his encounter with the city with that of another famous Catholic convert, prominent English writer Gilbert Keith Chesterton (1874-1936). Chesterton took a very public baptism in 1922, and visited Wilno with his wife in 1927 during a well-organised and lavish tour of Poland. The conversion brought Chesterton closer to the political realm and cultural milieus of the newly emerged Catholic nation-states. So, in contrast to Döblin, Chesterton was officially invited to visit Poland as a prominent champion of Polish interests. The Chestertons received a grand welcome: at the train station in Warsaw they were greeted by a large group of Polish dignitaries, including several cavalry officers representing Marshal Piłsudski.

During the trip, Chesterton expressed an unrestrained enthusiasm for Poland. At the Polish PEN Club guest album, he left a flattering inscription: "If Poland had not been born again, all the Christian nations would have died."[23] He also praised Piłsudski, whom he described as being "very sympathetic with Lithuania; though Lithuanians and Poles were quarrelling at the time. He was enthusiastic for Wilno; and I afterwards found on the frontier a historic site where Poles and Lithuanians are at peace – even when they are at war."[24] In contrast, Döblin had described Piłsudski as a much more ambiguous figure: "a revolutionary a la Mazzini ... anti-clerical ... radical leftist ... [who] resolutely organized the army in his own way ... fascinating, deeply passionate man, a thorough anti-parliamentarian."[25]

Chesterton was clearly delighted by Wilno, a Baroque "city of concord" in the *Kresy* (borderland) region of Poland. A few years after the trip, in an autobiographical story, he made the city the highlight of the Polish trip. Predictably, the writer did not notice or chose to ignore all signs of national animosity. In his memory, Wilno remained a city of innocent playfulness:

> I was driving with a Polish lady, who was very witty and well-acquainted with the whole character of Europe, and also of England (as is the barbarous habit of Slavs); and I only noticed that her tone changed, if anything to a sort of cool-ness, as we stopped outside an archway leading to a side-street, and she said: "We can't drive in here." I wondered; for the gateway was wide and the street apparently open. As we walked under the arch, she said in the same colourless tone: "You take off your hat here." And then I saw the open street. It was filled with a vast crowd, all facing me; and all on their knees on the ground. It was as if someone were walking behind me; or some strange bird were hovering over my head. I faced round, and saw in the centre of the arch great windows standing open, unsealing a chamber full of gold and colours; there was a picture behind; but parts of the whole picture were moving like a puppet-show, stirring strange double memories like a dream of the bridge in the puppet-show of my childhood; and then I realised that from those shifting groups there shone and sounded the ancient magnificence of the Mass.[26]

Bewitched by the magic of the site and the pleasant company, Chesterton's curiosity (or his memory) did not venture beyond the gate. Döblin, on the other hand, displays a greater interest in the everyday life of the city. Lost but no less enchanted, he goes deeper into the city, only to stumble upon another local mystery:

The street is named Ostra-brama. It lies almost mute, the worshipers barely emitting a sound. At the corner, men are burying drainpipes in the ground. I amble up the street with its small houses, woefully paved. It is ten a.m. But the shops are still closed. A few are open. And then I look at the names on the signs and realize it is the Jewish stores that do not open. The Feast of Tabernacles is still in progress.

The street widens like a square. On the other side, an ancient stone box: it's the old theater, with carriages in front. Upon passing a movie house, I notice that the posters come in two languages: there are Polish posters and Yiddish ones. The signs of many shops are likewise in the Hebrew alphabet, in Yiddish. I often encountered this in Warsaw, in the Nalewki district; but here, it's spread throughout the city. There seems to be a very large or very courageous Jewish population here. Yet I don't see any Jews, and that's the second thing. Individual Jews must be standing around, even if it's a holiday. And now I notice that I do see them but don't notice them. They stand next to me outside the movie house, walk about in white caps, young men and girls; older ones slowly cross the bumpy square, conversing in their language. No one wears a caftan! I see no one in a black "capote." They all wear European clothes – and yet do not speak Polish. This is a different breed of Jews than in Warsaw.[27]

Once again, Döblin is confronted with his own inability to place Jews within their living environment. Only this time, his imperceptiveness is even more embarrassing. Where in Warsaw he became over-stimulated by his exaggerated imagination, in Wilno he is blinded by the lack of it. Soon, Döblin realises that in order to see the Jewish world of Vilne/Wilno in its entirety, he needs to enter into an unmapped terrain of Yiddish culture.

Haim Sloves (1905-1988), a Yiddish writer and playwright, describes the cultural landscape of Yiddish – Yiddishland – as a territory permanently marked by a geographical fluidity: "There is a land which figures on no map of the world, a strange, unknown land of almost unreal immensity, whose ever-changing frontiers traverse continents and oceans. It is the land of Yiddish. How many claim this language as their own, from New York to Moscow, from Buenos Aires to Warsaw, from Jerusalem to Paris, from Melbourne to Johannesburg? Millions."[28] Because of its pluralistic nature, Yiddishland did not have a centre. Still, contemporary Jewish observers "often viewed Vilna as the exemplar of an East European Jewish community, a locale where the rich traditions of the past could serve as the basis of an innovative new culture. As a speaker at the 1930 YIVO [the Yiddish Scientific Institute] conference put it: 'for us Vilna is not simply a city, it is an idea.' "[29]

Vilne's status as an ideal cultural nexus for Yiddishland was based on the city's unsettled geopolitical and linguistic location within the fragmented nation-state map of Europe. Since no single national, linguistic, religious or ideological force could reign unchallenged in the city, the Yiddish-speaking Jews were able to carve their own urban cartography, which outlived most of the ruling regimes:

> Indeed, if Vilna had a specifically Jewish geography, it was largely created through the use of a distinct language. While the city officially changed from Vilna to Wilno to Vilnius, Jews called the city *Yerushalayim d'lite* [the Jerusalem of Lithuania], a name that never appeared on any official map. Moreover, Jewish residents employed their Yiddish vernacular to stake a claim to particular parts of the city, both formally and informally. Just as Jews had their own name for Vilna, certain parts of the city, particularly those in the Jewish quarter, had distinctive Yiddish appellations. Most buildings were organized around the courtyards [*hoyfn*] which were called after their owners; for example, the courtyard with an entrance at 7 Yidishe Street was known as Reb Shaul Shiske's Hoyfn and 8 Yatkever Street as Urel-Feygl Hoyfn. Some streets also had their own names in Yiddish, such as St. Nicholas Street, known to Jewish residents as Gitkes-toybes zavulek [Gitke-Toybe's Alley]. Since the designation of thoroughfares changed frequently as successive Russian, German, Lithuanian, and Polish regimes came to power, Jewish street names were sometimes older and better known than their official counterparts.[30]

However, few non-Jewish visitors or, for that matter locals, were interested in the Jewish topography of the city. In Warsaw, Döblin was warned by "a very intelligent very down-to-earth National Polish politician" about the "energetic, sly, hated Litvaks" (Lithuanian Jews) whom he identified as being the main cause of Polish anti-Semitism.[31] Many came and left Wilno with a hardened feeling of racial and religious intolerance. In 1938, for instance, Robert McBride, a Catholic American, toured the city chaperoned by an ultra-nationalist Polish priest and military chaplain. His itinerary and subsequent impressions of the city betray a disdain of everything Jewish:

> In every Polish city, save those of the extreme west, the ghetto is an integral part of the community. In Wilno it is more proportionately an entity than in any other important town. Here forty per cent of the population is Jewish and here, as elsewhere, they prefer the seclusion and exclusively racial character of the ghetto to life elsewhere. In these modern days no attempt had been made at segregation; the Jews prefer to live together in their huddled quarters in the same way as they dress in their orthodox black and allow their faces to remain unshaven. Their racial characteristics and orthodoxy are carefully guarded and they enjoy no social intercourse with their Polish neighbors. Seemingly unassimilable, if present customs hold they will continue to remain a race apart and be regarded by the Poles as a foreign element in their community. Why they wish to remain segregated in the narrow, ill-smelling streets of their ghettos is difficult to understand. Doubtless

66. A map of Vilne in Yiddish, circa 1940.

they are influenced by considerations of economy, of convenience and of habit arising from the days in which they were compelled to live separate from their Christians neighbors. The Hebrew population in Wilno engages in all the trading occupations – shopkeeping, vending in the market places, driving droshkies, and, I doubt not, taking in each other's washing.[32]

Döblin, of course, is different. After his initial puzzlement, he bravely walks into the busy maze of the impoverished old Jewish quarter. He accepts its overcrowded vitality as a sign of a dynamic life:

I find German Avenue, the Jewish street. Here, I understand the language. Store by store, countless people. Jews, hauling, lugging, standing in groups. A rare caftan,

usually European provincial garb. Very narrow lanes, street peddlers all the way
to the courtyards. The shops are open, often windowless, rows of meat and poultry
stores cheek by jowl. Arches span a few streets. They mark the boundaries of the
old ghetto. This is energetic life, here and at the castle hill, on the water, where
soldiers exercise.[33]

The writer's fast-paced acclimatisation to the Jewish street life proceeds alongside a more relaxed discovery of the city. He finds the city hard to grasp,
in part because of its unresolved national and political identity. He rejects
cartography as an obstructive imprint of the state, but finding no sensible
answers on the ground, becomes restless:

> I have a map of Wilno from the Russian period and a more recent map. Nearly all
> the streets and squares have been renamed. In Warsaw, this renaming delighted
> me, elated me; strange: here, I don't really care for it. It seems to have been in-
> flicted upon the city from above. It did not issue from within, as in Warsaw. The
> main thoroughfare in the center used to be called Bolshaya, the one in the north-
> west Georgievsky Prospekt; now Bolshaya is called Wielka and Zamkowa, and
> Georgievsky Prospect is renamed after Adam Mickiewicz. Then there is Slowacki
> Avenue, a Pilsudski, a Sigmund, a Kosciuszko Avenue.
>
> An educated woman whispers to me: the Pole is polite, sentimental, and deceit-
> ful; the Russian has a free nature, he is honest and charming. Oh, she misunder-
> stands me. I am a friend of the Polish people. The Poles had bad luck for centuries,
> they were forced to hide their feelings, they couldn't be open – under those very
> Russians, the honest, charming ones. Suppression makes you crooked and feeble.
> And Poland does not lie free like Russia, not vast like Russia; it is wedged in east
> and west, between north and south. This produces anything but simple people. A
> bridge: is that land or water? I feel distressed.
>
> The Wilno territory is a burning issue. The Lithuanians claim Vilnius as their
> capital. The Poles have occupied it. The Polish-Lithuanian border is closed. A
> permanent state of war exists between the two young states.[34]

Like any tourist, Döblin climbs up the steep Castle Hill to get a better view
and, possibly, a more detailed understanding of the place. By this time, the
wonders of the panoramic tableaux had already become a cliché. The German occupying forces, nonetheless, were the first to make it a lesson in the
pleasures of historical amnesia, albeit without drawing any undesirable con-
clusions. Monty, in his wanderings through Wilna, described the hill as the
mythological cornerstone of the place. "From these heights, Gedimyn [Gedi-
minas] ruled his vast domain and, according to a legend, his grave is located
somewhere near the ruins of the castle. On this elevated point, the history
of the city begins; but today," adds Monty imperiously, "there is no need to
remember its past." Instead of memory, the spectator should follow his aes-

67. Street scene in the Jewish Quarter of Vilne.

thetic instincts and enjoy "the most beautiful view in all of Lithuania" with the eye of an unburdened mind, "gliding above snowy roofs, fields and hills towards the seemingly endless horizon." This magic site itself dictates these rules of engagement, for "the darkened, distant hills perfectly frame the town with its countless spires and domes, creating a remarkable sense of rhythm and motion in this picture of the place."[35]

Despite its ideal location and idyllic framing (or because of them), the panorama fails to mesmerise Döblin, who looks down below and immediately writes history into the picture. With the historical narration comes personal annotation, which turns the picture-perfect scene into farce:

> But looming autumnally, in a blaze of yellow and brown foliage, the castle hill stands there, with the oldest of old Wilno. There once lived a Lithuanian grand prince, Gedymin, who built his castle up there. Down below, a fire burned in a pagan temple. The man whom the beautiful, delicate Jadwiga of Poland had to marry, the first Polish-Lithuanian Jagiello, became a Christian – by contract, I believe – and destroyed the temple. He replaced it with the Cathedral of St. Stanislaw, to wreak vengeance on Christianity. When a Christian sees this dreadful edifice, he reverts to paganism. Nothing comes of these shotgun marriages. The church looks like a Greek temple or a Polish municipal theatre. Vistula antiquity.

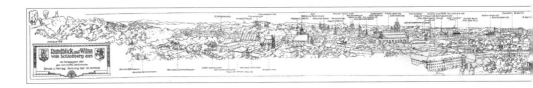

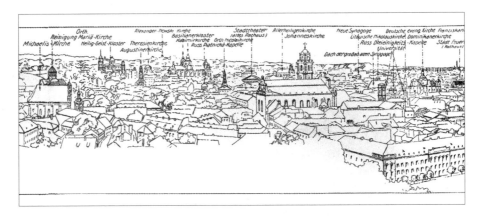

68. A panoramic view of Wilna from Castle Hill, 1917.

The marriage was dissolved by death, Poland and Lithuania are asunder again, the cathedral could not be rescinded. Supposedly, St. Kazimierz has a silver coffin here, weighing two thousand five hundred pounds; eight silver statues of Polish kings stand here, but all the perfumes of Araby … A campanile stands free, next to this Greek temple or municipal theater. I walk by at noon, a blare comes from the top. The man up there blares in all four directions. I hear it: he's a soldier, and this is a Polish custom in the garrisons. The Russians took along the monument to their Pushkin from the park at the foot of the castle hill. They must have been after the metal. German headquarters were housed here after Rennenkampf's retreat; German music was played at the town park in the afternoon. Rows of benches are lined up as in a resort park.[36]

Haunted by shards of war memories, Döblin quickly loses interest in the numerous architectural landmarks of Wilno: "I am taken to a number of churches; I follow obediently, but cautiously shut my eyes and ears inside. At one church, I see a chubby Polish peasant face hewn in a stone pillar. At another church, I am told, Napoleon stood in front of it and said he'd like to take this church to Paris. I can't stand these goddamned old artworks."[37] Out of boredom, Döblin initiates a casual game. He assumes the narrative responsibility of a guide who seizes and shapes the history of the place.

On the hill. Red brickwork; legend has it that a tunnel runs from here to Troki, the neighboring village. Red barracks below, yellow bushes down the slope, the shiny black surface of the river: the Wilja. Masses of small red-roofed houses down below, a rolling of wagons, a hammering. Behind me, to the side, stand – oddly enough – three adjacent tall white crosses: Poles, I hear, who were killed by General Muraviev in 1863. During the occupation, the Poles, forgetting nothing, already got to work putting up these crosses. A cannon: the Russians used to fire it at twelve noon as a midday signal. So many old customs: doctoral graduation in the church, the blowing of trumpets, the shooting of cannon. Clocks have been circulating recently, but how slow do such things come to the notice of the authorities. I delight for a long time in the shiny water of Wilja; behind it, the wreath of forests.

After looking down at what is known as Castle Square, with a small old church next to it, and the castle itself, I am down below again, unable to make up my mind about entering. After all, it's only for the old breed of tourists, and I belong to the new breed. My companion would love to see it; he's from Wilno; so I've decided to show him the castle.

'The Russian governor-general lived there?'

'Yes.'

'I knew it; it was obvious. Later on, the Germans turned it into either an officer's mess or an army hospital – the general command was over there, wasn't it?'

'A hospital.'

'The marble plaque with the gold inscriptions says that Napoleon stayed here during his retreat from Russia. He had to leave town in disguise during the night of November 24, 1812.'

A gypsy woman passes the entrance, she's holding a child by the hand. The gypsies have a camp outside the town; lots of them coming from Russia. My companion says they're fleeing the Bolsheviks.

'They're not fleeing the Bolsheviks, my son. When poor people come to power, they strike only at the rich. The gypsies always flee, or rather, do not flee, they wander.'

I impress the word 'wander' on my companion. Then we enter the courtyard of the castle. It is almost one p.m. We can walk undisturbed. Napoleon has fled, the Russians have left, the Germans are gone. Now we are here. My companion and I ponder whether we should hoist a flag, issue a proclamation in Polish and Yiddish, explaining that we have come as friends and that the inhabitants should assist us and our troops in every way. But he first wants to ask the caretaker, and I have no objection. The caretaker noticed us, and he was so startled that he instantly took off for lunch. My companion catches up with him. They speak – what do they speak? Russian. They admire Napoleon and speak Russian or Polish. I do not admire him and I speak French. When I address the porter in French, he replies that he doesn't know Yiddish. Crestfallen, I wander along, climb stairs. A waiting room comes my way; its carpet has vanished in the course of centuries. We work our way through to a ballroom; ragged rococo furniture mourns for Napoleon. There are rooms that are whitewashed, and they contain the usual tiled stoves. They ask themselves and me what they are doing in a castle. Muraviev, the dreadful man, lived in a very horrible room. It has no windows, not a single window. A mere cubbyhole. Muraviev was so afraid that he never slept in a room with a window. And now I noticed a smell that cuts me to the quick, a smell that I have never encountered in a castle. But I do not regret coming here; this is an unusual castle. Muraviev has to be here; I smell his presence, you can smell him here. The caretaker answers calmly: First of all, he doesn't know Yiddish; secondly, Muraviev is not here. What I smell is the sewage system, which isn't here. He says it hasn't been here since Napoleon's time, and ever since, it's been making itself felt with an intensifying smell. This condition is preserved, for this is a castle, a historic sight and smell. I am relieved, the dreadful Muraviev is not here. The caretaker shows me a real vestige of the Russians: a winding staircase to which several stairways lead. The secret stairways that the great tyrant used for his emergency escape.[38]

Once Döblin's tour comes across relics of the Great War, his historical imagination takes flight into a realm of intimate reflection. Within sight of the recent violence, his retrospective insight fleshes out as introspective emotion, with the city becoming the site of personal shame:

I hear pleasant things about the German occupation. The Germans, I'm told, left three cemeteries behind: one for civilians, one for officers, one for rank and file. The Good German Lord holds court according to civil and military laws. Then, out in the Zakret Woods, I see their graves in long, long rows: simple wooden crosses, as well as the strange Greek Orthodox crosses of Russians: the horizontal beams slant. The hush is profound. Below lie countless dead men who left this world amid the roaring of cannon, amid the moans in a hospital. Poor creatures; not one of them could have left this dreadful life without complaint. I feel tormented and abashed as I walk along these rows. I sense that I must ask forgiveness. Because they lie here and I live. I do not want to ask, I must not ask how they are. I would like to: they feel so good, as snug and comfy as the long green grass that rises from their graves.[39]

Social commitments and political curiosity drive Döblin back to the present. He wants to explore the mechanics of the ruling ideology of the day: "I get to see the changing, loosening forces. In Eastern Europe, the emancipation of the masses is taking place within a national framework – indeed, the strongest accent is on nationalism."[40] He sees that "the Jewish millions are developing a new sense of a free European nation, throwing off the weight of the old bondage and contempt. They want to be national minorities or else have the old Asiatic homeland borrowed from their religion."[41] Armed with such insight, the writer dives into the zeitgeist of Jewish Vilne.

The writer visits Zionist and Bund organisations, goes to Hebrew and Yiddish schools, and, after that, identifies the key Jewish dilemma of the modern age: "not just the Baal-Shem vs. the state, but also Orient vs. Occident. The first rift in the Jewish nation: Gaon, Baal-Shem vs. secular politics. The second rift among the emancipated Jews: supporters of the bourgeois state vs. Socialists. The Socialists – universal, humanistic, international – are better at holding the old Gaon line, the great supranational idea." He also discovers the ideological similarities between the promoters of Yiddish and the advocates of Hebrew: "Both are modern, national, Western." He is full of mistrust towards Zionist groups, but immediately feels at ease with the Bund, the socialist proponents of the Yiddish language.[42]

Döblin was clearly impressed by the cultural diversity and political vitality of the city's Jewish world. He saw the Gaon of Vilne as a role model for modern Jewry – rational and diligent, yet with an unwavering commitment to the spiritual life. But he feared that the idea of a Jewish state would work against the principles of the Gaon's teachings. Nationalism, in his opinion, might obliterate the spirituality of the Jews:

> I can't help thinking as I go out: What an impressive nation the Jews are. I didn't know this nation: I believed what I saw in Germany, I believed that the Jews are industrious people, the shopkeepers, who stew in their sense of family and slowly get too fat, the agile intellectuals, the countless insecure unhappy refined people. Now I see that those are isolated examples, degenerating, remote from the core of the nation that lives here and maintains itself. And what an extraordinary core is this, producing such people as the rich, inundating Bal-Shem, the dark flame of the Gaon of Wilno. What events occurred in these seemingly uncultured Eastern areas. How everything flows around the spiritual!
>
> ... What if history were turned backwards and the Jews were really given Zion? And this is becoming an urgent issue. The old artificial conditions can no longer be maintained, their rigor is slackening. The modern age, economic necessities, are driving the Jews out of their seclusion. The backward movement is rolling. The tragedy of fulfilment is rolling. The temple that they will find if they seek it will not be the Temple. The religious ones, the spiritual ones know it. They say: Only the Messiah can give us the Temple. The most genuine Jews stopped waiting for the 'state' long ago. One can preserve oneself only in the spiritual; that's why one

must remain in the spiritual. Politics cannot bring about heaven, politics produces nothing but politics. The 'modern' era presents no problems for those Jews.

However, today's external circumstances, political, economic, and the plight of the masses are facts. The old organism will put up a strong resistance to all change. 'State,' and 'Parliament' loom on the horizon—against the Gaon and the Baal-Shem.[43]

During the last day of the four-day visit, Döblin is taken to the old Jewish cemetery located directly across the river from the Castle Hill. "A Jewish cemetery," writes Israel Cohen in his 1943 history of Vilne, "in the traditional parlance of orthodox Jewry, is *Bet 'Olam*, a 'House of Eternity,' a term that may be said to combine a love for euphemisms with a belief in immortality. Vilna has two such 'houses,' situated at a considerable distance from one another. The old cemetery, which lies beyond the River Vilia ... stretches over a very large area, looking for most part like a deserted field, with grass growing wild; for the number of gravestones is comparatively small."[44] These cemeteries had an important function – they chronicled and encircled the local Jewish past. "Most Vilna Jews," remembers Lucy Dawidowicz, an American-Jewish resident of the city, "knew their history not so much from reading books as from visiting the two Jewish cemeteries, where their history was literally entombed. ... Tradition has it that Jews used [the old cemetery] as a burial ground as far as back as 1487, but the first historical records begin in 1592. The Russian authorities closed that cemetery in 1830 for lack of space."[45]

Graveyards entice Döblin: he went to the Jewish one in Warsaw on the Day of Atonement. The cemetery was packed with a restless mass of lamenting women and praying men. Döblin was aghast: "Cold shivers run up and down my spine when I see and hear these things. ... It is something primordial, atavistic. Does it have anything to do with Judaism? ... It is the remnant of a different religion, animism, a cult of the dead."[46] The visit to the old cemetery in Wilno provides a contrasting memorial to Jewish life.

Döblin goes to the old burial ground with two young guides, activists in the Yiddish youth movement. The gated cemetery is locked and, like three mischievous teenagers, they have to break in. The middle-aged writer is joyfully amused: "it's a terrible thing to say – we laugh, laugh as we step into the cemetery, bolt the gate behind us."[47] The deserted place mesmerises him with its commonplace piety, its mundane closeness to God and its melancholic loneliness. For the first time – in fact, the only time throughout his impressionistic account of Poland – Döblin leaves his thoughts unfinished. He abandons the narrative flow in front of the tomb of the Goan, as if waiting for an encouraging thought after the endless cycle of resettlements and chaotic exiles:

69. The old Jewish cemetery in Vilne.

Here, we find a vast lawn with several trees and, irregularly, here and there, alone and in clusters, low stone slabs. Withered leaves lie everywhere, even piled up in a few hollows. A fine drizzle is coming down. The stone tablets bear long inscriptions, red and yellow square Hebrew scripts. Lions are often depicted on the slabs. Shards, stone fragments lie about. Terrible the neglect of the cemetery. Bits of bricks, small stones on many headstones. Straw under the small stones, also slips of paper with Hebrew writing. These are memorial tokens of pious Jews who have prayed here. For they travel from far away to pray at the graves of famous men, holy men. That deep and dark feeling drives them to come here. Somehow – they think, they feel – the holy man is still by his grave, by his body, and they can approach him as their forebears did during his lifetime. The dead man is tied to his grave, his vanished soul to the corpse, and his soul can be evoked by prayer. And the pious man, the rebbe, the saints stand closer to God and can obtain more than a normal man from God, perhaps by way of God. How dilapidated everything is here. I hear shouts, orders, soldiers singing, and once, a mooing. I climb over a small rise on which shattered stone plaques are strewn. When I stand on top, I see a cow grazing below. Pasturing on the graves. Its pats lie around.

… The Jews of Wilno, I find, are proud, but only partially and in a very Eastern manner. The grass runs wild and high. On the mounds, you keep stepping on shattered headstones. They often bear the beautiful, tail-lashing lions, the ancient symbols of strength. The tomb of the Gaon of Wilno. A low stone house with fences of irons bars, it's locked. It contains his grave and the graves of his kith and kin. He lies here together with these people, who he didn't know so well during his lifetime. When his wife died, he said "I had to go hungry very often, but I did it for the sake of Torah and God. But you went hungry because of me, a human being." Whole piles of small written notes lie on his stone plaque and on the adjacent ground. They even hang outside, on the iron fence, tied to the bars with straw and tussocks. ...[48]

Döblins's Wilno is a collage of jagged impressions, juxtaposed thoughts and descriptive contradictions. But this literary style reflects his modern expressionist narrative spirit. One should read his picture of the city not as an unequivocal portrait, but as a cartographical imprint. A map is never a full or reliable representation of a place: it is a projection of a factual imagination, which only makes sense if one can read, understand and follow its specific cartographical legend.

The writer's admiration of the Jews of Vilne lasted his entire life. After the Holocaust, he placed his encounter with their vanished world alongside his most cherished experiences: "I went to Poland. I have written a book about it. I went there and for the first time in my life I saw Jews. I was deeply touched by the sight of them. I have never forgotten what I saw in the ghettos of Warsaw, of Wilna and Krakow..." Still, Döblin believed he failed to breach the gap between himself and their ideals. In the end, the cost to him for surviving the great resettlement was another form of estrangement. He summarised his brief flirtation with the Yiddish modernity of Wilno with a defeatist statement: "My words meant nothing. I felt nothing. It was yet another flag I could not carry."[49]

DISTANCES FROM VILNIUS

Border Countries
Kaliningrad 318km
Minsk 215km
Riga 300km
Warsaw 450km

Other Major Cities
Berlin 1,035km
London 1,751km
Moscow 875km
New York 6,929km
Paris 1,690km

70. Vilnius at the centre of Europe.

CHAPTER EIGHT:

Maelstrom Europe

> And once again I see that it is easier for a human being to change than for
> a city. A human being can transform himself. A city falls apart.
>
> Alfred Döblin

While I was writing this book, the exact location of the geographical centre of
Europe moved again. According to a new scientific conclusion reached (again)
by the French National Geographical Institute, the continental centre is now
located at 54 degrees and 50 minutes latitude, 25 degrees and 18 minutes
longitude. The new calculation is based on the exclusion of various political
protrusions of Europe, such as the islands of the Azores, the Canary Islands
and Madeira, which, in terms of their geotectonic base, belong to Africa, and
some of the Greek islands on the Asian side of the Aegean Sea. These minor
cartographic adjustments tightened up the tenuous boundaries of Europe
and also relocated the continental epicentre a bit closer to Vilnius, just six
kilometres north of its Old Town. Despite this shift, the commemorative
significance of the old centre remains unchanged. The monument erected
to mark Lithuania's entry into the European Union still adorns the previous
centre, even if its symbolic message was engineered based on a short-lived
scientific miscalculation.

Vilnius in the twentieth century is just like the geographical centre of
Europe: always shifting, recalculating, remapping, and yet never able to reach
a fixed meaning or a stable location. The modern age brought to Vilnius not
just wars, foreign occupations, revolutions, conflicting ideologies, massacres,
depopulation, economic depressions and irregular cycles of modernisation;
it also created perfect conditions for conversions and misinterpretations of
memory. Modern Vilnius has been built on a historical pretence, a deliberately
constructed idea that the past has no remaining eyewitnesses, only relics that
can be broken down, reassembled and then dispersed again. Contemporary
Vilnius is a restless city – not in terms of its present, or even its future, but its
own past. It is a place of relics, like an old graveyard where the ancient dead
compete for space and memory with more recent arrivals. By sheer chance,
the new centre of Europe fell on a fallow site that has recently been revived

to serve the needs of the ever-growing commemorative market of Vilnius. A derelict farmhouse, turned into a busy workshop producing gravestones, blots the heart of Europe.

Vilnius residents respect their *own* dead. It is a deeply engraved custom arising from a variety of religious and cultural traditions. A death without a marked grave is considered a pitiful and even cruel fate. Modern practices of cremation, grave-less funerals, burial plot leasing, the transposition of remains and depersonalised graveyards, traditions popular in most of Europe and North America, are simply seen by the locals as barbaric. Vilnius's cemeteries are still planned for and taken care of as eternal sites, allocated to the dead and their living family members for perpetuity. As a result, the expanding cemeteries take up a good part of the city's green spaces, making it one of the most necro-friendly places in Europe.

During the twentieth century, the necropolis of Vilnius gained great prominence among local people and the city's visitors alike. Relics might not talk, but they grind incomplete and unfinished parchments of history deep into the local terrain. In the absence of a coherent historical narrative and stable geographical location, the dead became the most identifiable markers of the city's current identity. In 1938, an American visitor was given a tour of one of the oldest Catholic cemeteries of the city on the first morning of his visit:

> Breakfastless, we were whisked off to see the combined tomb of Pilsudski and his mother and after it to early Mass at Ostra Brama, one of the most famous shrines in Poland. It was only a few minutes' drive from the station to the so-called Rossa cemetery at the edge of which lies the tomb, reached by a broad staircase. A slab of polished black marble set in the concrete platform marks the memorial of mother and son, impressive in its extreme simplicity. A phalanx of white crosses – two hundred of them – flank the grave on either side, silent epitaphs of the heroes who fell before Wilno defending the country. One standing on each side of the memorial, two soldiers of the Polish army keep perpetual vigil over the dead. So immovable were they in their khaki uniforms and so closely resembling bronze statues that it was some time before we realized they were living soldiers of the Republic. ... We strolled through the cemetery studying the tombs, early and recent, of Wilno's deceased townsfolk. In spite of the crowded quarters of its acres, the cemetery has many elements of natural beauty; it occupies a hillside and its natural features have all been retained. Miniature hills and valleys clad with trees and shrubs, diminutive cliffs and crags bright with wild flowers and alpine plants contribute their share to the charm of this unusual burying ground. We are not experts on cemeteries and perhaps the custom followed there is not exclusively a Polish one, but we were somewhat startled by the realism employed by the relatives of these dead: a photograph of the departed, framed and protected from the elements, is attached to many a headstone.[1]

In the cathedral crypt the American tourists were shown the recently un-covered body of Sigismund Augustus, the sixteenth-century king of Poland and grand duke of Lithuania, and his beloved wife, Barbara Radziwiłłowa (Radvilaite). Then they were taken to an even more morbid spectacle hidden in the subterranean passages of the old town:

> We had heard of a remarkable collection of mummies in the crypt of the Church of the Holy Spirit, part of a Dominican monastery founded in 1597. But we were hardly prepared for the gruesome sight which greeted us when we arrived at the church. In the gloomy crypt reached by a stone staircase in the old monastery yard, we were brought face to face with a multitude of the mummified bodies and skeletons of saints and sinners who had departed this life hundreds of years ago. These bodies had once reposed in their coffins in orderly array within the church's catacombs. But now they were ranged in complex disarray in the gloom of the underground vaulting. Such disregard of the sanctity of the dead is one charge laid against the inhumanity of the Russians; for long before the World War, in one of the sporadic outbreaks of Polish revolutionary activity, political prisoners were arrested in such number as to tax the maximum facilities of the city prisons. The Dominican crypt, large, roomy, well underground and suitably dark, appealed to the Muscovite overlords as quarters for the living rather than a resting place for the dead. The coffins were removed and placed in ranks on the unpaved floor of the rough vaulted cellar. However, the wood of the coffins was weakened from age and unable to stand the strain of removal. As a result many of them opened up and exposed their occupants, which were in a surprising state of preservation. Space in the cellars evidently gave out, and as more prison room was needed the crypt continued to disgorge its silent inhabitants. Obviously the Russian authori-ties were too indifferent to the welfare of the long-departed to construct shelves against the walls for accommodating the inflow of coffins. Selecting a deep recess in the vaulting, they removed the bodies from their coffins and unceremoniously tossed them in heaps into this dark opening. There they remain, literally hundreds of them, mostly unadorned skeletons now, lying chaotically in a gigantic mound; those on top have assumed fantastic postures, their heads, arms, legs, hands and feet protruding at all angles in gruesome array.

> The bodies which have been graciously permitted to remain in their coffins are well mummified and many are identifiable as to age, sex, and position. We inspected a woman belonging to the nobility, recognizable by fragments of garment and jewelry; another of an elderly lady; a gentleman adorned with tufts of hair and the remnants of a mustache, but otherwise unclothed; and still another woman, the bearer of a gold ring which had been stolen from her lifeless hand and later returned by the conscience-stricken pilferer. Displayed on tables was century-old clothing of priests and nuns, for this building enjoyed a long history as an ecclesiastical center; boots from the feet of Napoleon's soldiers who died on the retreat from Moscow; and miscellaneous articles found in the rubble of the burial vault.[2]

WILNO. Ul. Zamkowa.

71. Zamkowa (Castle) Street in Wilno, circa 1930.

By the middle of the twentieth century, Wilno came to be seen as the embodiment of an anachronistic Europe where an ancient, forgotten past had lingered into the modern age. Lucy Dawidowicz's first impression of the city was that of a romantic place coloured by historical exoticism. "Even more attractive to the American tourist smitten with history were Vilna's medieval relics, visible everywhere in its streets as on its hills. It was a city whose history receded into the mist of time. To me Vilna was the very epitome of the Old World, a storied place with a storied past."[3] The palimpsest features of the city were not to everyone's liking. In July of 1940, Ann Louise Strong, a young British labour union activist, made a stopover in the city on her journey to Moscow. She summarised the peculiarly framed geopolitical location of the place: "Whoever solves the problem of Vilna can solve the problem of Europe. Vilna is an insoluble mixture of national hates [and] a world example – there are many such in Europe – of the insolubility of the problem of national hates under capitalist rule."[4] At the same time, she was cynically advised by an American diplomat that the "only thing to do with Vilna is to pick it up and take it a long way off and squeeze the people out into their respective nations and then put the town itself in a museum."[5]

The change of labels came first. The city was plunged into the Second World War on September 1, 1939, as the Polish city of Wilno; it emerged from it in 1945 as Vilnius, the capital of the Soviet Republic of Lithuania. Local place-name changes followed suit, as the cultural and demographical dominance of the Polish and Yiddish languages was replaced by the ideological and administrative supremacy of the Russian and Lithuanian languages. This transformation was punctured by a few occupations of different national and ideological colours. In accordance with the secret protocols of the Nazi-Soviet Pact of 1939, the city, along with eastern parts of Poland, was occupied by the Soviet Union, which, for strategic reasons, returned it to Lithuania. For a half year, Vilnius, suddenly the legal but not yet administrative capital of neutral Lithuania, stayed in a surreal geopolitical limbo. Isolated from the rest of Europe by the engulfing war, the city became a precarious haven for thousands of Jewish and Polish refugees from the Nazi and Soviet occupations of Poland. Herman Kruk, a Jewish doctor from Warsaw, was among those who were able escape the Nazi bombardments and reached the city by crossing into the Soviet-controlled zone:

> The hundreds and thousands who arrived in Vilna were huddled together, terrified, hungry, and exhausted. Stooped – with a habit of bending over at the sound of every exploding bomb. Terrified of all that happens around them with such lightning speed, such terror and tragedy. ... The sea overflowed and flooded Vilna. A place to lie down is a dream. A piece of bread is rare. A shirt – who thinks of shirts? ... Soap is a luxury. Warm food a fantasy. Every room that looks normal makes you tremble: a room!? Do people still have rooms? ... Are people still sleeping in beds? ... Are they sleeping? Every refugee trembled when he saw that normal life is still going on somewhere and not everything is destroyed and crushed. ... Thus they trudged over the streets of Vilna, refugees from all over Poland. Workers from Warsaw, yeshiva students from Lublin, merchants from Katowice, engineers, doctors – plodding through the medieval alleys of Vilna, seeking refuge. Searching for an open door, some water to wash with, a board to lie down on. Over it all, the siren of alarm. Everyone responded in his own way and everyone wanted to help somehow, but ... Vilna was busy with its own troubles, its own anguish and suffering. Vilna had just shaken off the nightmare of war, the German bombardment, the dark nights and mortal days. Cut off from the world, Vilna was hungry and no one in those days had a mind for refugees.[6]

The Lithuanian control of Vilnius was short-lived. On June 15, 1940, a day after the German army entered Paris, Lithuania was occupied by Soviet troops. Within two months, Soviet Lithuania with its capital, Vilnius, became a member-state of the USSR, but the German army took the city in a blitzkrieg on June 24, 1941, three days after the beginning of the Nazi invasion of the Soviet

Union. At night, Yitskhok Rudashevski, a fourteen-year-old local Jewish boy with ties to the Communist party, observed "the empty, sad streets" of the old town. "A Lithuanian with a gun goes through the streets. ... At dawn a motorcycle rides through the street. A gray square-rimmed helmet, spectacles, a greatcoat and a rifle. Unfortunately the first soldier of the German usurping army that I have caught sight of. The helmet flashes coldly and evilly. At little later I go down to the street [where] I meet a comrade. And we walk like strangers over wide streets. The German army is marching. We both stand with bowed heads. A black mirage of tanks, motorcycles, machines." On July 8, "the decree was issued that the Vilna Jewish population must put on badges front and back – a yellow circle and inside it the letter J. It is daybreak. I am looking through the window and see before me the first Vilna Jews with badges. It was painful to see how people were staring at them. ... I was ashamed to appear in them on the street not because it would be noticed that I am a Jew but because I was ashamed of what [they were] doing to us." Two months later, "a beautiful, sunny day has risen. The streets are closed off by Lithuanians. The streets are turbulent. Jewish workers are permitted to enter. A ghetto is being created for Vilna Jews." In the turmoil, Rudashevsky was pushed through the ghetto gate: "I feel that I have been robbed, my freedom is being robbed from me, my home and the familiar Vilna streets I loved so much. ... I hear the restless breathing of people with whom I have suddenly been thrown together, people who just like me have suddenly been uprooted from home." On the first day of the ghetto, German officers came to photograph "the crooked streets, the frightened people. They take pleasure in the Middle Ages which they have transported into the twentieth century!!!!"[7]

The ghetto, writes Kruk, established in the old part of the city, "swarms like a beehive. An area for 3,000-4,000 people is occupied now by tens of thousands. Heads upon heads. One lies on top of another. Less than a meter per person, worse than a cemetery." The claustrophobic denseness of jammed buildings bursts into the open. "Every yard is a street. Every street is a city. A swarming anthill: pushing, chasing, rushing – pain of pain." Despite hunger, diseases and the recurring German *Aktions* of murder, the ghetto never becomes depopulated. The dead and murdered are replaced by new arrivals from other Jewish communities. While in 1943 only a handful of local Jews remained in the ghetto, "there was a mishmash of people driven out of the surrounding towns, or escapees from slaughters, from execution squares, from purges, from holes and hiding places. They have gone through horror and grief, have been purged in pain, have returned from hell. They are wild and wanton. Death is nothing to them, but they won't commit suicide." For them Vilne "is the last refuge. A place of challenges, of not letting go."[8] Despite the daily dread, a surreal feeling of normalcy makes life easier. "I am busy for hours at a time," writes Rudashevski in his diary. "It is hard to accomplish something at school and in the club, and at the same time to be involved with cooking and cleaning. At school we are now covering the theme Vilna in geography."[9]

A vast majority of the Vilne Jews were killed by the Germans and local collaborators in Ponary (Paneriai), the forested hill overlooking the city where the Napeolonic Army met its end in 1812. The ghetto was liquidated on September 23, 1943, with most of its eleven thousand remaining inhabitants sent to concentration camps in Estonia, where few survived the hard labour and starvation. Out of sixty thousand local Jews no more than three thousand saw the end of the war. When in the summer of 1944, soon after Vilnius was taken over from the Nazi occupation by the Soviet Army, Yiddish writer Chaim Grade (1910-1982) came back from his forced exile in Central Asia to his childhood neighbourhood in Vilne, he instantly felt like a stranger. Vilne was no more: the Jewish town was not even a museum or graveyard, but a ghost, a restless memory without a place to call home, a spirit without a body. "Since my return to Vilna," writes Grade, "I have roamed through the seven little alleys that once made up the Ghetto. The narrow alleyways enmeshed and imprisoned me, like a subterranean passages, like caves filled with ancient graves. Orphaned, they cast a spell upon me; their emptiness hovers in my brain, they attached themselves to me like seven chains of stone. Yet I have no desire to free myself of them. I want them to carve themselves still deeper into my body, into my flesh. I feel the dark, icy stiffness of bolted gates and doors creep under my skin. Shattered windows stare out through my eyes, and someone inside me cries aloud: 'So be it! I want to become a ruin!' "[10]

While Vilne became entombed in the flesh of the survivors who carried its memory to all corners of the earth, Vilnius was quickly populated by new residents. Some came from other Lithuanian cities and the demoralised and violence-ridden countryside (the Lithuanian resistance against the Soviet occupation continued for years after the end of the World War II, and massive deportations of the local population ended only with the death of Stalin in 1953). Others arrived from further afield, mostly Russia. The Sovietisation and Lithuanisation of local place-names aided the acclimatisation of the newcomers. But while the prewar dominance of the Polish and Yiddish languages was replaced by the administrative authority of Russian and Lithuanian, the city's new inhabitants never felt at ease in their home. Lithuanian poet Tomas Venclova remembers arriving in Vilnius after the war as a child. "It was a thoroughly unfamiliar city" to most Lithuanians,

72. The postwar ruins of Vilnius with its Baroque churches unscathed, circa 1947.

and "life in Vilnius at the beginning was an arduous sinking of roots into a new soil. In general, it was chaos."[11]

The historical metamorphosis veils the human breakdown of the city: in the decade during and after the war (1939-1949), through murder, deportation, exile, repatriation and emigration, Vilnius lost close to ninety percent of its population. With its Jewish community annihilated and many of its Polish residents forced to leave the town for the newly reconfigured Poland, Soviet Lithuanian Vilnius became a vacuous place, not unlike a museum, except without any acknowledgment of its recent past. With time, and out of the Stalinist terror, a new city emerged. Still multinational despite a dramatic change in its ethnic composition, Vilnius grew as the comatose heart of the downtrodden Lithuanian nationhood, and, just before the collapse of the Soviet Union, the Lithuanian speaking population, for the first time in modern history, gained a demographic majority.

One of the tragic paradoxes of the World War II period was that Vilnius not only lost most of its residents, but also mislaid most of its narratives and memories. For decades there were more natives of the city, that is, people who were born and lived in Vilnius before the war, living outside the city than in the city itself. Soviet Vilnius was largely a city of immigrants, whose family attachments to the city were weak and whose personal knowledge of the place was shallow. Undeniably, many of its new residents, mostly Lithuanians and Russians but also some Poles and Jews, loved the city and were proud of its past, but under the restrictive Soviet regime, their memory of the city could never fully cross the political boundaries of the divided world. The dislocation resulted in a shift of local identities: a generation of immigrant residents of Vilnius knew very little of its recent past, while the old residents and their offspring, removed from the place, often felt they were still part of the city. In a way, the line separating indigenous from foreign was inverted: a native became a stranger – a newcomer turned into a local. This demographical inversion altered the personality of the city, making contemporary Vilnius, in the words of a Lithuanian poet, an androgynous, constantly changing, yet at the same time barren place:

> This city
> changes its sex
> after a rupture
> and every time escapes
> from the trap
> of continuous serenity
> . . .
> how many poets have kissed
> the baroque silk halter
> but they learned
> only one thing –
> to depart.

"The Iron Dog: to Vilnius"[12]

Most of the city's former Polish inhabitants were resettled in the "recovered lands" of western and northern Poland, the former eastern provinces of Prussia. The Stefan Batory University of Wilno, with its Polish faculty, was replanted in the city of Torun, but a vast majority of the repatriates were given homes in Wrocław and Gdańsk, where the folk traditions of Wilno were woven into the cultural fabric of the new Poland. The nostalgia of the former residents of Wilno was captured by the German writer Günter Grass in the novel *The Call of the Toad*, describing a love affair between two expatriates: a German widower with his roots in Danzig and a Polish widow from a Wilno family. They first met on November 2, in the year of the collapse of the Soviet bloc, while each was visiting family graves in the cemetery of Gdańsk. "They called each other Herr Reschke and Frau Piątkowska. Relaxed after their exchange of views, they suddenly noticed that all around them other celebrants of All Souls' Day were paying their respect to their dead with flowers and hurricane lamps. And only then did the widow make the remark that the widower noted verbatim in his diary: 'Naturally, Mama and Papa would prefer to lie in Wilno cemetery than here, where everything strange was and is.' "[13] The Polish (and Lithuanian) spirit of the city was also seized by the countless immigrant Catholic parishes around the world carrying the names of Ostra Brama or Aušros Vartai, and Saint Casimir.

While the postwar memory of Vilne was extremely melancholic, it nonetheless helped to strengthen the spirit of Jewish national resistance, cultural continuity, religious traditionalism and social change. Vilne has been kept alive in the stories and recollections of Jewish families with their ancestral roots in Lithuania. In Israel, Vilne has been foremost invoked through the epic deeds of the ghetto partisans and the spiritual resilience of its yeshiva traditions. In the United States, Vilne is enshrined as an intellectual and cultural centre of the Jewish diaspora, through such academic and communal institutions as YIVO (founded in Vilne in 1925 but relocated to New York during the war years) and the restored historical *Vilna Shul* (Vilna Synagogue) in Boston. In France, the city's Jewish intellectual and political traditions were picked up by French academics and activists of the sixties, such as the eminent philosopher Emmanuel Levinas (1906-1995), who summarised them with the slogan "*le droit à la différence*" (the right to be different). The phrase, challenging the ideal of a single and centralised French culture, echoes the social sophistication of the Yiddish milieu of inter-war *Wilno,* which mesmerised Döblin with its ability to integrate local cultural plurality into the universal principles of modernity. Judith Friedlander, an American scholar, captured the spirit of the changing intellectual climate of France in a book, *Vilna on the Seine.* In post-1968 Paris, notes Friedlander, "Jewish Vilna seems to be everywhere: in the cinema and theater; in books and journals; and in the ways the young have recently chosen to return to Judaism, to make a *teshuva.* Inspired by symbolic, not historical, truth, Vilna (on the Seine) reaches beyond the walls of the Jerusalem of Lithuania. It gathers together the old Jewish communities that once stood along the Rivers Neris and Neman and across Lithuania's thick forests ... embracing an area, known as 'Lite' in Yiddish," which, after the war, was cut off from the rest of Europe by the Iron Curtain.[14]

Behind the ideological and political wall of Cold War separation, the ghosts of bygone days were exorcised by the spirit of socialist progress. Soviet Vilnius, now adorned as "Lithuania's breath and life," was declared to be "a city of contrasts, but not the sort of contrasts met with in the cities of the capitalist West – not the contrast between the luxury of the aristocracy and the poverty of the working-class districts; the city of Vilnius is unique in its rare combination of modern architecture and monuments of the hoary past." The cityscape of Vilnius, boasted Soviet propaganda, "is so unusual that at first you get the impression that you are in a theatre and all this is the decor carried out by an artist in love with the past."[15] Not unlike its capitalist counterpart, Soviet modernity was a future-oriented development of universal values and standards, but with a slight nod to local, vernacular aesthetics. Hence, Soviet Vilnius was envisioned as "the capital of tomorrow" where "elements of Lithuanian national architecture are organically blended in the socialist architecture of the new buildings." Such an innovative town had "no companions and no predecessors" and "anybody who has not been in Vilnius for the last three or four years will not recognize many corners of this ancient and at the same time youthful city. In a few years the view from the top of the Castle Hill will be a new and still more beautiful one. But no matter what changes may be made in Vilnius, it will always remain a monument to many centuries of Lithuanian history, the pride and glory of its people."[16] The homelike feeling of Lithuanian Vilnius, however, was built on a memory void, a spectral cartographical condition, which, in the words of Judita Vaičiūnaitė (1937-2001), a Lithuanian poet, helped the newcomers to domesticate the place. In the poem "Museum Street" (the post-war designation for German Street in Vilnius's Old Town which was, in part, remodeled in the showcase Soviet-style), she exposes the amnesiac ordinariness of the city's newly-found identity:

On the table – white dishes, bread and yellow apples.
And summer – beyond the opened window on the fifth floor.
Thunder and rain quieted.
    And the sun sketches
Itself round…
And a woman approaches the plaza – lighthaired and tall.
Drops of water on the roofs flashed for her.
Photographs of the holidays are ready.
These noisy, weary streets were laid with hot hands –
And the window,
  calling pigeons from towers
    and sparrows,
Bread-feeders,
Rising like a high melody
   above ghetto fires,
     requiems and ashes…[17]

In the process of modern beautifications and spatial expansion, the city narrowed its history to Lithuanian and Soviet themes. In both cases, many local relics were censored and destroyed in order to cleanse the topographical surface of the city. Often the unwelcome local dead of ideologically or nationally suspicious origins were replaced with relics of heroic Soviet figures. Immediately after the end of World War II, the German war cemeteries holding the military dead of both world wars were the first to go. Next came the elimination of old Protestant cemeteries, where many local European (mostly German) expatriates, including numerous professors from the university, were buried. The bodies and graves of many professional colleagues of Georg Forster and Josef Frank were desecrated by the orders of the Soviet Lithuanian administration, and a large part of the biographical past of the university was erased. The small Muslim cemetery near the main city prison melancholically encountered by Paul Monty during the Great War was also levelled. With the destruction of that cemetery and the adjacent mosque, the last vestiges of the historic Tartar neighbourhood were eliminated from the cityscape. In addition, the Soviet civic authorities severely diminished the visibility of various Polish and Lithuanian religious and national historical figures by removing their bodies to less prominent sites. The silver casket containing the relics of Saint Casimir, for instance, was moved from the Cathedral to Saint Peter and Paul Church. Another devastating blow to the city's historical topography came with the ruthless destruction of the two Jewish cemeteries – which, after the Nazi annihilation of the local Jewish population and Soviet repression of the greatly diminished Jewish community, were the most evidential reminders of the centuries-long history and geography of Jewish Vilne. The civic and ideological monuments of the new Vilnius were often built on the ground of these destroyed cemeteries. Indeed, many of the tombstones from the Jewish and Protestant cemeteries were used by local authorities in various construction sites as building materials. Some of the Jewish headstones ended up as stepping-stones in a stairway leading to the top of a hill offering a panoramic view of the altered topography and skyline of post-war Vilnius.

In general, Soviet Vilnius was an isolated, ideologically and politically caged town. But while the city had no direct road, railway or air connections with western Europe, it often appeared in the fantasy world of Soviet propaganda, if not as the centre of the continent, then at least as a vibrant hub of international travel. In a typical fashion, a Soviet travel book from the 1950s makes Vilnius a spectacular entryway into the Soviet dream-world, whose airport can barely handle the planes flowing in from Paris, Prague, Moscow, Warsaw, Berlin, etc. In the airport hall, "porters bustle about carrying bags

LENINO
AVENUE
Giros Str.
Cvirkos Str.
Kapsuko Str.
Gedimino Sq.
Pilies Mnt.
Pionieriu Str.
Sruogos Str.
M. Antokolskio Str.
Muziejaus Str.
Traku Str.
"Tiesos" Str.
SUBAČIAUS STR.
GORKIO STR.
ARKLIU STR.
KOMJAUNIMO STR.
1. Bust to Stanislaw Moniuszko
2. Church of St. Catherine
3. Monument to Salomeja Neris
4. Church of the Dominicans (of the Holy Spirit)
5. Senasis Rusys Restaurant
6. Memorial to Vincas Mickevičius-Kapsukas
7. Art Museum (Town-Hall building)
8. Palace of Art Exhibitions
9. Museum of Atheism (building of the Church of St. Kazimieras)
10. State Philharmonic of the Lithuanian SSR
11. Bazilian Gates
12. Church of the Holy Spirit
13. Church of St. Tereza
14. Medininku (Aušros) Gates
15. Church of Sts. Peter and Paul

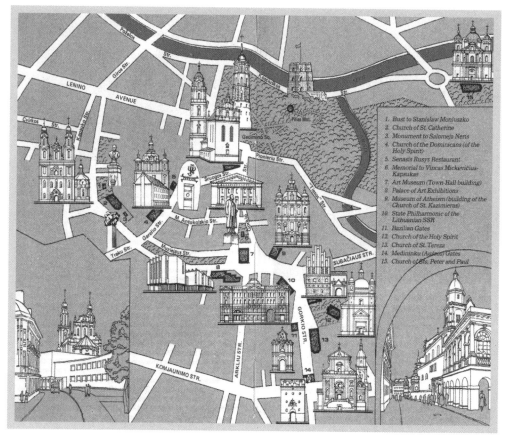

73. A tourist plan of Soviet Vilnius, 1981. During the Soviet years, Saint Casimir Church, marked on the map as number 9, was turned into the Museum of Atheism.

with hotel labels from many countries, people are speaking Chinese, English, Polish, German. ... For many people arriving from abroad Vilnius is the aerial gateway to the Soviet Union and their first acquaintance with the land of socialism is through the building of the international airport."[18] Moscow, however, was never keen on Vilnius, seeing both its recent Polish-Jewish past and its budding Lithuanian future as an ideological challenge to the Soviet present. So despite its architectural beauty and historical significance, Vilnius was rarely put on the officially sanctioned *Intourist* itineraries, specially designed for foreign tourists. Further, independent travelling in the Soviet Union, especially in border regions such as Lithuania, was so dreaded and controlled by the authorities that even former residents of Vilnius who had left the country could visit their relatives still living in the city only by joining a packaged tour group. Foreigners in Vilnius were rare birds, easily spotted by their dress or unrepressed social behaviour, but avoided by most locals out of fear of the KGB. Under the watchful eye of the Soviet authorities, an unofficial or unrestrained fraternisation with foreigners could easily be turned into an ideological and social vice. Aside from sporadic family reunions, only members of the cultural elite, high-ranking Communist party officials, dissidents and prostitutes could periodically mingle with passing foreigners.

Some visitors, such as Simone Beauvoir and Jean-Paul Sartre, who passed through Lithuania in 1965, carried an aura of philosophical (if not always ideological) independence. Alas, it was a singular event, and their visit, monitored by the party, made a long-lasting impact in the minds of those who were allowed to be acquainted with the highbrow couple. Those who were allowed by the Soviet authorities to stay for a longer period were more or less sympathetic to the socialist regime, but even their encounters with the city were circumvented by official censorship and ideological guardianship. One such visitor was Phillipe Bonosky, born in 1916 of Lithuanian parents in a Pennsylvanian steel town, who later became a self-described American proletarian writer. Bonosky, who was also a Moscow correspondent of *The Daily Worker*, a newspaper published by the Communist party of the USA, visited Vilnius in the mid-1960s. He assembled his impressions of the city in 1967 in a book entitled *Beyond the Borders of Myth: from Vilnius to Hanoi*. Bonosky certainly had a friendly if not fully supportive disposition towards the socialist regime of the Soviet administration. His encounter with post-Stalinist Vilnius, however, had a strikingly personal resonance, rarely detected in the propaganda-driven accounts of the place. At the height of the Cold War, Bonosky was one of the first foreign visitors to openly admit to the illusory powers of such an encounter:

> There is one Vilnius: the Vilnius visible to the eyes, the ears, the nose, and other senses. This is a Vilnius which the whole world agrees is one of the lovely cities of Europe. It has suffered too much, as a city, but its suffering has been so closely intertwined with human suffering that one thinks of it as half-human, as having feelings, as humanly enduring.
>
> There is another Vilnius which is one's own, and which one makes for himself. That Vilnius becomes part of one's autobiography.
>
> I came to Vilnius for the first time as though I had been there many times before, as though 'I had lost thee.' It was already as familiar as a dream."[19]

As his contact with the city deepened, Vilnius transmuted from a mesmerising vision into a horrible sight. For Bonosky, this conversion led to a recognition of the universality of the city, of Vilnius as representation of both old and new Europe:

Old Vilnius is a living museum, though it leads a double life. The Nazis destroyed almost all of it. But literally from its ruined foundations the Lithuanians rebuilt the city just as it had been where that was possible. Only atomic fire could melt these stones now.

That is one reason why it's possible to view this old Vilnius without a too-over-powering sense of nostalgia. For no feeling person can forget the pain here. There are many who have a far better right to be walking, this very moment, on these very stones, but lie in still and unknown graves.

You too walk with ghosts here – along this road to Panerai, where tens of thousands walked before you. This will lead to a gully over which no birds fly – even the dead here are completely reduced to dust.

So leave it! Come instead to visit beautiful old Vilnius, forgetting, you hope, all that. And suddenly – you are brought face-to-face with the Ghetto!

These stones you are now walking on flinch from your feet. No 'art,' with all its coyness, can silence them. No time is long enough to grow a crust of forgetfulness over them. For only yesterday they ran with living blood, and this should not be forgotten, not only because the dead should always be remembered but the reasons for the tragedy should be remembered even more. ... So this is a bit of Vilnius, not all of it, and not everybody's Vilnius, and very little of the new part of it, but the city that history knows, which reveals itself to the visitor. This writer comes and connects to what has endured here, for this is universal.[20]

Despite its universal appeal, most writers, foreign or local, paid little attention to Soviet Vilnius. Those in the west, except for its former residents, had no opportunity or desire to explore an unfamiliar town indistinctly located at the cultural and political fringes of the Soviet empire. The local ones lacked either curiosity about its past or were afraid to venture into its perplexing history, fearing unwanted attention from the ideological censors of the regime. Lithuanian writers and artists of the period might have led an urban life, but coming from a rural milieu, they were mostly preoccupied with the representation of the massive post-war social and cultural changes that consumed the Lithuanian countryside. The Russian intelligentsia of the Soviet era also demonstrated no particular interest in the provincial town with no significant Russian population or cultural memory. Poets, on the other hand, were much less constrained, if not in their ability to speak freely, then at least in their aspiration to see, capture and place difference within the ideologically monotonous imagination of the Soviet reality.

During the last two decades of Soviet oppression, Vilnius offered an imperfect and risky opportunity of intellectual escape. In contrast to many Soviet cities, Vilnius retained the shattered relics of its past, not just in stones, but also in spirit. Many new residents of the city felt a religious affinity to

74. Palm Sunday in Vilnius with Aušros Vartai in the background, 1967; a photograph by A. Kunčius.

local shrines, and despite the unyielding religious oppression, the domes and spires of the Baroque churches still dominated the skyline of Soviet Vilnius. (While the Soviet authorities destroyed the remains of the Great Synagogue and reassigned many other religious buildings to different social functions, only one or two churches were demolished in the post-war period.) The modern aesthetics of Vilnius, especially in architecture, theatre, jazz music, design and fashion, were a bit more western-oriented than anywhere else in the Soviet Union. Unnoticeable, perhaps, to a foreign eye, the nuanced cultural differences of Vilnius were quickly discerned by visitors coming from other parts of the Soviet Union. For Joseph Brodsky (1940-1996), the Russian poet and Nobel prize winner from Leningrad, an affable encounter with the new Vilnius stimulated a poetic detour into the biographical realm of historical possibilities. Brodsky, who traced his family's origins from Lithuanian Jewry, visited Vilnius after his internment in the gulag for "social parasitism." Persecuted and dispossessed, he lived a nomadic life until his expulsion from the Soviet Union in 1972. In his wandering state, he was able to re-imagine Jewish life in old Vilnius as an opening chapter of modern human estrangement. In the poem "Liejyklos" (the Lithuanian name for Foundry Street), from his 1971 poetic cycle *Lithuanian Divertissement*, Brodsky echoes the words of Döblin, describing the personal cost of the resettlement, forced or voluntary, of his ancestors:

> To be born a century ago
> and over the down bedding, airing,
> through a window see a garden grow
> and Catherine's crosses, twin domes soaring;
> be embarrassed for Mother, hiccup
> when the brandished lorgnettes scrutinize
> and push a cart with rubbish heaped up
> along the ghetto yellow alleys,
> sigh, tucked in bed from head to toe,
> for Polish ladies, for example;
> and hang around to face the foe
> and fall in Poland somewhere trampled –
> for Faith, Tsar, Homeland, or if not,
> then shape Jews' ringlets into sideburns
> and off, on to the New World like a shot,
> puking in waves as the engine churns.[21]

By the time of the revolutionary changes in Eastern Europe in the late 1980s, Vilnius's population had grown to almost six hundred thousand people. But the purge of the socialist inscriptions that followed stripped the city bare, and vacant squares, emptied of their sculptural residents (Lenin and other Soviet heroes), exposed the lack of a coherent vision of the place. Anatol Lieven, a Moscow correspondent for *The Times* of London, described local residents as dismissive of their city's historical beauty or its future market potential:

> In contrast to the Estonians in Tallinn and the Latvians in Riga, Lithuanians in old Vilnius are usually ignorant of the history and legends attached to the streets where they live. ... Around the remains of the Ghetto stretch the streets of the old city, a delightful maze of old houses and courtyards, mostly quite poor and plain but painted in lovely, faded colours of yellow, blue and light green. An English visitor compared one of them to a painting of de Chirico. Among them are the more ornate palaces of the old nobility, with Atlases and Caryatids propping up their gates. The fine architecture of much of Vilnius is not merely an asset for tourism, but can provide some fine offices for business.[22]

When Vilnius finally became the capital city of independent Lithuania in 1991, its ideologically contested and nationally challenged topography was turned once more into a symbolic battleground for the geographical and historical definition of Europe. "The free democratic Lithuania," states the Lithuanian-American writer, Venclova, "faces a task of creating a new identity for Vilnius without rejecting a single historical and cultural streak of the city. Having integrated its past and its entire cultural potential, Vilnius is turning into a European capital worthy of its founders and best citizens."[23]

Europe, however, holds different meanings for different people, and before Vilnius could be fully transformed into a dynamic capital of a revived European nation-state, it had to become acquainted with its former status as one of the graveyards of Europe. The first visitors who came to Vilnius after the collapse of the Soviet Union were the exiled natives (or their children) of the city. They were searching for the familiar but departed Jewish Vilne or Polish Wilno, but could only find Lithuanian Vilnius. There was little melancholy or even nostalgia in such sojourns, for both emotions require either a feeling of sorrow or of consolation. Lithuanian Vilnius could provide neither. The city did not recognise the estranged visitors as its own residents. The loss of language, culture, religion, place-names and most importantly people made its mark: Vilnius was foreign both to itself and Europe. Memory-less, or rather, amnesiac, the city appeared to be a rough and empty place.

Rose Zwi, who grew up in South Africa, came to Lithuania from Australia in 1993 in search of her family roots. As is frequently the case, she described the idea of visiting the country as a homecoming: "My desire to visit *der heim* lay dormant for years. The land of my forebears had become a desert of graves, curtained by iron. With Lithuanian independence in 1991, however, it became possible to go 'home.' "[24] She found her relatives living in Vilnius, in an apartment located in a typical old town building with "a stone arch" entrance "which leads into a cobbled courtyard overrun by mangy cats. The odour of catpiss follows one up the wooden steps into a small, dark entrance, where it mingles with a dank, familiar smell. ... The front door, barely visible in the murky light, opens into a different world. We walk directly into a tiny, spotlessly clean kitchen, which has two doors. The one on the left leads into a small bedroom; the door on the right takes us into the living room, which is large and high-ceiling."[25]

The communication between Zwi and the extended family in Vilnius was warm but testing. The customary Yiddish, the native language of Vilne, no longer provided a reliable link of communication: Zwi was more at home in English, her relatives in Russian and Lithuanian. Outside the intimate family realm, the city with its largely immigrant Lithuanian population appeared menacing:

> Vilnius is beautiful. Vilnius, not Vilna, which no longer exists. ... Ernest points out the TV tower in the distance, surrounded by blocks of modern buildings, where a fierce brief battle had raged between Lithuanian patriots and the Soviet army just eighteen months ago. I am unmoved by Ernest's fervour; the phrase "Lithuanian patriots" has a chilling ring. Vilnius's beauty is dimmed, suddenly, by a cold drizzle and icy winds that drive us from the tower.
>
> ... At Ernest's insistence I am taken to see the barricades which had been erected against the Soviet forces outside the Parliament building, and to the spot where crosses have been erected for those killed in the resistance.
>
> By this time I am in no mood for either Lithuanian patriotism nor the religious fervour which accompanies it. I am not warming to the severe-looking Lithuanians in the streets and in the church queues. I might have responded more warmly to their pagan ancestors who worshipped oak trees.
>
> I am perturbed by this reaction; I had prided myself on my tolerance. But perhaps too much troubled history lies between us to remain untouched by it.[26]

A compatriot of Zwi, the writer Dan Jacobson, visited Vilnius with his son for the same reason – to trace family roots within the dramatically transformed small town landscape of Lithuania. Vilnius was a stepping stone in this search, but an important one nonetheless. From this city, most Jews, including Jacobson's ancestors, left Lithuania to escape from almost certain death at the hands of the SS paratroopers and their local Lithuanian auxiliaries. Despite being an integral part of the family memory, Lithuania and Vilnius were distant places. "I've never before been in a country I know so little about," remarked Jacobson's son.[27]

The unfamiliar Vilnius greeted the Jacobsons with naked emptiness; the road from the airport to the city led through the Rasos cemetery, foreshadowing a sense of loss:

> A car. Another car. At last, a couple walking. Another couple waiting at a bus stop. The huge red ball of the sun stands proud of the serrated tree tops on the horizon. Some blocks of flats appear. Even they look unpeopled. Only when the road passes through the middle of a heavily wooded cemetery within an elaborate, miniature topography of hills, hollows and rocky knolls do we come on anything resembling a throng. It is made up entirely of stone and bronze figures: angels, life-size images of Jesus carrying his cross or already mounted on it, many Marys with heads bowed or arms held out. There are also a few effigies of the human departed, in frock coats. The tallest of them are lit up momentarily in random rays from the

sun. Then a few more roads come together and sidle off from one another – and here we are, on the edge of the Old Town of Vilnius.

... Much the same, it seemed to me, could have been said of Vilnius as a whole. On our first outing it looked as if the city was inhabited by about fourteen people. We went up some narrow, cobbled alleyways and through irregularly sloping squares. Streetlamps with lights inside them were almost as rare as people. ... Amid the darkness and general depopulation there were a few large plate-glass windows, behind which one could make out displays of chairs or glassware aspiring to elegance and high modernity: to a positively Finnish finish. But most of the shops were meagrely and dirtily windowed, still under the Communist blight, as if nothing had changed since the death of the old order, or ever would.[28]

Wandering through this seemingly abandoned city of a half-million living souls without any deeper knowledge or memory compass, Jacobson came to a striking emotional conclusion: "A strange thought suddenly occurred to me. No wonder the city appeared to be empty! A quarter – no, a third eventually – of the people who had once lived here had been wiped out. All around us were the spaces they had occupied. We were in the midst of a vacancy their absence had created; the city's silence was that of the words they and their unborn children would never speak."[29]

Other visitors were less ignorant of the current status or history of the city, but even their encounter with it was defined by the presence of the dead. Anne Applebaum, an American journalist, visited Vilnius at the time of the revolutionary break-up of the Soviet Union. Foreign tourism was still an unheard-of rarity in Vilnius, and Applebaum, despite the brewing political upheavals surrounding her, could enjoy a moment of evocative solitude in an encounter with the city's missing present:

I went alone to the Polish cemetery. A vast slab of black marble engraved with the words "Mother of Pilsudski, and the Heart of Her Son" lay on the grass outside the main gate.

"And just as well that he didn't live to see the day when his heart would be buried in a foreign country."

A middle-aged Polish woman in a polka-dot silk top and blue, bell-bottomed silk trousers stood in front of the vast grave. Her midriff was bare. Her feet were squeezed into tiny, open-toed rhinestone-bedecked sandals. Her fingernails sparkled with gold paint, her wrists jangled with gold bracelets, and gold earrings dripped from her ears. She wore shiny red lipstick and big, round, American sunglasses. Oddly, she was quite beautiful.

Her companion, a thirty-ish looking country cousin in a dusty yellow shirt, was listening to her with dull attentiveness.

"They should have taken it to Krakow after the war, and buried it with the rest of his body. You see, Henryk, Pilsudski's body is buried in Krakow with the Polish

75. The Bernardine and Saint Anna Churches in Vilnius; a photograph by J. Bułhak.

kings, you must remember that he is almost like a king. His heart is buried here, in Wilno, Polish Wilno, and his mother is buried here, too. Look, oh, look, how poor the flowers are now."

... Since the war, she had only been in Wilno a few times: she could count her visits on one hand. The trip had been difficult for ex-residents to make, and not many had wanted to try; after all, she pointed out, "there isn't much left of old Wilno, is there?" Between the Soviets and Lithuanians (and she didn't know who was worse) they managed to destroy the city.

... "What would Grandmother and Grandfather think now, if only they could see Wilno, lovely Wilno now? What they would make of the street signs, all in Lithuanian?"[30]

Stan Persky, a Canadian writer with the credentials of a prolonged European residence, went to Vilnius from Berlin, because, as he put, "my father said he had been born there. Precisely when he had been born there, and when, as a baby, he had left Vilnius for Chicago, and the order and dates of the births of three brothers and four sisters, were matters of endless and rollicking dispute whenever his side of the family gathered."[31] Persky had no relatives in the city, but he entered the sleepy life of the city with the curiosity of a gay man searching for comradeship and, perhaps, some more corporeal adventure. He read almost everything about the city available in English at the time: memoirs of its former Jewish residents, essays of its famous native Polish literati and the fiction of its current Lithuanian authors. His contact with the city increased day by day, and gradually, the city became populated both by ghosts from the past and by the living. He paid due respect to the only semi-legal gay bar in the city, visited museums and met with the emerging political leaders of Lithuania. Inevitably, the path of memory led to the Paneriai forest, where most of the city's Jews, alongside many other victims of the German occupation, were killed:

> The small cottage that housed a museum was closed for renovations, and a couple of workmen were the only people we saw. In the forest, winding footpaths led to two or three unobtrusive monuments. Behind one of them there was a broad swath of burned pine trees, and an abandoned rusted-out bus. I wandered through the charred remains of the trees. But what happened in these woods had occurred long before the fire. There was, in a sense, nothing to be seen here. There was only the quiet, sunlit forest.[32]

After silent and sightless Paneriai, Persky and his Lithuanian guide went to hear the words of a survivor:

> "What did Vilnius look like in 1945?" I asked Grigory Kanowitsch. He was a Jewish novelist in his mid-sixties. His parents had somehow escaped Lithuania and made their way to Kazakhstan, in the Soviet Union. Kanowitsch had returned to Vilnius at the end of the Second World War as a sixteen-year-old.
> "It's in Kafka's novels," he replied, sitting across from us on a sofa in the large living room of the apartment where he and his wife lived. He was wearing a short-sleeved shirt and a tie slightly askew. "Everyone, not just Jews – soldiers, Lithuanians, Poles – seemed uprooted, flying between the heaven and earth. That's why I remembered Kafka."
> "When you returned, was the extent of the Holocaust apparent to you then?"
> "It was shouting. It was shouting," he said, and repeated that phrase a third time. "From every window, from every basement, from every hole."
> ... After we left the novelist's ... Standing towards the back of the street-car, catching an occasional glimpse of the sun on the river, I experienced an instant in which I felt both the comfort of being alive – just to see the powdery substance of falling maple and linden blossoms clogging the cracks between the black bricks – and the melancholy of our losses. Nothing returned the dead to us.[33]

Persky's daytime encounter with the city metamorphosed into an allegorical vision, a nightmarish tableau of modern Europe, or the entire world – muted, fragmented, and still violently restless, leading to an unknown future destination under the sign of annihilation. It was not a dream, but a contemporary version of a Baroque danse macabre, during which life and death are joined in an embracing circle of oblivion. As an escape from this cursed cycle of history, Persky ends his literary travelogue across the freshly demarcated (old) borderlands of Europe by proposing an impossible task. In Vilnius he calls for a conversation between the dead and living, thus, placing the city on the transmundane map of a shared human destiny. This conversational union between the departed and the present human worlds contains the promise of dispelling the fog of history, which could create a new type of geography dominated not by differences but similarities. On this eschatological chart, everything becomes local and everyone is a native to the place:

> During the night, I remembered what I had imagined that afternoon in the Paneriai forest. Some of the dead were sitting on chairs, others were standing around the charred woods, coffee cups and saucers in hand, wearing their death clothes – dark jackets and trousers, white shirts with slightly frayed collars, black hats on their heads; the women were in plain black dresses like the one I'd seen my grandmother wear, one or two of them absently smoothing wrinkles in the cloth. The dead children were farther off, among the trees.
>
> They were not all Jews, though Jews were prominent among them. Their ranks included contemporary combatants from places in Yugoslavia, Armenia, Afghanistan, and elsewhere, whose unfamiliar names we had forgotten as soon as the nightly news pronounced the unfamiliar names of new cities under siege. Perhaps I even imagined an ancient, sightless Bulgarian.
>
> They gazed at us, oddly but patiently, from the other side of a piece of time. They didn't speak among themselves, nor did we, the living. But I felt that both the living and the dead, separated by the piece of time, wanted to speak to each other. It seemed that there was everything to say.[34]

The eschatological map of the other world, in a way, is a reflection of a desirable yet unattainable geography. In this context, corpses and their resting sites – the relics of the corporeal – are often turned into flexible symbols of metaphysical currency; they become ideal markers of the specific ideological and geopolitical order of the place. In her study of the post-socialist "political lives" of the dead, anthropologist Katherine Verdery points to the representational elasticity and social profundity of relics. The presence, or for that matter, the absence of dead bodies is an essential part of a communal narrative of place:

> Remains are concrete, yet protean; they do not have a single meaning but are open to many different readings. ... Dead people come with a curriculum vitae or résumé – several possible résumés, depending on which aspect of their life is being considered. They lend themselves to analogy with *other people's* résumés.

That is, they encourage identification with their life story, from several possible vantage points. Their complexity makes it fairly easy to discern different sets of emphasis, extract different stories, and thus rewrite history. Dead bodies have another great advantage as symbols: they don't talk much on their own (though they did once.) Words can be put into their mouths – often ambiguous words – or their own actual words can be ambiguated by quoting them out of context. It is thus easier to rewrite history with dead people than with other kinds of symbols that are speechless.

Yet because they have a single name and a single body, they present the illusion of having *only one* significance. Fortifying that illusion is their materiality, which implies their having a single meaning that is solidly "grounded," even though in fact they have no such single meaning. Different people can invoke corpses as symbols, thinking those corpses mean the same thing to all present, whereas in fact they may mean different things to each. All that is shared is everyone's *recognition* of this dead person as somehow important.[35]

Traditionally, Vilnius's dead have been essential participants in the reframing of the city's location within Europe. The turbulent and contested regional history has supplied a constant flow of multivocal dead with contrasting résumès and antagonistic post-mortem loyalties. Hence, as I see it, Vilnius's cemeteries and memorial spaces are threshold sites where, in the Bakhtinian sense of the word, various narrative knots of Europe are simultaneously tied and untied. To enter these both physically and allegorically metamorphosing spaces of Vilnius is to witness the changing local representational possibilities of Europe.

In the process of turning post-Soviet Vilnius into a European capital, the local dead became key participants of the geo-narrative drama. A German voluntary association restored the destroyed military cemeteries of Vilnius in a geographically and ideologically inclusive way: the graves of the German soldiers were resurrected in parallel to those of the Russian soldiers. In fact, the restored German and Russian military cemeteries from the Great War lost their historical authenticity by gaining a few symbolic headstones commemorating the German soldiers of Jewish origins and the Russian soldiers of the Muslim faith. Today, among the rising forest of Protestant/Catholic crosses, one can find a patch of Orthodox crosses interspersed with tombstones bearing the Star of David or the Islamic Crescent. (The original German cemeteries contained only Christian and secular nationalistic commemorative symbols.) Yet other destroyed cemeteries have not been restored, thus deepening a memory fissure within the commemorative topography of modern Vilnius.

Furthermore, Polish war cemeteries – including the one containing the cenotaph with the heart of Piłsudski – exist in a commemorative national limbo. While these monuments in general are well attended and taken care of by various local and external Polish associations, often supported by the government of Poland, rarely they are included in the list of officially protected monuments of Lithuanian history. This makes the Polish burial places private rather than national memorials, thus essentially excluding them from the dominant Lithuanian version of the city's history. In a similar fashion, the graves of the Red Army soldiers and Soviet functionaries are rarely put on the post-socialist tourist maps of Vilnius. Despite this absence from the official narrative, these and other "foreign" burial sites often share the same space with the graves of various dead honoured by the Lithuanian state. This memorial melange – the spatial intimacy between ideologically accredited and discredited dead – creates an undulating topography of local history, with the high peaks of remembrance alternating with deep valleys of amnesia; and in between the two extremes – vast plateaus of a commonplace memory delineated by the rows of native dead of various persuasions. A walk though a contemporary Vilnius graveyard (Rasos or Antakalnis cemetery, for instance) is like listening to an atonal composition in which a musical discord splits up into different harmonies, each with its own rhythm and refrain, but each born out of the same basic accord. In such a musical or memorial oeuvre, unity is achieved not through agreement but dissonance, which keeps melody or memory in a constant state of defiance. In this sense, the cemeteries of Vilnius are sites of anti-memory, challenging every version of local history. Unable to fit within the memorial perimeters of Vilnius's soil, the local dead reach for the map of Europe.

The historical burden of Europe in Vilnius has increased dramatically with the unanticipated unearthing of a few thousands of human remains on a vast commercial and residential development site in the fall of 2001. Initially, this discovery created only a minor local sensation, not just because of the high number of corpses, but mostly because of their mysterious origin and sinister location. The mass grave was in the territory of a former Soviet military base; so, understandably, its whereabouts raised memories of countless crimes committed by the Stalinist regime. After all, seven years before this discovery, just a few hundred meters away from the newly found mass grave, hundreds of bodies of NKVD (KGB) victims were recovered from the park of the former Tuskulėnai (Tusculanum) estate. The newly uncovered burial ground could have easily been an extension of the first site. It was also suspected that the remains could have belonged to Polish soldiers killed at the beginning of World War II and hastily buried en masse. Very soon, however, with the help of metal detectors, workers and anthropologists found more mundane and easily identifiable objects, such as coins and buttons, scattered among the bones. Many metal artefacts had French inscriptions and bore recognisable portraits of Napoleon. Immediately, it became obvious that the human remains were once soldiers of the Grande Armée, those who had died in Vilna in 1812.

Although the historical factuality of ten thousand French soldiers buried in Vilna had never been disputed, there was no evidence of where, since the Russian authorities seemed to bury them in deliberately unmarked (and soon forgotten) locations. Even Frank, for instance, who returned to the city in the summer of 1813, could find no traces of the massive burial grounds that should have contained thousands of human remains. Therefore, the recently discovered remains provided the first archaeological proof of the tragic role Vilna played in the Napoleonic history of Europe. As soon as the "national" identity of the bodies was established, the municipal authorities contacted the French Embassy in Vilnius. The French government quickly responded to the news from Vilnius by sending an anthropological team, and assumed an immediate administrative responsibility for the military relics.

Still, the national association of the thousands of corpses with contemporary and historical France has become a matter of international genealogical debate, since a vast majority of the soldiers, officers and accompanying personnel that formed the Grande Armée were not of French origin. In fact, soldiers from at least twenty contemporary European nations participated in the fateful march on Moscow, so alongside the French, there were Germans (Bavarians, Prussians, Westphalians, Saxons), Dutch, Flemings, Italians, Spaniards, Portuguese, Austrians, Poles, Lithuanians, Swiss, Croatians, Hungarians, etc. Furthermore, according to limited archaeological evidence, most of the three thousand bodies that have been so far uncovered in Vilnius were identified as belonging to the non-French military units of the Grand Armée.

Because the mass grave in Vilnius is the largest burial site from the Napoleonic wars ever to be uncovered and examined, it provided enormous scientific value and political capital. From a scientific point of view, the diverse ethnic composition of the remains has been an anthropological treasure, for it provides an anatomical cross-section of the European male population (only a few women were found among the dead), bonded together by the deadly winter of 1812-1813: "Now, crammed between construction cranes and stacks of concrete brick a corps of archaeologists and anatomists is mining a mass grave of Napoleon's soldiers, reconstructing the army's final days – and taking a remarkable measure of what it was like to be a man in Europe nearly two centuries ago."[36]

The disclosure of the remains also offered an opportunity for the world-wide media to come to Lithuania, which rarely makes international headlines. The mayor of Vilnius invited journalists from all major national and international news corporations to witness the discovery. And subsequently two television networks – BBC and Discovery Channel – have been directly involved in the anthropological exploration of the site. In the mass graveyards of Vilnius, BBC found plenty of material for its series "Meet the Ancestors," and the Discovery Channel collected footage for its documentary "Moments in Time." In addition to the media exposure and the exclusive rights to record it, both companies provided some additional funding for future exploration of the site. The anticipated media-driven scientific disclosure of other funereal sites has been also heralded by the civic administration as a long-overdue foreign discovery of the city. "It puts us on the map," declared the mayor of Vilnius, because it "confirms how important a role the city has played in the struggle over the historical destiny of Europe."[37]

Yet these European – international – bodies conveniently camouflage the contested and ambiguous location of Vilnius both within 'united' Europe and the modern Lithuanian state. Usually Vilnius's dead are historically controversial and geographically problematic, because, metaphorically and literally speaking, they segment, segregate, and divide the city according to different national identities and destinies. The relics of the NKVD victims found on the Tuskulėnai estate posed a typical challenge. According to the NKVD records, all victims were killed between 1944 and 1947, and many of them were members of the Lithuanian resistance movement. Notwithstanding, among the remains there were also German military officers accused of crimes against civilians; some local Nazi collaborators, who were persecuted for their participation in the Jewish genocide; numerous deserters from the Soviet Army, who had committed serious criminal offences; and local civilians charged with homicide.[38] Considering such a wide array of criminal offences and personalities, no single memorial can encompass the contradictory conduct and memory of the executed individuals. A memorial to all NKVD victims has been strongly opposed by the local Jewish community, which objects to a commemoration that would include some Nazi executioners. These remains, like many other local corpses, raise extremely sensitive historical and moral questions: do all remains deserve the same commemorative treatment? Should they be reburied together, or split apart according to their documented life deeds? Since the badly decayed bodies have no clear identity marks, is it even feasible to correctly identify them? (So far, only about fifty bodies have been identified.)

In contrast to the local dead, the "foreign" remains of the Grande Armée, perhaps reassuringly, map the historical march towards the unity of Europe. In fact, it became clear from the beginning that the local post-mortem of the international assemblage of distant and muted Europeans could become one of the greatest tourist attractions of Vilnius. Soon after the discovery, the Vilnius tourist office started to plan for so-called "Napoleon tours" of the country. "Vilnius," proudly declared a headline in *Lietuvos rytas*, the national daily, "will also be celebrated for the dead of Napoleon's army."[39] Because close to eighty percent of the soldiers who served in the army were not French, their collective profile, in a strange way, fits the international characteristics of the enlarged European Union. Consequently, both French and Lithuanian authorities have insisted that while the remains found on Lithuanian soil make "a part of the collective French memory," they belong to the trans-national heritage of Europe.[40]

Despite the fact of "belonging" to Europe, the remains were taken into joint Paris-Vilnius custody. Bringing the multinational remains to France was ruled out, and since French law does not permit cremation of French soldiers, it was decided to rebury them in Lithuania. After a detailed scientific analysis, the ceremonial reburial of the remains took place on June 1, 2003. The remains were put to rest in the most diverse (ideologically and nationally) cemetery of Vilnius. Appropriately, this large cemetery, known as the Soldiers' Cemetery, contains the remains of soldiers of many wars and nationalities. But alongside German, Russian, Polish and Soviet, and now, Napoleonic, troops, there are also the graves of Lithuanian Communist party officials, local cultural and academic elites, and the victims of the Soviet army attack on Vilnius in 1991. The French government paid about sixty thousand euros for the memorial, and while the reburial ceremony was orchestrated by the Vilnius Municipality, it closely followed the official French instructions concerning the burial procedures for fallen French soldiers. Many Lithuanian state officials, members of the diplomatic corps from most European countries and representatives of the Napoleon Society from France attended the ceremony. Priests blessed the ground and in his eulogy, Jean Bernard Harth, the French ambassador in Lithuania, drew a parallel between 1812 and 2003, referring to Lithuania's ninety percent backing in a referendum held three weeks prior for joining the EU. The attendees of the reburial ceremony were also cautiously reminded about the fallacies of war and the dangers of forced integration of Europe: "Napoleon was on a quest for a united Europe," remarked the ambassador, "but it failed because it attempted to unite a continent by force. ... Today, we see this dream of a united Europe coming true because it is done peacefully."[41]

Subsequently, this sombre commemorative ritual bounced back into the city as a pageant celebrating war as an important component of the European political consolidation. The burial of the remains became an integral part of the official celebration, "Vilnius 1812", which was meant to familiarise the citizens of Lithuania with the history of the brief French occupation of the city. The three-day event was also meant to celebrate Vilnius as a pivotal geo-political site that had altered Lithuanian and European history. The primary benefactor and organiser of the celebration was the Lithuanian Ministry of Defence, and the climax of this urban festivity was the re-enactment of a battle between "French" and "Russian" forces on the right bank of the Neris River (the site of the new municipal building and a modern business and entertainment centre located next to Europe Square). Since in 1812 there was no battle between the two armies in or around Vilnius, the performance of the battle was not just a costume drama, but a historical farce. Still, before the festival, the Lithuanian Minister of Defense boldly declared that "the march of Napoleon's army through Lithuania brought a breeze of freedom and the possibility of liberation. Moreover, it offered a chance for Lithuania to come closer to Europe."[42]

In a reverse gesture, some local dead refuse to take Vilnius to Europe without a taint of shame. A new commercial development made the vicinity of the eradicated Jewish cemetery – one of the oldest graveyards in Europe and the site of the tomb of the Vilne Goan – prime real estate. The graveyard, located across the river from Castle Hill, was cleansed by the Soviet authorities decades ago, but there is no clear evidence that all the relics were removed. Yet even if no single corpse still inhabits the site, it nevertheless speaks of the Jewish presence in the city with its bare, violated memory of annihilation. For obvious reasons, various Jewish groups raised global awareness about the development, and in response, the Congress of the United States threatened Lithuania with political censure. The Lithuanian government called for geologists (specialists in natural phenomena) to set down the exact location of the cemetery, since the city's authorities thought the work of Lithuanian archaeologists (social scientists) inadequate and misleading. The history of the city became a question of geophysical processes, as if human memory and loss were a part of the natural, topographical world. This scientific "return to nature" echoes the first cultural inscriptions of the city as a site lost in the wilderness of Europe. The truth, of course, is less allegorical: in the drive to profit local real estate, the city turned the Jews into local strangers, dead nomads with no place to call home.

Vilnius's geo-narrative interplay between "local strangers" and "foreign natives" is best captured by Johannes Bobrowski (1917-1965), a German poet whose relationship to the mythological land of Sarmatia was shaped by an intense sense of personal and historical atonement. In 1961, he published his first cycle of poems entitled *Sarmatische Zeit (Sarmatian Time)*, dedicated to his life-long encounters with Sarmatia. In a nutshell, the poetic cycle captures the poet's vast geographical and emotional experiences as a Wehrmacht soldier on the Eastern Front and prisoner of war in the Soviet Union. Yet Bobrowski, in his own words, envisioned his lyrics as a meditative and mediating atonement for the historical German encounters with their eastern neighbours: "This became a theme, something like this: the Germans and the European East – because I grew up around the river Memel, where Poles, Lithuanians, Russians and Germans lived together, and among them all, the Jews – a long history of misfortune and guilt, for which my people is to blame, ever since the days of the Order of Teutonic Knights. Not to be undone, perhaps, or redeemed, but worthy of hope and honest endeavour in German poems."[43]

For Bobrowski, European history and local geography fuse in Sarmatia, creating a narrative space that opens up as a threshold, a swelling terrain of images, experiences, place-names, languages, memories, stories, biographies, faces, voices and natural features. It is a time-space of discoveries and evocations, but also of losses and irrevocable changes. Hence he starts to draw his map of Sarmatia with a poem that begins with a toponymic trace of the city and ends with a prophesy:

> Vilna, you
> oak –
> my birch,
> Novgorod –
> once in the woods the cry
> of my springs flew up, my days'
> step sounded over the river.
>
> O, it is the bright
> glitter, the summer constellation,
> given away; by the fire
> squats the teller of tales,
> those who listened nightlong, the young ones,
> went away.

76. Vilna by an unknown seventeenth century artist.

Lonely he will sing:
Across the steppe
wolves travel, the hunter
found a yellow stone,
It flared in the moonlight. –

What is holy swims,
a fish,
through the old valleys, the wooded
valleys still, the fathers'
words still sound:
Welcome the strangers!
You will be a stranger. Soon.

"Call"[44]

Notes

PROLOGUE: *Departures*

1. Renate Lachmann, *Memory and Literature: Intertextuality in Russian Modernism*, trans. Roy Sellars and Anthony Wall (Minneapolis: University of Minnesota Press, 1997), 164.
2. Jan Bułhak, *Vilniaus peizažas: fotografo kelionės* (Vilnius: Vaga, 2006), 21-23.

CHAPTER ONE: *The Brink of Europe*

1. Gediminas's letter to Pope John XXII in V. Pašuta and I. Štal, eds., *Gedimino laiškai* (Vilnius: Mintis, 1966), 22.
2. Gediminas's letter to the burghers of Lubeck, etc., ibid., 28-35.
3. For more on the mythological meanings of Vilnius see Vladimir Toporov, "Vilnius, Wilno, Vil'na: miestas ir mitas" in *Baltų mitologijos ir rituralo tyrimai* (Vilnius: Aidai, 2000), 35-98.
4. The report of the papal delegates in Pašuta and Štal, op. cit., 127.
5. Ibid., 128.
6. Ibid., 128-131.
7. Ibid., 145.
8. As quoted in Eric Christiansen, *The Northern Crusades* (London: Penguin Books, 1997), 156.
9. Jonathan Riley-Smith, *The Crusades: A History* (New Haven: Yale University Press, 2005), 253.
10. As quoted in James Charles Roy, *The Vanished Kingdom: Travels through the History of Prussia* (Boulder: Westview Press, 1999), 69.
11. As quoted in Christiansen, op. cit., 176.
12. Ghillibert de Lannoy in Juozas Jurginis and Algirdas Šidlauskas, eds., *Kraštas ir žmonės* (Vilnius: Mokslas, 1983), 49.
13. Ibid., 49-50.
14. Zacharias Ferrerius, *Vita S. Casimiri*, in Mintautas Čiurinskas, ed., *Ankstyvieji Šv. Kazimiero „gyvenimai"* (Vilnius: Aidai, 2004), 75.
15. Ibid., 79.

16. Jacobus Piso, "De Lithuania," in Eugenija Ulčinaitė, ed., *Gratulatio Vilnae* (Vilnius: Lieuvių literatūros ir tautosakos institutas, 2001), 27.

17. Ferrerius, op. cit., 81.

18. Ibid., 69.

19. Ibid., 51.

20. Ibid., 75.

21. Ibid.

22. Ibid., 83-85.

CHAPTER TWO: *Mapping Sarmatia*

1. See Aldona Bieliūnienė et all, eds., *Lithuania on the Map* (Vilnius: Lietuvos nacionalinis muziejus, 1999), 24-25.

2. On historical variations of the name Vilnius, see Jonas Jurkštas, *Vilniaus vietovardžiai* (Vilnius: Mokslas, 1985) and also Aleksandras Vanagas, "Miesto vardas Vilnius" in *Gimtasis žodis*, nr. 11(59) November, 1993.

3. Hartmann Schedel, *Sarmatia*, the Sarmatian chapter from *Liber chronicarum* printed in Nuremberg by Anton Koberger in 1493, trans. and ed. B. Deresiewicz (London: Oficyna Stanisław Gliwa, 1973), 86.

4. Sigismund Herberstein, *Notes upon Russia: being a translation of the earliest account of that country, entitled Rerum Moscoviticarum commentarii*, trans. and ed. R.H. Major (New York: Burt Franklin, 1963), 87.

5. Ibid., 86.

6. Ibid., 94.

7. Ibid., 99.

8. Quoted in Norman Davies, *God's Playground: A History of Poland, vol.1* (New York: Columbia University Press, 1982), 45.

9. Schedel, op. cit., 85.

10. Thomas Da Costa Kaufmann, *Court, Cloister and City: The Art and Culture of Central Europe, 1450-1800* (Chicago: University of Chicago Press, 1995), 288.

11. Harry E. Dembkowski, *The Union of Lublin: Polish Federalism in the Golden Age* (Boulder: East European Monographs, 1982), 210-211.

12. Schedel, op. cit., 88.

13. Alexander Gwagnini, as quoted in Artūras Tereškinas, *Imperfect Communities: Identity, Discourse and Nation in the Seventeenth-Century Grand Duchy of Lithuania* (Vilnius: Lietuvių literatūros ir tautosakos institutas, 2005), 237.

14. In Juozas Jurginis and Algirdas Šidlauskas, *Kraštas ir žmonės* (Vilnius: Mokslas, 1983), 78-79.

15. Ibid., 79.

16. Schedel, op. cit., 91.

17. Petri Royzzi Maurei, "Facies Urbis Vilnae" in Eugenija Ulčinaitė ed., *Gratulation Vilnae* (Vilnius: Lietuvių literatūros ir tautosakos institutas, 2001), 86.

18. In Jurginis and Šidlauskas, op. cit., 82.

19. Boemus Joannes, *The manners, lawes and customs of all nations with many other things...* (London: 1611), 221-222.

20. Lawrence Korvin Novotarski, "Sapphic Ode on Poland," trans. Kenneth Mackenzie, in Schedel, op. cit., 111-112.

21. John Hale, *The Civilization of Europe in the Renaissance* (New York: Atheneum, 1994), 38.

22. Ibid., 20.

23. Ibid., 24.

24. In Jurginis and Šidlauskas, op. cit., 85.

25. Daniel Stone, *The Polish-Lithuanian State, 1386-1795* (Seattle: University of Washington Press, 2001), 211-213.

26. Davies, op. cit., 367.

27. As quoted in Larry Wolff, *Inventing Eastern Europe: The Map of Civilization on the Mind of the Enlightenment* (Stanford: Stanford University Press, 1994), 30. For more information on the Sarmatian style, see Marija Matušakaitė, *Apranga XVI-XVIII a. Lietuvoje* (Vilnius: Aidai, 2003), 95-222; also Gražina Marija Martinaitienė, "At the crossings of western and eastern cultures: the contush sashes" in *Lietuvos Didžiosios Kunigaikštystės barokas: formos, įtakos, kryptys*, Acta Academiae Artium Vilnensis 21 (2001), 167-175.

28. Aivas Ragauskas, *Vilniaus miesto valdantysis elitas: XVII a. antrojoje pusėje* (Vilnius: Diemedžio leidykla, 2002), 448.

29. Algimantas Miškinis and Vytautas Jurkštas, in *Vilniaus architektūra*, ed. A. Jankevičienė (Vilnius: Mokslas, 1985), 9. More specifically, there were 233 brick and 163 wooden houses owned by the citizens, 53 owned by nobles and 49 (brick and wooden) Jewish houses.

30. Kaufmann, op. cit., 421.

31. J. Jurginis, V. Merkys and A. Tautavičius, *Vilniaus miesto istorija: nuo seniausių laikų iki Spalio revoliucijos* (Vilnius: Mintis, 1968), 190.

32. Rosario Villari, "Introduction" in *Baroque Personae*, ed. Rosario Villari (Chicago: University of Chicago Press, 1995), 2.

33. Remy G. Saisselin, *The Enlightenment against Baroque: Economics and Aesthetics of the Eighteenth Century* (Berkeley: University of California Press, 1992), 6.

CHAPTER THREE: *Enlightenment Shadows*

1. Georg Forster to Samuel Thomas Sömmerring, 12-13 December, 1784, *Georg Forsters Werke: Sämliche Schriften, Tagebücher, Briefe (Briefe 1784 – Juni 1787)*, vol. 14,

ed. Brigitte Leuschner (Berlin: Akademie Verlag, 1978), 232. German physiologist and anatomist Sömmerring (1755-1830) was one of Forster's closest friends.

2. George Forster, *A Voyage Round the World, vol. 1* (Honolulu: University of Hawai'i Press, 2000), 6.

3. Friedrich Schlegel, *Kritische Schriften*, as quoted in Thomas F. Saine, *Georg Forster* (New York: Twayne Publishers, 1972), 13.

4. Alexander von Humboldt, *Kosmos*, as quoted in Forster, *A Voyage Round the World, vol. 1*, op. cit., xl.

5. Forster to Sömmerring, 2 July 1784, *Georg Forsters Werke 14*, op. cit., 114.

6. Ibid., 113-114.

7. Forster, as quoted in Saine, op. cit., 163.

8. Goethe, as quoted in Wolff, op. cit., 333.

9.   Louis-Phillipe de Ségur, *Mémoires, souvenirs, et anecdotes, par le comte de Ségur, vol.1*, as quoted in Wolff, op. cit., 19.

10. Ibid., 19-20.

11. William Coxe, *Travels in Poland, Russia, Sweden and Denmark* (London: J. Nicholas, 1784), 148.

12. Ibid., 226.

13. Ibid., 211.

14. Ibid., 226.

15. Ibid., 230-31.

16. Ibid., 234.

17. Friedrich Schulz in Jurginis and Šidlauskas, op. cit., 106.

18. Ibid., 97.

19. Georg Forster to Friedrich Heinrich Jacobi, 17 December 1784, *Georg Forsters Werke 14*, op. cit., 248-249.

20. Ibid., 249.

21. Georg Forster to Therese Heyne, 12 November 1784, *Georg Forsters Werke 14,* op. cit., 205.

22. Georg Forster to Joachim Heinrich Campe, 9 July 1786, ibid., 503.

23. Forster to Jacobi, 17 December 1784, ibid., 249.

24. Georg Forster, *Georg Forster Werke: Sämliche Schriften, Tagebücher, Briefe, vol.12*, ed. Brigitte Leuschner, (Berlin: Akademie Verlag, 1978), 189.

25. Forster to T. Heyne, 13 December 1784, *Georg Forsters Werke 14*, op. cit., 242.

26. Forster to T. Heyne, 24 January, 1785, ibid., 267.

27. Ibid., 269.

28. Georg Forster to Maria Wilhelmina von Thun, 24 November 1784, ibid., 215-216.

29. Forster to Sömmerring, 3 February, 1785, ibid., 271.

30. Ibid., 273.

31. Forster to Sömmerring, 12 December, 1784, ibid., 232.

32. Georg Forster to Christian Gottlob Heyne, 10 August, 1786, ibid., 521.

33. Georg Forster to Johann Gottfried Herder, 21 July, 1786, ibid., 513.

34. Forster to Campe, 9 July 1786, ibid., 502-503.

35. Therese Forster, *Johann Georg Forster's Briefwechsel*, as quoted in Saine, op. cit., 43.

36. Forster to Sömmerring, 8 October 1786, *Georg Forsters Werke 14*, op. cit., 561.

37. Georg Forster to Johann Karl Phillip Spener, 17 June, 1787, ibid., 699.

38. Forster to T. Heyne, 16 February, 1785, ibid., 282.

39. Forster to Sömmerring, 12-13 December, 1784, ibid., 236.

40. The doctor was probably Judah ben Mordechai ha-Levi Hurwitz, although Forster never mentioned his name in his correspondence.

41. Georg Forster to Petrus Camper, 7 May, 1787, *Georg Forsters Werke 14*, op. cit., 677-680.

42. Georg Forster to Georg Christoph Lichtenberg, 18 June, 1786, ibid., 491-492. (English translation from Wolff, op. cit., 338.)

43. Forster to Sömmerring, 3 February, 1785, ibid., 271.

44. Forster to Herder, 21 July, 1786, ibid., 512.

45. Therese Forster to Spener, 19 February, 1786, ibid., 793.

46. Forster to Herder, 1 September, 1787, *Georg Forsters Werke, vol. 15*, ed. Horst Fiedler (Berlin: Akademie Verlag, 1981), 32.

47. Georg Forster to Johann Georg von Zimmermann, 4 May, 1788, *Georg Forsters Werke 15*, op. cit., 151.

48. Forster as quoted in Saine, op. cit., 147.

49. Goethe to Sömmerring, 17 February, 1794, as quoted in Saine, op. cit., 155.

CHAPTER FOUR: *Napoleon's Curse*

1. Jozefas Frankas (Josef Frank), *Atsiminimai apie Vilnių*, trans. Genovaitė Druč-kutė (Vilnius: Mintis, 2001), 42.

2. Ibid., 44.

3. Ibid., 46.

4. Ibid., 44-45.

5. Tomas Venclova, *Vilnius: City Guide* (Vilnius: R. Paknio leidykla, 2001), 37. The 1795 census failed to give statistics on the residents of non-Christian confessions.

6. Frank, op. cit., 49.

7. Ibid.

8. Norman Davies, *Heart of Europe: the Past in Poland's Present* (Oxford: Oxford University Press, 2001), 173.

9. Subsequently this seventeenth-century building came to be known as the Frank House, and today it houses the French Embassy.

10. Frank, op. cit., 49.

11. Ibid., 49-52.

12. Ibid., 50.

13. Ibid.

14. Ibid., 65-68.

15. Ibid., 110-111.

16. Davies, op. cit., 142.

17. In general, the French military seemed to have a very poor geographical understanding and cartographical knowledge of Lithuania. Nevertheless, before the beginning of the Russian campaign, Napoleon familiarized himself with the works of C. Malte-Brun, a French geographer who in 1807 published a geo-historical study of Poland entitled *Tableau de la Pologne ancienne et modern*, which also covered Lithuania.

18. As quoted in Paul Britten Austin, *1812: the March on Moscow* (London: Greenhill Books, 1993), 31.

19. Phillipe-Paul de Segur, *Napoleon's Russian Campaign*, trans. J. David Townsend (London: Michael Joseph, 1959), 16-17.

20. Ibid., 18.

21. Louis-François Lejeune, *Mémories du Général Lejeune*, as quoted in Austin, *1812: the March to Moscow*, op. cit., 44.

22. H. A. Vossler, *With Napoleon in Russia in 1812: the Diary of Lt. H. A. Vossler, a Soldier of the Grand Army 1812-1813*, trans. Walter Wallich (London: Constable, 1998), 45.

23. Segur, op. cit., 17.

24. Carl von Martens, *Dänkwürdigkeiten aus dem Leben eines alten Offiziers*, as quoted in Austin, *1812: the March to Moscow*, 57.

25. Segur, op. cit., 19-20.

26. Vossler, op. cit., 50-51.

27. Bourgogne, *Memoir of Sergeant Bourgogne* (London: Jonathan Cape, 1940 [1896]), 16.

28. Roman Soltyk, *Napoleon en 1812. Mémoires Historiques et militaires sur la Campagne de Russie*, as quoted in Austin, *1812: the March to Moscow*, 98.

29. As quoted in Austin, *1812: the March to Moscow*, 98.

30. Soltyk, op. cit., 71.

31. François Dumonceau, *Mémoires du Général Comte François Dumonceau*, as quoted in Austin, *1812: the March to Moscow*, 74.

32. Segur, as quoted in Austin, *1812: the March to Moscow*, 71.

33. Armand de Caulaincourt, *Mémoires du Général de Caulaincourt, Duc de Vizence, Grand Ecuyer de l'Empereur,* as quoted in Austin, *1812: the March to Moscow,* 73.

34. Ibid.

35. Ibid., 77.

36. M. de Fezensac, *The Russian Campaign, 1812,* trans. Lee Kennett (Athens: University of Georgia Press, 1970), 10.

37. Lois-Flarimond Fantin des Odoards, *Journal du general Fantin des Odoards,* as quoted in Austin, *1812: the March to Moscow,* 101.

38. Dumonceau, *Mémoires du Général Comte François Dumonceau,* as quoted in Austin, *1812: the March to Moscow,* 73.

39. Vincent Bertrand, *Mémoires du capitaine Vincent Bertrand,* as quoted in Austin, *1812: the March to Moscow,* 77.

40. Choiseul-Gouffier, as quoted in Adam Zamoyski, *Moscow 1812: Napoleon's Fatal March* (New York: Harper Collins, 2004), 162.

41. Dumonceau, op. cit., 74-75.

42. Vossler, op. cit., 2, 53.

43. Eugene Labaume, *The Campaign in Russia* (London: Samuel, Leigh, in the Strand, 1815), 34. Most likely the Jews described by Labaume were local Karaites.

44. Segur, op. cit., 29-30.

45. Ibid., 30.

46. Ibid., 205.

47. Vossler, op. cit., 52.

48. Stendhal, *To the Happy Few: Selected Letters of Stendhal* (New York: Grove Press, 1952), 139.

49. Bourgogne, op. cit., 27.

50. Stendhal, op. cit., 144.

51. Bourgogne, op. cit., 66-67.

52. Vossler, op. cit., 89.

53. Ibid., 73.

54. Ibid., 90.

55. Segur, op. cit., 205-206.

56. Ibid., 226.

57. Bourgogne, op. cit., 201.

58. Segur, op. cit., 243.

59. Bourgogne, op. cit., 203.

60. Ibid., 209.

61. C. F. M. Le Roy, *Souvenirs de Leroy, major d'infanterie, veteran des armies de la République et de l'Empire,* as quoted in Austin, *1812: the Great Retreat* (London: Greenhill Books, 1996), 312.

62. Vossler, op. cit., 92.

63. Bourgogne, op. cit., 217.

64. Vossler, op. cit., 93.

65. Segur, op. cit., 261.

66. Bourgogne, op. cit., 220-21.

67. Jean-Marc Bussy, in *Soldats Suisses au service de la France*, as quoted in Austin, *1812: the Great Retreat*, 365.

68. As quoted in Austin, *1812: the March to Moscow*, 76.

69. Stendhal, op. cit., 136.

70. Marie Charlotte Oudinot, *Récites de guerre et de Foyer*, as quoted in Austin, *1812: the March to Moscow*, 70.

71. Bangowski, as quoted in Austin, *1812: the Great Retreat*, 367.

72. Austin, *1812: the Great Retreat*, 367.

73. Porphyre Jacquemont, as quoted in Austin, *1812: the Great Retreat*, 368.

74. Segur, op. cit., 253.

75. Stendhal, op. cit., 152.

76. Fezensac, op. cit., 109.

77. Dumonceau, as quoted in Austin, *1812: the Great Retreat*, 380.

78. Segur, op. cit., 261-262.

79. Vossler, op. cit., 84.

80. Louise Fussil, *Souvenirs d'une Femme sur la retraite de Russie*, as quoted in Austin, *1812: the Great Retreat*, 377.

81. Dumonceau, as quoted in Austin, *1812: the Great Retreat*, 376.

82. Roch-Godart, *Mémoirs du general-baron, Roch Godart, 1795-1812*, as quoted in Austin, *1812: the Great Retreat*, 367.

83. Fezensac, op. cit., 108.

84. Vossler, op. cit., 87.

85. Segur, op. cit., 262.

86. Nicholas Louis Planat de la Faye, *Vie de Planat de la Faye*, as quoted in Austin, *1812: the Great Retreat*, 380.

87. Segur, op. cit., 262.

88. Choiseul-Gouffier, as quoted in Austin, *1812: the Great Retreat*, 383.

89. Bourgogne, op. cit., 222.

90. In Austin, *1812: the Great Retreat*, 384-385.

91. Bourgogne, op. cit., 222-223.

92. Ibid., 230.

93. Segur, op. cit., 265.

94. Jean Rapp, *Mémoires écrits par lui-méme et publiés par sa famille*, as quoted in Austin, *1812: the Great Retreat*, 382.

95. Segur, op. cit., 264.

96. Charles François, *Journal du Capitaine François*, as quoted in Austin, *1812: the Great Retreat*, 393.

97. Segur, op. cit., 266-267.

98. In Zamoyski, op. cit., 513.

99. Fezensac, op. cit., 112.

100. Denis Davidov, *In the Service of the Tsar against Napoleon: the Memoirs of Denis Davidov, 1806-1814*, ed. and trans. Gregory Troubetzkoy (London: Greenhill Books, 1999), 156.

101. Boris Uxkull, *Arms and the Woman: the Intimate Journal of a Baltic Nobleman in the Napoleonic Wars*, trans. Joel Carmichael (New York: The Macmillan Company, 1966), 105.

102. Davidov, op. cit., 156.

103. Uxkull, op. cit., 105.

104. Ibid., 106-109.

105. Robert Wilson, *General Wilson's Journal, 1812-1814*, ed. Anthony Brett-James (London: William Kimber, 1964), 92-94. The Earl of Tyrconnel was an attaché at the British embassy in Saint Petersburg, but joined the Russian army in the adventurous pursuit of Napoleon.

106. Ibid., 96.

107. Ibid., 97.

108. Ibid., 96.

109. Aleksandr Chicherin, *Dnevnik Aleksandra Chicherina*, ed. S.G. Engel, M.I. Perper, L.G. Beskrovnyi (Moskva: Nauka, 1966), 67-68.

110. Ibid., 74.

111. Uxkull, op. cit., 107.

112. Chicherin, op. cit., 93.

113. Ibid., 75.

114. Ibid., 94.

115. Ibid., 95.

116. Uxkull, op. cit., 111.

117. Frank, op. cit., 415.

118. Ibid., 416-17. The painting was made into a lithograph and was widely reproduced in Vilna and abroad throughout the nineteenth century.

119. Ibid., 398.

120. Ibid., 419.

121. Ibid., 418.

122. Ibid., 419.

123. Ibid., 577-578.

CHAPTER FIVE: *Russian Intrigue*

1. Leo Tolstoy, as quoted in Birutė Masionienė, *Levas Tolstojus ir Lietuva* (Vilnius: Vaga, 1978), 11-12.

2. Leo Tolstoy, *War and Peace*, trans. Constance Garnett (New York: The Modern Library, 2002), 1252-1256.

3. Benjamin Harshav, "Preface" in Herman Kruk, *The Last Days of the Jerusalem of Lithuania: Chronicles from the Vilna Ghetto and the Camps, 1939-1944*, ed. Benjamin Harshav, trans. Barbara Harshav (New Haven: Yale University Press, 2002), xxx – xxxiii.

4. J. Jurginis, V. Merkys and A. Tautavičius, op. cit., 275-276.

5. Age Meyer Benedictsen, *Lithuania, "The Awakening of a Nation" – a Study of the Past and Present of the Lithuanian People* (Copenhagen: Egmont H. Petersens, 1924), 139-141.

6. *Handbook for Travellers in Russia, Poland and Finland* (London: John Murray, 1867), 173.

7. Aleksandr Ostrovsky, *Polnoje sobranije t. 10,* eds. G. I. Vladykina, et al. (Moskva: Isskustvo, 1978), 379-381.

8. "Pamiati grafa Mikhaila Nikolaevicha Muravieva" in *Russkaja literature v Litve XIV-XX v.,* ed. Pavel Lavrinec (Vilnius: Lietuvos Rašytojų Sąjungos Leidykla, 1998), 218-219.

9. "Polskij Vopros" in *Severnaya Pchela* (May 5, 1863), 3.

10. A. Sas., "Poezdka v Vilno" in *Severnaya Pchela* (May 5, 1863), 1.

11. *Handbook for Travellers in Russia, Poland and Finland*, 51-52.

12. Joseph Frank, *Dostoevsky: the Miraculous Years, 1865-1871* (Princeton: Princeton University Press, 1995), 161.

13. Ibid., 184.

14. Anna Dostoevskaya, as quoted in Frank, *ibid.,* 185.

15. Ibid., 184.

16. Ibid., 189.

17. Joseph Frank, ibid., 191.

18. Ibid.

19. Ibid.

20. Anna Dostoevskaya, *Dnevnik 1867 goda*, ed. S. Zhitomirskaya (Moskva: Nauka, 1993), 4-6.

21. David Goldstein, *Dostoevsky and the Jews* (Austin: University of Texas Press, 1981), 57.

22. Ibid., 56.

23. Joseph Frank, op. cit., 47.

24. Ibid., 48.

25. Ibid., 50.

26. For more on the Lithuanian origins of the Dostoevsky family, see Birutė Masioni-enė, "F. Dostojevskio kilmės klausimu" in *Literatūrinių ryšių pėdsakais* (Vilnius: Vaga, 1982), 7-35.

27. Joseph Frank, *Dostoevsky: the Seeds of Revolt, 1821-1849* (Princeton University Press, 1976), 8.

28. Ibid.

29. Ibid.

30. Ibid., 9.

31. F. Dobryanski, *Staraja i Novaja Vilna* (Vilna: Typografia A.G. Syrkina, 1904), 10-11.

32. "Pamiati grafa Mikhaila Nikolaevicha Muravieva" in Lavrinec, op. cit., 221-224.

33. A. A. Vinogradov, *Putevoditel po gorodu Vilna i evo okrestnosiam* (Vilna: Tipo-grafia Shtaba Vilenskavo Voenava Okruga, 1908), 41.

34. Benedictsen, op. cit., 174-177.

35. Venclova, op. cit., 53.

36. Katerina Clark and Michael Holquist, *Mikhail Bakhtin* (Cambridge: Harvard University Press, 1984), 22.

37. Ibid., 25.

38. Mstislav Dobujinsky, *Vospominaniya, vol. 1* (New York: Put' Zhizni, 1976), 72.

39. Ibid., 150.

40. Ibid., 169.

41. Ibid., 152.

42. Ibid., 213.

43. Ibid., 256.

44. Ibid., 289-290.

45. Feodor Tyutchev, "Nad Russkoj Vilnoj starodavnej" in Lavrinec, op. cit., 330.

46. The hundredth anniversary of the 1812 War also spurred the publication of various books, including Russian memoirs, about Vilna's role during the war; for instance, see C.F. Dobryanski, *K istorii otechestvenoi voiny. Sostoyania Vilny v 1812 g. – Za-piski Sev.-zapadnovo otdeleniia imperatorskovo russkovo geografichestkovo o-va*, book 3 (Vilna: 1912); and O. A. Kudrinskii, *Vilna v 1812 godu* (Vilna: 1912).

47. Bernard Pares, *Day by Day with Russian Army, 1914-1915* (London: Constable & Company, 1915), 17.

48. Stanley Washburn, *On the Russian Front in the World War I: Memoirs of an Ame-rican War Correspondent* (New York: Robert Speller and Sons, 1982), 41.

49. Valery Bryusov, *Sem' tsvetov radugi: stikhi 1912-1915* (Moskva: Izdatelstvo K.F. Nekrasova, 1916), 116.

50. Stephen Graham, *Russia and the World* (New York: The Macmillan Company, 1915), 145-147.

51. Ibid., 90.

52. Ibid., 160-161.

53. Ibid., 167-168.

54. Ibid., 110.

55. Bryusov, op. cit., 115.

CHAPTER SIX: *German Intrusion*

1. Hayyim Schauss, *The Jewish Festivals: History and Observance* (New York: Schocken Books, 1975), 154.

2. Joseph Roth, *The Wandering Jews*, trans. Michael Hofmann (New York: W. W. Norton, 2001), 40-43.

3. Vejas Liulevicius, *War Land on the Eastern Front: Culture, National Identity and German Occupation* (Cambridge: Cambridge University Press, 2001), 19.

4. Erich Ludendorff, *My War Memories, vol. 1* (London: Hutchinson & Co., 1919), 175.

5. Ibid., 243.

6. Ibid., 210-212.

7. Ibid., 221-222.

8. Ibid., 211.

9. Ibid., 211-212.

10. Ludendorff, *My War Memories, vol. 2*, (London: Hutchinson & Co., 1919), 154.

11. Alfred Brust, *Die verlorene Erde,* as quoted in Dietmar Albrecht, *Wege nach Sarmatien – Zehn Kapitel Preußenland: Orte, Texte, Zeichen* (München: Martin Meidenbauer, 2006), 174.

12. Richard Dehmel, *Zwischen Volk und Menschheit: Kriegstagebuch,* as quoted in Albrecht, op. cit., 173.

13. Petras Čepėnas, *Naujųjų laikų Lietuvos istorija, t. II* (Vilnius: Mokslo ir enciklopedijų leidykla, 1992), 27.

14. Wiktor Sukiennicki, *East Central Europe during World War I: from Foreign Domination to National Independence, vol. 2.* (New York: Columbia University Press, 1984), 161.

15. Ludendorff, op. cit., *My War Memories, vol. 2*, 153-155.

16. Petras Klimas, *Iš mano atsiminimų* (Vilnius: Lietuvos enciklopedijų redakcija, 1990), 45.

17. Israel Cohen, *Vilna* (Philadelphia: The Jewish Publication Society of America, 1992), 366.

18. Paul Fechter died in West Berlin in 1958.

19. Paul Monty, *Wanderstunden in Wilna* (Wilna: Verlag der Wilnaer Zeitung, 1918), 76.

20. Ibid., 9.

21. Ibid., 10.

22. Ibid., 10-12.

23. Ibid., 17.

24. Ibid., 13.

25. Ibid., 15.

26. Ibid., 16.

27. See, for instance, Paul Weber, *Wilna: eine vergessene Kunstsstätte* (Wilna: Verlag der Zeitung der 10. armee, 1917).

28. Modris Eksteins, *Rites of Spring : The Great War and the Birth of the Modern Age* (New York: Anchor Books, 1990), 211.

29. Monty, op. cit., 81.

30. Ibid., 28.

31. Ibid., 27.

32. Ibid.

33. Ibid., 28.

34. Ibid.

35. Ibid.

36. Ibid., 14.

37. Ibid., 40.

38. Ibid., 27.

39. Ibid., 87.

40. Ibid., 79.

41. Ibid., 82-84.

42. Ibid., 20.

43. Ibid., 22-23.

44. Ibid., 59.

45. Ibid., 59-60.

46. Hirsz Abramowicz, *Profiles of a Lost World: Memoirs of East European Jewish Life before World War II,* ed. Dina Abramowicz and Jeffrey Shandler, trans. Eva Zeitlin Dobkin (Detroit: Wayne University Press, 1999), 193.

47. Monty, op. cit., 62.

48. Abramowicz, op. cit., 202.

49. Monty,op. cit., 62-67.

50. Ibid., 68-71.

51. Ibid., 73.

52. Ibid., 74.

53. Ibid.

54. Ibid., 75-76.

55. Eksteins, op. cit., 212.

56. Monty, op. cit., 78-79.

57. Thomas Mann, *Buddenbrooks: the Decline of a Family*, trans. John E. Woods (New York: Knopf, 1993), 643.

58. Monty, op. cit., 79-82.

59. Ludendorff, *My War Memories, vol. 1*, op.cit., 137.

60. Jean-Noel Grandhomme, "Vilnius 1915-1918 m. seno kareivio iš Elzaso prisiminimai" in *Metai* (July, 2000), 130.

61. Ibid., 136.

CHAPTER SEVEN: *The Absent Nation*

1. Mykolas Römeris, *Dienoraštis*, trans. Vaiva Grigaitienė (Vilnius: Versus Aureus, 2007), 183.

2. Alfred Döblin, *Destiny's Journey*, trans. Edgar Passler (New York: Paragon House, 1992), 105.

3. Heinz Graben, "Introduction," in Alfred Döblin, *Journey to Poland*, trans. Joachim Neugroschel. New York: Paragon House, 1991), xv.

4. Döblin, as quoted in Graben, op. cit., xv.

5. Ibid.

6. Döblin, *Destiny's Journey*, op. cit., 105-106.

7. Ibid., 110.

8. Benedictsen. op. cit., 212-214.

9. David Brenner, *Marketing Identities: the Invention of Jewish Ethnicity in 'Ost und West'* (Detroit: Wayne State University Press, 1998), 34.

10. Ibid., 83.

11. Döblin, *Journey to Poland,* op. cit., 7.

12. Ibid., 191.

13. Ibid., 240.

14. Ibid., 9.

15. Ibid., 31.

16. Ibid., 151.

17. Ibid., 187.

18. Ibid., 70-71.

19. Ibid., 84.

20. Ibid., 84-85.

21. Döblin, *Destiny's Journey*, op. cit., 109.

22. Ibid., 322.

23. Gilbert Keith Chesterton, as quoted in Michael Ffinch, *G.K. Chesterton* (London: Weidenfeld and Nicholson, 1986), 312.

24. Gilbert Keith Chesterton, *Autobiography* (London: Hutchinson and Company, 1936), 317.

25. Döblin, *Journey to Poland*, op. cit., 33.

26. Chesterton, *Autobiography,* op. cit., 317-318.

27. Döblin, *Journey to Poland*, op. cit., 86.

28. Haim Sloves, as quoted in Henri Minczeles, "A journey into the heart of Yiddishland" in *Yiddishland,* ed. Gerrard Silvain and Henri Minczeles (Corte Madera, California: Gingko Press, 1999), 7.

29. Cecile E. Kuznitz, "On the Jewish Street: Yiddish culture and the urban landscape of interwar Vilna" in *Yiddish Language and Culture: Then and Now* (Creighton: Creighton University Press, 1998), 66.

30. Ibid., 67.

31. Döblin, *Journey to Poland*, op. cit., 37.

32. Robert Medill McBride, *Towns and People of Modern Poland* (New York: McBride and Company, 1938), 137-138.

33. Döblin, *Journey to Poland*, op. cit., 98.

34. Ibid., 89-90.

35. Monty, op. cit., 23.

36. Döblin, *Journey to Poland*, op. cit., 94.

37. Ibid., 97.

38. Ibid., 95-96.

39. Ibid., 97-98.

40. Ibid., 103.

41. Ibid., 109.

42. Ibid.

43. Ibid., 102-103.

44. Cohen, op. cit., 415.

45. Lucy Dawidowicz, *From That Place and Time: A Memoir, 1939-1947* (New York: W.W. Norton & Company, 1989), 48-49.

46. Döblin, *Journey to Poland*, op. cit., 66.

47. Ibid., 111.

48. Ibid., 111-113.

49. Döblin, *Destiny's Journey*, op. cit., 110-111.

CHAPTER EIGHT: *Maelstrom Europe*

1. Robert Medill McBride, op. cit., 113-117.
2. Ibid., 130-132.
3. Lucy Dawidowicz, op. cit., 28-29.
4. Anne Louise Strong, *Lithuania's New Way* (London: Lawrence & Wishart, 1940), 31.
5. Ibid.
6. Herman Kruk, *The Last Days of the Jerusalem of Lithuania: Chronicles from the Vilna Ghetto and the Camps 1939-1944*, ed. Benjamin Harshav, transl. Barbara Harshav (New Haven: Yale University Press, 2002), 28-29.
7. Yitskhok Rudashevski in Laurel Holliday ed., *Children in the Holocaust and World War II: Their Secret Diaries* (New York: Pocket Books, 1995), 140-147.
8. Kruk, op. cit., 656-657.
9. Rudashevski, op. cit., 181.
10. Chaim Grade, *My Mother's Sabbath Days*, trans. Channa Kleinerman Goldstein and Inna Hecker Grade (New York: Alfred A. Knopf, 1986), 335.
11. Tomas Venclova in Czesław Miłosz, *Beginning with My Streets*, trans. Madeline G. Levine (New York: Farrar Straus Giroux, 1991), 40.
12. Romas Daugirdas, "The Iron Dog, to Vilnius" trans. Antanas Danielius in *Vilnius: Lithuanian Literature, Culture, History* (1997 summer), 67.
13. Günter Grass, *The Call of the Toad,* trans. Ralph Manheim (New York: Harcourt Brace & Company, 1992), 17.
14. Judith Friedlander, *Vilna on the Seine: Jewish Intellectuals in France since 1968* (New Haven: Yale University Press, 1990), 5-6.
15. G. Metelsky, *Lithuania: Land of the Niemen* (Moscow: Foreign Languages Publishing House, 1959), 33.
16. Ibid., 75-76.
17. Judita Vaičiūnaitė, "Museum Street," trans. Jonas Zdanys in *Contemporary East European Poetry: An Anthology*, ed. Emery George (Oxford: Oxford University Press, 1993), 85.
18. Metelsky, op. cit., 36.
19. Phillipe Bonosky, *Beyond the Borders of Myth: from Vilnius to Hanoi* (New York: Praxis Press, 1967), 79.
20. Ibid., 84-89.
21. Joseph Brodsky, *A Part of Speech* (New York: Farrar, Straus, Giroux, 1980), 37-38.
22. Anatol Lieven, *The Baltic Revolution: Estonia, Latvia, Lithuania and the Path to Independence* (New Haven: Yale University Press, 1993), 12.
23. Venclova, *Vilnius*, op. cit., 9.
24. Rose Zwi, *Last Walk in Naryshkin Park* (North Melbourne: Spinifex, 1997), 61.

25. Ibid., 125.

26. Ibid., 142-145.

27. Dan Jacobson, *Heshel's Kingdom* (London: Penguin Books, 1998), 114.

28. Ibid., 111-113.

29. Ibid., 115.

30. Anne Applebaum, *Between East and West: Across the Borderlands of Europe* (New York: Pantheon Books, 1994), 63-65.

31. Stan Persky, *Then We Take Berlin: Stories from the Other Side of Europe* (Toronto: Alfred Knopf, 1995), 350.

32. Ibid., 380.

33. Ibid., 381-382.

34. Ibid., 384.

35. Katherine Verdery, *The Political Lives of Dead Bodies: Reburial and Postsocialist change* (New York: Columbia University Press, 1999), 28-29. Italics in original quote.

36. Michael Wines, "Baltic soil yields evidence of a bitter end to Napoleon's Army" in *New York Times* (September, 14, 2002), A5.

37. As quoted in M. Tarm, "The Napoleon graves" in *City Paper: The Baltic States* (November, 2002), 11.

38. For more, see Severinas Vaitiekus, *Tuskulėnai: egzekucijų aukos ir budeliai* (Vilnius: Lietuvos gyventojų genocido ir rezistencijos tyrimo centras, 2002), 106-134.

39. "Vilnių garsins ir Napoleono palaikai" in *Lietuvos rytas,* section Sostinė (September 13, 2002), 1.

40. "Rasti palaikai – daugelio tautų paveldas" in *Lietuvos rytas* (March 30, 2002), 7.

41. As quoted in Ian Traynor, "Frozen victims of 1812 get final burial" in *The Guardian* (June 2, 2003) www. guardian.co.uk, accessed June 2, 2003.

42. Linas Linkevičius, quoted from "Vilnius 1812" press conference at the Lithuanian Ministry of Defense, May, 22, 2003.

43. Johannes Bobrowski as quoted in Michael Hamburger, "Introduction" in Johannes Bobrowski, *Shadow Lands: Selected Poems,* trans. by Ruth and Matthew Mead (New York: New Directions Books, 1984), 16.

44. Ibid., 23.

Illustrations

1. Frontispiece from S. Muenster, *La cosmographie universelle*, Basel 1556. (Vilnius University Library)   p. 10.

2. Wilno. Photograph by J. Bułhak, circa 1939 (Library of the Lithuanian Academy of Sciences)   p. 13.

3. Vilnius in many languages. A detail of "Lithuania," prepared by M. V. Coronelli, Venice, 1696. (Vilnius University Library)   p. 15.

4. "New map of Europe," from S. Muenster, *La cosmographie universelle*, Basel, 1556. (Vilnius University Library)   p. 18.

5. Gediminas builds a castle on the site of his dream. Woodcut by M.E. Andriolli and B. Puc, 1882. (Lithuanian Art Museum)   p. 23.

6. Pagan Lithuanians worshiping fire, the oak tree and the garden snake, from S. Muenster, *La cosmographie universelle*, Basel 1556. (Vilnius University Library)   p. 25.

7. A Teutonic knight, from S. Muenster, *La cosmographie universelle*, Basel, 1556. (Vilnius University Library)   p. 28.

8. "Lithuania" from H. Schedel, *Weltchronik*, Nürnberg, 1493. (Vilnius University Library)   p. 31.

9. Ostra Brama. Lithograph by J. Hoppen, 1924. (Vilnius University Library)   p. 33.

10. Saint Casimir. Copper engraving by F. Balcewicz, 1749. (Vilnius University Library)   p. 37.

11. "Sarmatia, the threshold province of Europe," from S. Muenster, *Cosmographiae Universalis*, Basel, 1572. (Private collection of L. Briedis)   p. 40.

12. Lithuanian moose, from S. Muenster, *La cosmographie universelle*, Basel, 1556. (Vilnius University Library)   p. 42.

13. Sarmatia in Europe and Asia, from C. Ptolemy, *Geographia*, Strasbourg, 1513. (Vilnius University Library)   p. 46.

14. Frontispiece from A. Gwagnini, *Sarmatiae Europeae Descriptio ...*, Cracovie, 1578. (Vilnius University Library)   p. 48.

15. "Wilna or Wilda, the capital city of Lithuania," G. Bodenehr, Augsburg, circa 1720. (Vilnius University Library)   p. 50.

16. Saint Christopher, from *Staroe Vilno*, circa 1906. (Vilnius University Library)   p. 52.

17. The resurrection of Vilnius. Frontispiece from A. Pozniak, *Senator septem consulabris ...*, Vilnae, 1666. (Vilnius University Library)   p. 56.

18. The triumph of Poland. Illustration from N. Kiszka De Ciechanowiec, *Triumphale Solium Serenissimae Regine Poloniarum ...,*Vilnae, 1637. (Vilnius University Library)   p. 57.

19. "Plague in Vilnius in 1710." Copper engraving by X. Karęga after a drawing by F. Pelikan, 1799. (Lithuanian Art Museum)   p. 60.

20. Roads to Vilnius. Detail from "Neueste Karte von Polen und Litauen," F.Müller and C. Schütz, Wien, 1792. (Vilnius University Library)   p. 62.

21. "Plan of Willda or Willna in Lithuania," author unknown, 1737. (Lithuanian Art Museum)   p. 65.

22. The great courtyard of the university in Wilna. Drawing by F. Smuglewicz, 1786. (Vilnius University Library)   p. 66.

23. Jewish merchants near Wilna. Chromolithograph by L.Bichebois, I. Deroy and K. Kukiewicz, from J. L. Wilczyński, *Album de Wilna*, Paris, 1848. (Vilnius University Library)   p. 69.

24. The city wall of Wilna. Drawing by F. Smuglewicz, 1785. (Lithuanian Art Museum)   p. 72.

25. A view of the university's botanical garden. Watercolour by J. Pezska, 1808. (Vilnius University Library)   p. 77.

26. Erasing Sarmatia from the map of Europe. "Division of Poland-Lithuania," engraved by J.E. Nielsen, 1773. (Lithuanian National Museum)   p. 80.

27. Vilna: the city cordon. Lithograph by K. Bachmatowicz from *Przypomniene Wilna (Memories of Wilna)*, 1837. (Vilnius University Library)   p. 83.

28. The Imperial University of Vilna in the first part of the nineteenth century. Chromolithograph by P. Benoist and A. Bayot, from J. K. Wilczyński, *Album de Wilna*, Paris, 1850. (Lithuanian Art Museum)   p. 85.

29. A street scene in Vilna. Lithograph by K. Bachmatowicz from *Przypomniene Wilna (Memories of Wilna)*, 1837. (Vilnius University Library)   p. 86.

30. The Grand Armée crossing the Niemen (Nemunas) River in 1812. Lithograph by I. Klauber after a painting by Bagetti, printed in Saint Petersburg, circa 1850. (Lithuanian National Museum)   p. 92.

31. Map of Poland and Lithuania. A detail from "Regni Poloniae, Magni Ducatus Lituaniae...," J. J. Kanter, sheet 7, Regiomonti, 1770. (Vilnius University Library)   p. 95.

32. The palace of the governor-general in Vilna. Chromolithograph by P. Benoist, from J. K. Wilczyński, *Album de Wilna*, Paris, circa 1850. (Vilnius University Library)   p. 97.

33. A graph representing the collapse of the Napoleonic army during the Russian campaign of 1812 by C.J. Minard, 1869. (Private collection of L. Briedis)   p. 105.

34. French officers in Vilna rescued by a Samaritan monk from the hands of local assailants. "An assault on De Bissy," lithograph by J. Oziebłowski, 1844. (Lithuanian Art Museum)   p. 109.

35. The retreat of the Grand Armée through Vilna in 1812. Lithograph by V. Adam and L. Bichebois after a painting by J. Damel, from J. K.Wilczyński, *Album de Wilna*, Paris, 1846. (Vilnius University Library)   p. 111.

36. Alexander I reviews the troops after the capture of Vilna by Russian forces in December of 1812. Drawing by A. Chicherin, from *Dnevnik Aleksandra Chicherina*, Moskva: Nauka, 1966. (Vilnius University Library)   p. 114.

37. The view of Vilna from the surrounding hills in the 1820s. Lithograph by J. Hoppen, 1925. (Lithuanian Art Museum)   p. 119.

38. Ostrabrama Street in Vilna in the first part of the nineteenth century. Chromolithograph by L. Bichebois and V. Adam after a painting by M. Zaleski, from J. K. Wilczyński, *Album de Wilna*, Paris, 1846. (Vilnius University Library)   p. 122.

39. A plan of the Saint Petersburg to Warsaw railway, from A. H. Kirkor, *Przewodnik: Wilno*, Wilna, 1863. (Library of the Lithuanian Academy of Sciences)   p. 124.

40. Saint Casimir Catholic Church in Vilna turned into Saint Nicholas Russian Orthodox Cathedral after the 1863-1864 Polish-Lithuanian insurrection against tsarist rule. Photo by S. F. Fleury, circa 1896. (Lithuanian National Museum)   p. 129.

41. The entrance to the courtyard of the Old Synagogue in Vilne, circa 1900. (Postcard courtesy A. Kubilas)   p. 130.

42. A plan of Vilna, 1882. (Lithuanian National Museum)   p. 133.

43. The interior of the Church of Our Lord Jesus (Trinitarian) in Vilna. Chromolithograph by I. Deroy after V. Sadovnikov, from J. K. Wilczyński, *Album de Wilna*, Paris, 1847. (Lithuanian Art Museum)   p. 136.

44. Vilna as the ancient gateway to the Russian Empire, 1872. Frontispiece from P.N. Batyushkov, *Pamiatniki Russkoi stariny*, Vilna, 1872. (Library of the Lithuanian Academy of Sciences)   p. 140.

45. "Greetings from Vilna: Bolshaya [Great] Street," circa 1900. (Postcard courtesy A. Kubilas)   p. 143.

46. Swimming in the Viliya River. Photography by S.F. Fleury, 1900. (Library of the Lithuanian Academy of Sciences)   p. 148.

47. A street in Vilna; postcard from a drawing by M. Dobuzhinsky, circa 1914. (Postcard courtesy A. Kubilas)   p. 153.

48. Saint Casimir Chapel in Vilna; postcard from a photograph by J. Bułhak, circa 1910. (Postcard courtesy A. Kubilas)   p. 156.

49. Russian Vilna, circa 1900. (Postcard courtesy A. Kubilas)   p. 158.

50. A statistical map of Lithuania, designed by the German occupational forces to highlight the ethnic division of the country, titled as "Verwaltungsbezirk der Militärverwaltung Litauen," 1918. (Vilnius University Library)   p. 162.

51. "The capture of Wilna, the Russian city of government, August, 1915." (Postcard courtesy A. Kubilas)   p. 165.

52. Wilna: the view from Castle Hill, 1916. (Postcard courtesy A. Kubilas) p. 167.

53. German soldier-flaneur in Wilna, 1916 (Postcard courtesy A. Kubilas) p. 172.

54. A plan of Wilna and its environs with highlighted main thoroughfares cutting through the city, titled as "Garnison-Umgebundgskarte von Wilna," 1917. (Lithuanian National Museum) p. 175.

55. The waiting hall of Wilna train station. Drawing by W. Buhe from *Bilderfschau der Wilnaer Zeitung*, 3 April, 1916. (Library of the Lithuanian Academy of Sciences) p. 177.

56. Wilna Labour House Exhibition. Poster by M. Bühlmann, 1916. (Library of the Lithuanian Academy of Sciences) p. 179.

57. Wilna: a wartime scene at a busy flea market, circa 1916. (Postcard courtesy A. Kubilas) p. 180.

58. "Christmas greetings from Wilna: a picturesque corner," 1916. (Postcard courtesy A. Kubilas) p. 183.

59. A holy day in the Old Synagogue of Wilna. Drawing by W. Buhe from *Bilderfschau der Wilnaer Zeitung*, 29 March, 1916. (Library of the Lithuanian Academy of Sciences) p. 185.

60. The wooden mosque of Wilna, 1916. (Postcard courtesy A. Kubilas) p. 187.

61. Wilna: the fourth year of war, 1917. (Postcard courtesy A. Kubilas) p. 190.

62. Map of Poland and Lithuania, published by G. Freytag & Berndt, Vienna, circa 1923. (Vilnius University Library) p. 192.

63. Wilno: St. George Avenue, circa 1920. (Courtesy A. Kubilas) p. 196.

64. Wilno reads in many languages. Photo from *The National Geographic Magazine* 74-6 (June, 1938), 779. p. 202.

65. Ostra Brama gate; photograph by J. Bułhak, circa 1920. (Postcard courtesy A. Kubilas) p. 205.

66. A map of Vilne in Yiddish, circa 1940, from Leyzer Ran, *Jerusalem of Lithuania*, New York, 1974. (Printed with permission of the Judaic Centre at the University of Vilnius) p. 209.

67. Street scene in the Jewish Quarter of Vilne, circa 1925. (Postcard courtesy A. Kubilas) p. 211.

68. A panoramic view of Wilna from Castle Hill, by J. Grutzka, printed by *Zeitung der 10. Armee*, 1917. (Vilnius University Library) p. 212.

69. The old Jewish cemetery in Vilne, circa 1920. (Postcard courtesy A. Kubilas) p. 217.

70. Vilnius at the centre of Europe. Illustration from *Vilnius: Unforgettable Harmony and Charm*, Vilnius Municipality Economic Department Tourism Division, 2002. (Printed with the permission of Vilnius Municipality) p. 220.

71. Wilno: Zamkowa (Castle) Street, circa 1930. (Postcard courtesy A. Kubilas) p. 224.

72. The postwar ruins of Vilnius with its Baroque churches unscathed, circa 1947. Photography from *Tarybų Lietuva, 1940-1950*, Vilnius: Vaga, 1950. (Vilnius University Library)   p. 228.

73. A tourist plan of Soviet Vilnius. Illustration from A. Papšys, *Vilnius: a guide*, Moscow: Progress Publishers, 1981, pp. 88-89.   p. 233.

74. Palm Sunday in Vilnius, 1967. Photograph by A. Kunčius. (LATGA-A, Vilnius 2008)   p. 236.

75. The Bernardine and Saint Anna Churches. Photograph by J. Bułhak, circa 1930. (Postcard courtesy A. Kubilas)   p. 241.

76. Vilna by an unknown seventeenth century artist. Facsimile by Barousse, from J. K. Wilczyński, *Album de Wilna*, Paris, circa 1850. (Lithuanian National Museum).   p. 251.

Cited works

Abramowicz, Hirsz. *Profiles of a Lost World: Memoirs of East European Jewish Life before World War II*, ed. Dina Abramowicz and Jeffrey Shandler. Trans. Eva Zeitlin Dobkin. Detroit: Wayne University Press, 1999.

Albrecht, Dietmar. *Wege nach Sarmatien – Zehn Kapitel Preußenland: Orte, Texte, Zeichen.* München: Martin Meidenbauer, 2006.

Applebaum, Anne. *Between East and West: Across the Borderlands of Europe.* New York: Pantheon Books, 1994.

Austin, Paul Britten. *1812: the March on Moscow.* London: Greenhill Books, 1993.

Austin, Paul Britten. *1812: the Great Retreat.* London: Greenhill Books, 1996.

Benedictsen, Age Meyer. *Lithuania, "The Awakening of a Nation" – a Study of the Past and Present of the Lithuanian people.* Copenhagen: Egmont H. Petersens, 1924.

Bieliūnienė, Aldona et all, eds., *Lithuania on the Map.* Vilnius: Lietuvos nacionalinis muziejus, 1999.

Bobrowski, Johannes. *Shadow Lands: Selected Poems.* Trans. by Ruth and Matthew Mead. New York: New Directions Books, 1984.

Bonosky, Phillipe. *Beyond the Borders of Myth: from Vilnius to Hanoi.* New York: Praxis Press, 1967.

Bourgogne, *Memoir of Sergeant Bourgogne.* London: Jonathan Cape, 1940 [1896].

Brenner, David. *Marketing Identities: the Invention of Jewish Ethnicity in 'Ost und West.'* Detroit: Wayne State University Press, 1998.

Brodsky, Joseph. *A Part of Speech.* New York: Farrar, Straus, Giroux, 1980.

Bryusov, Valery. *Sem' tsvetov radugi: stikhi 1912-1915.* Moskva: Izdatelstvo K.F. Nekrasova, 1916.

Bułhak, Jan. *Vilniaus peizažas: fotografo kelionės.* Vilnius: Vaga, 2006.

Campbell, Thomas. "Poland." In *English Romantic Writers*, ed. David Perkins. New York: Harcourt, Brace, Janovich, 1967.

Čepėnas, Petras. *Naujųjų laikų Lietuvos istorija, t. II.* Vilnius: Mokslo ir enciklopedijų leidykla, 1992.

Chesterton, Gilbert Keith. *Autobiography.* London: Hutchinson and Company, 1936.

Chicherin, Aleksandr. *Dnevnik Aleksandra Chicherina.* Ed. S.G. Engel, M.I. Perper, L.G. Beskrovnyi. Moskva: Nauka, 1966.

Christiansen, Eric. *The Northern Crusades.* London: Penguin Books, 1997.

Čiurinskas, Mintautas. ed., *Ankstyvieji Šv. Kazimiero „gyvenimai."* Vilnius: Aidai, 2004.

Clark, Katerina and Holquist, Michael. *Mikhail Bakhtin.* Cambridge: Harvard University Press, 1984.

Cohen, Israel. *Vilna.* Philadelphia: The Jewish Publication Society of America, 1992.

Coxe, William. *Travels in Poland, Russia, Sweden and Denmark.* London: J. Nicholas, 1784.

Daugirdas, Romas. "The Iron Dog, to Vilnius" trans. Antanas Danielius in *Vilnius: Lithuanian Literature, Culture, History*, 1997 (summer), 67.

Davidov, Denis. *In the Service of the Tsar against Napoleon: the Memoirs of Denis Davidov, 1806-1814.* Ed. and trans. Gregory Troubetzkoy. London: Greenhill Books, 1999.

Davies, Norman. *God's Playground: A History of Poland, vol.1.* New York: Columbia University Press, 1982.

Davies, Norman. *Heart of Europe: the Past in Poland's Present.* Oxford: Oxford University Press, 2001.

Dawidowicz, Lucy. *From That Place and Time: A Memoir, 1939-1947.* New York: W.W. Norton & Company, 1989.

Dembkowski, Harry E. *The Union of Lublin: Polish Federalism in the Golden Age.* Boulder: East European Monographs, 1982.

Döblin, Alfred. *Destiny's Journey.* Trans. Edgar Passler (New York: Paragon House, 1992.

Döblin, Alfred. *Journey to Poland.* Trans. Joachim Neugroschel. New York: Paragon House, 1991.

Dobryanski, C.F. *K istorii otechestvenoi voiny. Sostoyania Vilny v 1812 g. – Zapiski Sev.-zapadnovo otdeleniia imperatorskovo russkovo geografichestkovo o-va, book 3.* Vilna: 1912.

Dobryanski, F. *Staraja i Novaja Vilna.* Vilna: Typografia A.G. Syrkina, 1904.

Dobujinsky, Mstislav. *Vospominaniya, vol. 1.* New York: Put' Zhizni, 1976.

Dostoevskaya, Anna. *Dnevnik 1867 goda.* Ed. S. Zhitomirskaya. Moskva: Nauka, 1993.

Dostoevsky, Feodor. *The Brothers Karamazov.* Trans. David Magarshack. London: Penguin Books, 1982.

Eksteins, Modris. *Rites of Spring : The Great War and the Birth of the Modern Age.* New York: Anchor Books, 1990.

Fezensac, M. *The Russian Campaign, 1812.* Trans. Lee Kennett. Athens: University of Georgia Press, 1970.

Ffinch, Michael. *G.K. Chesterton.* London: Weidenfeld and Nicholson, 1986.

Forster, Georg. *Georg Forster Werke: Sämliche Schriften, Tagebücher, Briefe, vol.12.* Ed. Brigitte Leuschner. Berlin: Akademie Verlag, 1978.

Forster, Georg. *Georg Forsters Werke, vol. 15.* Ed. Horst Fiedler (Berlin: Akademie Verlag, 1981).

Forster, Georg. *Georg Forsters Werke: Sämliche Schriften, Tagebücher, Briefe (Breife 1784 – Juni 1787), vol. 14.* Ed. Brigitte Leuschner (Berlin: Akademie Verlag, 1978).

Forster, George. *A Voyage Round the World, vol. 1.* Honolulu: University of Hawai'i Press, 2000.

Frank, Joseph. *Dostoevsky: the Seeds of Revolt, 1821-1849.* Princeton: Princeton University Press, 1976.

Frank, Joseph. *Dostoevsky: the Miraculous Years, 1865-1871.* Princeton: Princeton University Press, 1995.

Frankas, Josefas (Josef Frank). *Atsiminimai apie Vilnių.* Trans. Genovaitė Dručkutė. Vilnius: Mintis, 2001.

Friedlander, Judith. *Vilna on the Seine: Jewish Intellectuals in France since 1968.* New Haven: Yale University Press, 1990.

Goldstein, David. *Dostoevsky and the Jews.* Austin: University of Texas Press, 1981.

Graben, Heinz. "Introduction." In *Journey to Poland,* Alfred Döblin, trans. Joachim Neugroschel. New York: Paragon House, 1991, i-xxviii.

Grade, Chaim. *My Mother's Sabbath Days.* Trans. Channa Kleinerman Goldstein and Inna Hecker Grade. New York: Alfred A. Knopf, 1986.

Graham, Stephen. *Russia and the World.* New York: The Macmillan Company, 1915.

Grandhomme, Jean-Noel. "Vilnius 1915-1918 m. seno kareivio iš Elzaso prisiminimai." In *Metai,* 2000 (July), 130-136.

Grass, Günter. *The Call of the Toad.* Trans. Ralph Manheim. New York: Harcourt Brace & Company, 1992.

Hale, John. *The Civilization of Europe in the Renaissance.* New York: Atheneum, 1994.

Handbook for Travellers in Russia, Poland and Finland. London: John Murray, 1867.

Harshav, Benjamin. "Preface." In Herman Kruk, *The Last Days of the Jerusalem of Lithuania: Chronicles from the Vilna Ghetto and the Camps, 1939-1944,* ed. Benjamin Harshav, trans. Barbara Harshav. New Haven: Yale University Press, 2002, xv-lii.

Herberstein, Sigismund. *Notes upon Russia: being a translation of the earliest account of that country, entitled Rerum Moscoviticarum commentarii.* Trans. and ed. R.H. Major. New York: Burt Franklin, 1963.

Jacobson, Dan. *Heshel's Kingdom.* London: Penguin Books, 1998.

Jankevičienė, Algė, ed., *Vilniaus architektūra.* Vilnius: Mokslas, 1985.

Joannes, Boemus. The *manners, lawes and customs of all nations with many other things* ... London: 1611.

Jurginis, J., Merkys, V. and Tautavičius, A. *Vilniaus miesto istorija: nuo seniausių laikų iki Spalio revoliucijos*. Vilnius: Mintis, 1968.

Jurginis, Juozas and Šidlauskas, Algirdas, eds. *Kraštas ir žmonės*. Vilnius: Mokslas, 1983.

Jurkštas, Jonas. *Vilniaus vietovardžiai*. Vilnius: Mokslas, 1985.

Kaufmann, Thomas Da Costa. *Court, Cloister and City: The Art and Culture of Central Europe, 1450-1800*. Chicago: University of Chicago Press, 1995.

Klimas, Petras. *Iš mano atsiminimų*. Vilnius: Lietuvos enciklopedijų redakcija, 1990.

Kruk, Herman. *The Last Days of the Jerusalem of Lithuania: Chronicles from the Vilna Ghetto and the Camps 1939-1944*. Ed. Benjamin Harshav, transl. Barbara Harshav. New Haven: Yale University Press, 2002.

Kudrinskii, O. A. *Vilna v 1812 godu*. Vilna: 1912.

Kuznitz, Cecile E. "On the Jewish Street: Yiddish culture and the urban landscape of interwar Vilna" in *Yiddish Language and Culture: Then and Now*. Creighton: Creighton University Press, 1998, 66-92.

Labaume, Eugene. *The Campaign in Russia*. London: Samuel, Leigh, in the Strand, 1815.

Lachmann, Renate. *Memory and Literature: Intertextuality in Russian Modernism*. Trans. Roy Sellars and Anthony Wall. Minneapolis: University of Minnesota Press, 1997.

Lavrinec, Pavel. ed. *Russkaja literature v Litve XIV-XX v*. Vilnius: Lietuvos Rašytojų Sąjungos Leidykla, 1998.

Lieven, Anatol. *The Baltic Revolution: Estonia, Latvia, Lithuania and the Path to Independence*. New Haven: Yale University Press, 1993.

Liulevicius, Vejas. *War Land on the Eastern Front: Culture, National Identity and German Occupation*. Cambridge: Cambridge University Press, 2001.

Ludendorff, Erich. *My War Memories, vol. 1-2*. London: Hutchinson & Co., 1919.

Mann, Thomas. *Buddenbrooks: the Decline of a Family*. Trans. John E. Woods. New York: Knopf, 1993.

Martinaitienė, Gražina Marija. "At the crossings of western and eastern cultures: the contush sashes." In *Lietuvos Didžiosios Kunigaikštystės barokas: formos, įtakos, kryptys*, Acta Academiae Artium Vilnensis 21, 2001, 167-175.

Masionienė, Birutė. "F. Dostojevskio kilmės klausimu." In *Literatūrinių ryšių pėdsakais*. Vilnius: Vaga, 1982, 7-35.

Masionienė, Birutė. *Levas Tolstojus ir Lietuva*. Vilnius: Vaga, 1978.

Matušakaitė, Marija. *Apranga XVI-XVIII a. Lietuvoje*. Vilnius: Aidai, 2003.

McBride, Robert Medill. *Towns and People of Modern Poland*. New York: McBride and Company, 1938.

Metelsky, G. *Lithuania: Land of the Niemen*. Moscow: Foreign Languages Publishing House, 1959.

Miłosz, Czesław. *Beginning with My Streets: Essays and Recollections*. Trans. Madeline G. Levine. New York: Farrar, Strauss and Giroux, 1991.

Minczeles, Henri. "A journey into the heart of Yiddishland." In *Yiddishland,* ed. Gerrard Silvain and Henri Minczeles. Corte Madera, California: Gingko Press, 1999, 7-32.

Monty, Paul. *Wanderstunden in Wilna*. Wilna: Verlag der Wilnaer Zeitung, 1918.

Ostrovsky, Aleksandr. *Polnoje sobranije t. 10*. Eds. G. I. Vladykina, et al. Moskva: Isskustvo, 1978.

Pares, Bernard. *Day by Day with Russian Army, 1914-1915*. London: Constable & Company, 1915.

Pašuta V. and I. Štal, eds. *Gedimino laiškai*. Vilnius: Mintis, 1966.

Persky, Stan. *Then We Take Berlin: Stories from the Other Side of Europe*. Toronto: Alfred Knopf, 1995.

"Polskij Vopros." In *Severnaya Pchela* (May 5, 1863), 3.

Ragauskas, Aivas. *Vilniaus miesto valdantysis elitas: XVII a. antrojoje pusėje*. Vilnius: Diemedžio leidykla, 2002.

"Rasti palaikai – daugelio tautų paveldas" in *Lietuvos rytas*. March 30, 2002, 7.

Riley-Smith, Jonathan. *The Crusades: A History*. New Haven: Yale University Press, 2005.

Römeris, Mykolas. *Dienoraštis*. Trans. Vaiva Grigaitienė. Vilnius: Versus Aureus, 2007.

Roth, Joseph. *The Wandering Jews*. Trans. Michael Hofmann. New York: W. W. Norton, 2001.

Roy, James Charles. *The Vanished Kingdom: Travels through the History of Prussia*. Boulder: Westview Press, 1999.

Rudashevski, Yitskhok. In *Children in the Holocaust and World War II: Their Secret Diaries,* Laurel Holliday ed. New York: Pocket Books, 1995.

Saine, Thomas F. *Georg Forster*. New York: Twayne Publishers, 1972.

Saisselin, Remy G. *The Enlightenment against Baroque: Economics and Aesthetics of the Eighteenth Century*. Berkeley: University of California Press, 1992.

Sas. A. "Poezdka v Vilno." In *Severnaya Pchela* (May 5, 1863), 1.

Schauss, Hayyim. *The Jewish Festivals: History and Observance*. New York: Schocken Books, 1975.

Schedel, Hartmann. *Sarmatia*, the Sarmatian chapter from *Liber chronicarum* printed in Nuremberg by Anton Koberger in 1493. Trans. and ed. B. Deresiewicz. London: Oficyna Stanisław Gliwa, 1973.

Segur, Phillipe-Paul. *Napoleon's Russian Campaign*. Trans. J. David Townsend. London: Michael Joseph, 1959.

Stendhal, *To the Happy Few: Selected Letters of Stendhal*. New York: Grove Press, 1952.

Stone, Daniel. *The Polish-Lithuanian State, 1386-1795*. Seattle: University of Washington Press, 2001.

Strong, Anne Louise. *Lithuania's New Way*. London: Lawrence & Wishart, 1940.

The Story of Wilno. The Polish Research Centre. London: The Cornwall Press, 1942.

Sukiennicki, Wiktor. *East Central Europe during World War I: from Foreign Domination to National Independence, vol. 2*. New York: Columbia University Press, 1984.

Tarm, M. "The Napoleon graves." In *City Paper: The Baltic States* (November, 2002), 9-13.

Tereškinas, Artūras. *Imperfect Communities: Identy, Discourse and Nation in the Seventeenth-Century Grand Duchy of Lithuania*. Vilnius: Lietuvių literatūros ir tautosakos institutas, 2005.

Tolstoy, Leo. *War and Peace*. Trans. Constance Garnett. New York: The Modern Library, 2002.

Toporov, Vladimir. *Baltų mitologijos ir ritualo tyrimai*. Vilnius: Aidai, 2000.

Traynor, Ian. "Frozen victims of 1812 get final burial." In *The Guardian* (June 2, 2003) www.guardian.co.uk, accessed June 2, 2003.

Ulčinaitė, Eugenija, ed., *Gratulation Vilnae*. Vilnius: Lietuvių literatūros ir tautosakos institutas, 2001.

Uxkull, Boris. *Arms and the Woman: the Intimate Journal of a Baltic Nobleman in the Napoleonic Wars*. Trans. Joel Carmichael. New York: The Macmillan Company, 1966.

Vaičiunaitė, Judita. "Museum Street," trans. Jonas Zdanys. In *Contemporary East European Poetry: An Anthology*. Ed. Emery George. Oxford: Oxford University Press, 1993.

Vaitiekus, Severinas. *Tuskulėnai: egzekucijų aukos ir budeliai*. Vilnius: Lietuvos gyventojų genocido ir rezistencijos tyrimo centras, 2002.

Vanagas, Aleksandras. "Miesto vardas Vilnius." In *Gimtasis žodis*, nr. 11(59) November, 1993, 4-7.

Venclova, Tomas. "Dialogue about Wilno with Thomas Venclova. In *Beginning with My Streets*, Czesław Miłosz, trans. Madeline G. Levine. New York: Farrar Straus Giroux, 1991, 36-57.

Venclova, Tomas. *Vilnius: City Guide*. Vilnius: R. Paknio leidykla, 2001.

Verdery, Katherine. *The Political Lives of Dead Bodies: Reburial and Postsocialist change*. New York: Columbia University Press, 1999.

Villari, Rosario. "Introduction." In *Baroque Personae*, ed. Rosario Villari. Chicago: University of Chicago Press, 1995.

"Vilnių garsins ir Napoleono palaikai" in *Lietuvos rytas,* section Sostinė (September 13, 2002), 1.

Vinogradov, A. A. *Putevoditel po gorodu Vilna i evo okrestnosiam*. Vilna: Tipografia Shtaba Vilenskavo Voenava Okruga, 1908.

Vossler, H. A. *With Napoleon in Russia in 1812: the Diary of Lt. H. A. Vossler, a Soldier of the Grand Army 1812-1813*. Trans. Walter Wallich. London: Constable, 1998.

Washburn, Stanley. *On the Russian Front in the World War I: Memoirs of an American War Correspondent*. New York: Robert Speller and Sons, 1982.

Weber, Paul. *Wilna: eine vergessene Kunstsstätte*. Wilna: Verlag der Zeitung der 10. armee, 1917.

Wilson, Robert. *General Wilson's Journal, 1812-1814*. Ed. Anthony Brett-James. London: William Kimber, 1964.

Wines, Michael. "Baltic soil yields evidence of a bitter end to Napoleon's Army." In *New York Times* (September, 14, 2002), A5.

Wolff, Larry. *Inventing Eastern Europe: The Map of Civilization on the Mind of the Enlightenment*. Stanford: Stanford University Press, 1994.

Zamoyski, Adam. *Moscow 1812: Napoleon's Fatal March*. New York: Harper Collins, 2004.

Zwi, Rose. *Last Walk in Naryshkin Park*. North Melbourne: Spinifex, 1997.

Index

A

Abramowicz, Hirsch, 182
Africa, 12, 201, 221
Alexander, Grand Duke of Lithuania and King of Poland, 32-34, 48
Alexander I, Tsar of Russia, 82, 84, 88, 90, 94-97, 114, 125, 127
Alexander II, Tsar of Russia, 134, 144
Alexander IV, Pope, 19
Alexanderplatz, in Berlin, 196-197
Alexei Mihailovich, Tsar of Russia, 55
Alsace-Lorraine, 190
Applebaum, Anne, 240
Armenians, 45
Asia, 12, 46-47 53, 76, 102, 146, 178, 215, 221
Asia Minor, 11, 38
Austria, 62, 76, 81-82, 86-87, 90-91, 97, 118, 121, 125, 157, 201, 246
Aušros Vartai, in Vilnius (*see also* Ostra Brama), 33, 230, 236
Avignon, 19-20, 24-25
Azores, 11, 221
Azov Sea, 47

B

Babylon, 45, 59, 131
Bakhtin, Mikhail, 150-151, 154, 244
Bakhtin, Nikolai, 150-151
Baltic region, 19-20, 22, 24, 26, 54, 113, 164
Baltic Sea (*see also* Mare Germanicum), 18, 29, 38, 45, 47, 54-55, 193, 197
Bangowski, Polish officer, 106
Baroque, 55-61, 63, 87, 116, 128, 131, 151-152, 154, 206, 228-229, 236, 242
Baudelaire, Charles, 151
Bavaria, 21, 91, 110, 246
Beauvoir, Simone, 234
Belarus, 12, 45, 145; *see also* Byelorussian
Benedictines, 25
Benedictsen, Age Meyer, 132, 148, 198
Benjamin, Walter, 12
Berezina River, 103-104, 107
Berlin, 16, 60, 70, 101, 126, 132, 137, 142, 144, 152, 165, 169, 171, 190, 196-198, 232, 241
Bernardine Church, in Vilnius, 135-136, 241

Bernotai, 11

Berthier, Louis-Alexandre, 107

Bertrand, Vincent, 98

Białystock, 68, 91

Black Sea, 38, 45, 47, 150, 193

Bobrowski, Johannes, 11, 250

Bohemia, 27-29, 32, 34, 47, 121

Bolshaya Street, in Vilnius (*see also* Great and Wielka Street), 142-143, 210

Bolsheviks, 195, 213

Bonosky, Phillip, 234

Borisov, 103

Borodino, battle of, 101

Bourgogne, Adrien-Jean-Baptiste-François, 94, 101-105, 109-110

Braun, Georg, 49-50

Bremen, 21

Brest-Litovsk, 81

Britain, 157, 193

British, 90, 115, 139, 155, 157, 159, 224, 240

Brodsky, Joseph, 236-237

Brust, Alfred, 168

Bryusov, Valery, 155, 160

Bug River, 81

Bułhak, Jan, 13, 156, 205, 241

Bund, 215

Burgundy, 30

Byelorussian, 14, 45, 54, 150, 154, 168, 195, 201

Byelorussian language, 14-15, 43, 45, 169, 179, 202

Byzantine Empire, 38

C

Calabria, 91

Calvary, in Vilnius, 131

Calvinist, 61, 83-84, 88

Cambridge, 131

Campbell, Thomas, 63

Canary Islands, 11-12, 221

Casimir, Prince and Saint, 34-39, 52, 55-56, 157, 228, 230, 232

Caspian Sea, 47, 84

Castle, in Vilnius, 22-23, 26, 30, 95, 148, 210-211, 213

Castle Hill, in Vilnius, 37, 43, 84, 167, 174, 178, 188, 210-212, 216, 231, 249

Castle (Pilies) Street, in Vilnius (*see also* Zamkowa Street), 49, 118, 224

Cathedral, in Vilnius, 29, 35, 37, 43, 55, 84, 87, 106, 135, 153, 171, 211-212, 223, 232

Cathedral Square, in Vilnius, 147-148, 174

Catherine II, (the Great), Empress of Russia, 62, 76, 147

Catholic, 19-21, 23-27, 29, 32, 34-35, 37, 39, 43-45, 55-56, 58, 61, 66, 71, 83-84, 87-88, 127-128, 131-132, 136-137, 139, 143-145, 149, 152, 154, 157, 169, 203-205, 208, 222, 230, 244

Caulaincourt, Armand, 96-97

Cedron, in Vilnius, 131

cemeteries, in Vilnius, 32, 90, 98, 143, 163, 184-186, 202, 214, 216-217, 222, 230, 232, 239, 240, 244-245, 248-249

Central Asia (see also Asia), 227

Charles IV, King of France, 24

Chaucer, Geoffrey, 28

Chesterton, Gilbert Keith, 205-206

Chicago, 241

Chicherin, Aleksandr, 114, 116-118

China, 164

Christendom, 19, 23-24, 43, 53-54

Christian,19, 21-22, 24-28, 30-33, 38, 43-45, 51, 54, 59, 67, 74, 83, 88, 132, 138, 183, 186, 204, 206, 209, 211, 244

churches, in Vilnius; see individual names

Cimarosa, Domenico, 101

Cisalpine Republic, 82

Clement V, Pope, 24

Cohen, Israel, 216

Cold War, 11, 230, 234

Commonwealth, Polish-Lihuanian, 46-47, 56-58, 67-68, 78, 82, 95, 125, 129, 145; see also Poland-Lithuania

Compans, Dominique, 94

Confederation of the Rhine, 82

Congress of Vienna (1814-1815), 125

Constantinople, 38, 73, 141

Cook, James, 63

Cossacks, 54, 56, 81, 110-113, 121, 134, 137, 148, 157, 164

Counter-Reformation, 58, 66

Coxe, William, 68-70

Cracow (see also Kraków), 68

Cresque, Abraham, 29

Crete, 11

Crimea, 45, 54, 186

Cusanus, Nicolus, 41

Cyrillic (alphabet), 43, 139

Czartoryski, Adam Jerzy, 85

D

Damel, J., 111, 118

Danish, 132, 199

Danzig (*see also* Gdańsk), 91, 106, 229

Davidov, Denis, 113

Dawidowicz, Lucy, 216, 224

Dehmel, Richard, 168

Diaghilev, Sergei, 151

Dnieper River, 47, 100, 103

Döblin, Alfred, 196-201, 203-212, 214-216, 218, 221, 230, 237

Dobuzhinsky, Mstislav, 151-154

Dominicans, 27

Dostoevo, 145

Dostoevskaya née Snitkina, Anna Grigoryevna, 141-144

Dostoevsky, Feodor, 125, 141-146

Dresden, 142, 152-153, 171, 174

Dumonceau, François, 98-99, 107-108

Duna (Daugava) River, 100

Dunaburg (Daugavpils), 132, 134

E

Eastern Front, in World War I, 166, 170, 176; in World War II, 250

Educational Commission of Lithuania, 66, 85

Egypt, 30, 130

Eydtkuhnen (Chernyshevskoye), 132, 137, 144

Eksteins, Modris, 163, 175, 188

Elbling (Elbląg), 91

Eliyahu ben Shlomo Zalman (known as Vilne Gaon), 130-131, 215-217

England, 30, 67, 91, 125, 206

English, 64, 68, 115, 121-122, 205, 237

English language, 28, 53, 64, 135, 171, 233, 239, 241

Enlightenment, 53, 60-61, 63-65, 67, 73, 82

Estonia, 45, 227, 237

Etruria, 82

Eurasia, 11, 47

Europa, 11

Europe, 11-16, 18-25, 27-31, 33-35, 37, 39-48, 53-55, 57-64, 66, 68-69, 75, 81-82, 84-91, 93, 96-99, 103-104, 106, 110, 123-127, 129, 134-135, 138, 142, 146, 157, 173, 179-180, 191, 193-195, 198, 206, 208, 220-225, 230, 234, 238, 242-251

Europe, central, 55, 81

Europe, centre of, 11-12, 220-221

Europe, eastern, 200, 214, 237

Europe, northern, 45, 47

Europe, southern, 54
Europe, western, 42, 54, 124, 126, 134, 153, 232
European Union, 11-12, 221, 248

F

Fantin des Odoards, Lois-Flarimond, 98
Fechter, Paul Otto Heinrich (*see also* Monty, Paul), 171
Ferreri, Zaccharia, 32-39
Fezensac (duke), 97, 108, 112
Finance, Lucien, 189-191
Finland, 97
Florence, 174
Forster, Johann Georg Adam, 63-68, 70-71, 73-78, 86-87, 171
Forster, Therese, 67, 71, 73-77
France, 20, 24, 28-29, 33, 61, 68, 77, 90-91, 106, 121, 125, 157, 191, 193, 230, 246, 248
Frank née Gerhardi, Christine, 81, 86-87, 90, 118, 120
Frank, Johann Peter, 81-82, 84, 87
Frank, Josef, 81-82, 84-90, 107, 118-123, 232, 246
Franz I, Emperor of Austria, 87
Freiberg, 64
French, 20-21, 24-25, 28, 64, 71, 74-75, 77, 82, 89, 91, 93-94, 96-98, 101, 104-107, 109-
    110, 112, 118-122, 130, 137, 166, 179, 214, 230, 246, 248, 249
French language, 15, 83, 100, 102, 106, 246
French National Geographical Institute, 11-12, 221
Friedlander, Judith, 89, 230

G

Galicia, 91

Ganges River, 91

Gdańsk (*see also* Danzig), 47, 229-230
Gediminas, Grand Duke of Lithuania, 19, 21-27, 29, 34, 45, 132, 150, 210
Gerhardi, Christine, *see* Frank née Gerhardi
George, Earl of Tyrconnel, 115
German, 20, 27, 29, 31, 45, 49, 53, 58, 64, 67, 70-74, 77, 84, 88, 99, 104, 113, 118, 120,
    133, 144, 146, 162-173, 175-176, 178-179, 180-182, 185, 187-189, 196-198, 200-201,
    208, 212-214, 227, 229, 232, 244, 246, 248, 250
German language, 14-15, 20, 28, 41-42, 45, 53, 59, 64, 67, 84, 89, 102, 132, 133, 144, 146,
    160, 167-168, 170, 174-176, 179, 181, 197, 199, 200-201, 229, 233, 250
German military, 157, 159, 162-166, 168-172, 175-177, 179, 181-182, 187, 189-191, 193,
    195, 198, 200, 208, 210, 212, 214, 225-226, 242, 244, 247
German Sea, 38, 47
German (Vokiečių) Street, in Vilnius, 49, 184, 209, 231

Germany, 63, 64, 73, 76, 84, 103, 112, 132-133, 141-142, 155, 157, 166, 168-169, 178-179, 186, 193, 215
Ghetto, *see* Vilne Ghetto
Goethe, Johann Wolfgang, 67, 77, 185
Göttingen, 67, 73, 85
Grade, Chaim, 227
Graham, Stephen, 157, 159
Grande Armée, 90-91, 93, 95, 97, 100-101, 106, 120-121, 125-126, 154, 246, 248
Grass, Günter, 229
Great (Didžioji) Street, in Vilnius (*see also* Bolshaya and Wielka Street), 86, 142-143
Great (Old) Synagogue, in Vilnius, 88, 130, 183-185, 236
Greece, 11, 38, 46-47, 53, 150-151, 211-212, 221
Greek Orthodox, *see* Orthodox, Greek
Green Bridge (Žaliasis Tiltas), in Vilnius, 147, 190
Grodno, 68, 71, 73, 91, 201
Guadalquivir, 91
Gwagnini, Alexander, 48-49

H

Haghia Sophia, in Constantinople, 38
Hale, John, 41, 53
Hamburg, 197
Harshav, Benjamin, 131
Harth, Jean Bernard, 248
Haussmann, G., 173
Haydn, Franz Joseph, 87
Hebrew language, 45, 59, 89, 131, 163, 181, 184, 199, 207, 215, 217
Helvetia, 82
Henekin (monk and Gediminas's translator), 27
Henry V, King of England, 30
Herberstein, Sigismund, 43-45
Herder, Johann Gottfried, 73, 76
Herodotus, 47
Heyne, Christian Gottlob, 67, 74
Heyne, Therese (*see also* Forster, Therese), 67
Hogenberg, Franz, 49
Holocaust, 218, 242
Holy Roman Empire, 21, 46
Horace, 71
Humboldt, Alexander, 64
Hungary, 27, 34, 47

I

Illyria, 82
India, 90-91
Israel, 181, 230
Istria, 91
Italy/Italians, 21, 32, 36, 38, 55, 58, 85, 91, 101, 104, 246

J

Jacobi, Friedrich Heinrich, 71
Jacobson, Dan, 239-240
Jadwiga, Queen of Poland, 29-30, 211
Japan, 76
Jawlensky, Alexey, 152
Jena, 131
Jerusalem, 19, 24, 30, 130-131, 141, 207
Jerusalem of Lithuania, 130-131, 208, 230
Jesuit Order, 55, 58, 66, 128, 145
Jewish Quarter, in Vilnius, 88-89, 157, 171, 180-182, 184, 208-209, 211
Jews, 31-32, 43, 45, 51, 58-59, 61, 63, 69-70, 84, 88-89, 99, 102, 108, 110, 120, 126, 129-131,
    136, 144, 149, 154-155, 159, 168, 181-182, 184, 195, 198-200, 207-209, 215-218,
    226-227, 229, 237, 239, 242-243, 249-250
Jogaila (Jagiełło), Grand duke of Lithuania and King of Poland, 29-30, 34, 48
John (also known as John the Blind), King of Bohemia, 27, 29
John XXII, Pope, 19-21, 24-25
Judaism, 45, 197, 216, 230
Julius Caesar, 75

K

Kaffa, 35
Kafka, Franz, 242
Kaluga, 102
Kamchatka, 76
Kandinsky, Vassilyi, 152
Kanowitsch, Grigory, 242
Karaites, 45, 59, 84
Karakozov, Dimitry, 144-145
Kassel, 64, 67
Katowice, 225
Kaunitz, Wenzel Anthon, 65
Kiev, 35
Königsberg (Kaliningrad), 23, 106, 190
Kops, Charlotte, 121-123

Korsakov, General, 120

Kovno (Kaunas; *see also* Kowno), 91, 93, 106, 113, 137

Kowno (Kaunas; *see also* Kovno), 164, 166, 168, 188

Kraków (*see also* Cracow), 42, 49, 65, 67-68, 73, 200, 218, 240

Kresy (Polish borderlands), 206

Kruk, Herman, 225-226

Kutuzov, Mikhail, 115, 126-127

L

Labaume, Eugene, 99

Lannoy, Guillebert, 30-32

Latin alphabet, 139

Latin language, 15, 19, 43, 45, 49, 53, 59, 74, 151

Latvia, 45, 132

Latvians, 45, 237

Lejeune, Louis-François, 92

Leo X, Pope, 33-34, 39

Leonardo de Vinci, 151

Levinas, Emmanuel, 230

Lieven, Anatol, 237

Litaliania, 38

Lithuania, Grand Duchy, 29-30, 41, 45-46, 49, 55, 64, 66, 83, 103, 125, 193, 195

Lithuania, nature, 29, 44, 75, 91

Lithuanian language, 22, 59, 84, 139

Lithuanian Statute, 51

Lithuanians, 19, 21, 25-29, 31, 36, 45-46, 52, 58, 64, 70, 92, 96, 98, 108, 110, 123, 125, 149-150, 154, 166-167, 169, 195, 206, 210, 226-227, 229, 235, 237, 239, 241-242, 246, 250

Livonia, 18, 20, 25, 45, 48

Lombardy, 121

London, 16, 60, 76, 155, 237

Louis XVI, King of France, 68

Lubeck, 21

Lublin, 46-47, 49, 225

Ludendorf, Erich, 165-167, 169, 176, 188

Ludwig IV of Bavaria, Emperor, 24, 34

Luther, Martin, 34, 36, 185

Lutheran, 34, 45, 61, 83-84. 88, 164

M

Madeira, 12, 221

Madrid, 101

Magdeburg, 21, 29, 146

Mainz, 43

Mann, Thomas, 189

Mare Germanicum (Baltic Sea), 18

Marie Louise, Empress of France, 106

Marx, Karl, 151

McBride, Robert, 208

Medici, 33

Mediterranean Sea, 20, 134

Memel River (*see also* Nemunas and Niemen), 250

Mendelssohn, Moses, 74

Mickiewicz, Adam, 128, 149, 210

Middle Lithuania, 195

Milan, 101

Miłosz, Czesław, 19

Mindaugas, King of Lithuania, 19

Mir, 151

modernity, 173, 178, 200, 218, 230-231, 240

Moldavia, 45

Montenegro, 170

Monty, Paul (*see also* Fechter, Paul), 171, 173-176, 178-189, 210, 232

Moscow, 16, 33-35, 38, 43-45, 49, 55, 81-83, 91, 94, 101-102, 104, 106-108, 110, 112, 121,
    135, 145, 168, 207, 223-224, 232-234, 237, 246

Mozart, Wolfgang Amadeus, 90

Munich, 152-153

Murat, Joachim, 91, 98, 107, 110, 112

Muraviev, Mikhail, 139, 145-147, 170, 213-214

Muscovy, 36, 47-48, 132

Muslims, 24, 33, 45, 51, 59, 88, 186, 232, 244

N

Naples, 32, 60, 110, 121

Napoleon, Emperor of France, 82-83, 85, 88, 90-97, 100, 102-103, 106-108, 110, 118,
    120-121, 127, 130, 152-154, 165-166, 212-214, 223, 246, 248-249

Napoleon II, King of Rome, 87

Narbonne, Louis, 91

Nassenhuben, 67

nation-state, 194, 198, 201-202, 205, 208, 238

Nazi-Soviet Pact of 1939, 225

Nemunas River (*see also* Memel and Niemen), 92

Neris River (*see also* Vilia), 43, 131, 230, 249

New York, 207, 230

New Zealand, 63, 75

Nicholas (Grand Duke, commander of the Russian army during WWI), 157-158

Nicholas I, Tsar of Russia, 125, 128, 134, 139
Nicholas II, Tsar of Russia, 155, 157, 170
Niemen River (*see also* Memel and Nemunas), 49, 90-92, 97, 100, 104, 166
Nietzsche, Friedrich, 151
North America, 68, 76, 222
North Sea, 38
Novgorod, 30, 45, 152, 250

O

Ober-Ost (Upper-Eastern territory), 166, 168, 171
Octavius Caesar, 75
Odessa, 150
Orel, 150
Orsha, battle of, 35
Orthodox, 24, 32, 34, 44, 58, 132, 147, 152, 157, 159, 244
Orthodox, Greek, 37, 43, 45, 84, 136, 169, 214
Orthodox, Russian, 25-27, 34-36, 38, 45, 55, 61, 83, 128-129, 144-145, 147, 154, 170, 203
Ostjuden, 200
Ostra Brama, in Vilnius (*see also* Aušros Vartai), 33, 98, 107, 122, 135-137, 149, 158, 204-205, 207, 222, 230
Ostrovsky, Aleksandr, 134-135, 137
Ottomans, 33, 38, 45, 56-57, 186
Oxford, 131

P

Pacific Ocean, 63, 65, 76-77
Padua, 32
pagans, 25-27
Palestine, 131, 159, 198
Paneriai (*see also* Ponari *and* Ponary), 134, 227, 242-243
Pares, Bernard, 155
Paris, 16, 60, 77-78, 81-83, 86, 97, 100-101, 106-107, 113, 125, 151-153, 195, 207, 212, 225, 230, 232, 248
Peace Conference of Paris (1919), 195
Persky, Stan, 241-243
Peter I, Tsar of Russia, 59
Peternelli (colonel), 121
Pfeil (general, German military commader of Wilna), 168
Picart (colonel), 109-110
Piłsudski, Józef, 206, 210, 222, 240, 244
Piso, Jacobus, 35-36
plica Polonica, 58, 70, 121

Podolia, 45, 145

Pohulianka, in Vilnius, 137

Poland, 29, 34-35, 42, 46, 48, 54-55, 57, 63-68, 71, 76, 84, 90, 93, 95, 137, 145, 157-159, 192-196, 198, 200-203, 205-206, 210-212, 216, 218, 222-223, 225, 228-229, 237, 245

Poland-Lithuania, 33-34, 46, 55, 61-62, 67, 78, 80-81, 129; see also Commonwealth of Poland-Lithuania

Poles, 27, 45, 47, 52, 58, 65, 70, 72, 91, 96, 98, 104, 111, 125, 128, 136, 138-139, 143-145, 149, 154-155, 157-159, 167, 169, 195, 206, 208, 210, 213, 229, 242, 246, 250

Polish language, 13-15, 29, 33, 45-46, 49, 53, 55, 67, 74, 85, 87, 89, 127-128, 133, 139, 149-150, 155, 158, 168-170, 179, 202, 207, 213-214, 222, 225, 227, 233, 241

Polish-Lithuanian insurrection (1794, 1830-1831, 1863-1864), 128-129, 137, 144

Ponari (*see also* Paneriai *and* Ponary), 112-113

Ponary (*see also* Paneriai *and* Ponari), 227

Ponary Hill (*see also* Paneriai), 111, 121, 134

Ponevezh (Panevėžys), 131

Poniatowski, Stanislaw (junior, nephew to the King of Poland), 64

Poniatowski, Stanislaw, King of Poland and Grand Duke of Lithuania, 76

Protestant, 34, 39, 43, 45, 58, 67, 164, 169-170, 232, 244

Prussia, 18, 20, 28, 30, 42, 45, 48-49, 62, 64, 68, 76, 78, 81-82, 90, 97, 104, 125-126, 132, 137, 144, 157, 167-169, 171, 201, 229

Prussians, 104, 246

Pskov, 30

Ptolemy, 47

Pushkin, Aleksandr, 147, 212

R

Radvila, Mykolas (Radziwiłł, Mikołaj), 55-56

Radziwiłłowa (Radvilaite), Barbara, 223

Reggio, 91

reysa, 28-30, 42

Rennenkampf, Paul, 163-164,

Renaissance, 32, 38, 41, 43, 47, 53-55, 59

Riga, 19, 21, 23, 25-26, 68, 87, 237

Rococo, 60, 153, 214

Romantic, 20, 64, 128

Rome, 16, 19-21, 33-34, 36, 38-39, 41, 55, 59, 173

Roth, Joseph, 163

Royzius, Petrus (Mauro), 51

Rudashevsky, Yitskhok, 226

Russia, 25, 28, 30, 43-46, 48, 55, 68-70, 76, 78, 81-83, 85, 90, 91, 93, 96, 100-102, 110, 113, 120-121, 123, 125-127, 129, 132-139, 144, 147, 152-153, 159, 166, 168, 178, 185, 188, 193, 195, 200, 210, 213, 227

Russian language, 128-129, 147

Russians, 19, 27, 31, 36, 83, 97, 107, 110, 112, 127-128, 131-133, 139, 146, 148-150, 154-155, 157-159, 164, 168-170, 180, 190, 210, 212-214, 223, 229, 250

Russian military, 35, 56, 59, 70, 78, 81, 93-96, 100, 103, 113-114, 125, 138-139, 155, 157-159, 164-165, 168, 244, 249

Ruthenian language, 59

S

Saint Anna Church, in Vilnius, 241

Saint Casimir Church, in Vilnius, 55, 128, 228, 233

Saint Nicholas Basilica, in Vilnius, 128

Saint Petersburg, 60, 68, 82-84, 91, 94, 124, 126, 128, 132, 135, 138-142, 144, 146-147, 151-154, 168

Saints Peter and Paul Church, in Vilnius, 135

Salieri, Antonio, 90

Samogitia, 48, 146

Sarmatia, 38-42, 46-49, 51-54, 57-59, 61-63, 68, 74-76, 78, 82, 121, 123, 194, 250

Sarmatian (Baltic) Sea, 38

Sarmatism, 47-48, 56, 58-59

Sartre, Jean-Paul, 234

Savoy, 121

Saxon era, 58

Saxony, 58, 65

Schulz, Friedrich, 70

Schytia, 38

Scotland, 67

Segur, Louis-Phillipe, 68

Segur, Phillipe-Paul, 91, 93, 95, 100, 103-104, 107-108, 110-111

Seleste, 190

Severo-zapadnyi krai (the North-Western Region of the Russian Empire), 139, 166

Sigismund, King of Poland and Grand Duke of Lithuania, 33-34, 43

Sigismund Augustus, King of Poland and Grand Duke of Lithuania, 49, 223

Simpson (Jewish merchant), 89

Skaryna, Francis, 43

Sloves, Haim, 207

Słowacki, Juliusz, 128

Smolensk, 45

Sniadecki (Śniadecki), Jan, 96, 120

Snitkina, *see* Dostoevskaya, Anna

Sobieski, Jan, King of Poland and Grand Duke of Lithuania, 56

Socialists, 215

Soholnicki (Polish general), 94

Soltyk, Roman, 94

South Africa, 238

Soviet Union, 11, 225-226, 228, 233, 236-238, 240, 242, 250
Spain/Spanish 29, 30, 32, 51, 102
Spiritualists, 21
Spitsbergen, 11
Stendhal (Henri Beyle), 100-101, 106-107
Stettin, 197
Stralsund, 21
Strong, Ann Louise, 224
Suvorov, Alexander, 81
Sweden, 45
Symbolism, 151, 154
Syria, 30, 151, 159

T

Tacitus, 47
Tahiti, 63
Tallinn, 23, 237
Tarquini (singer), 121
Tartars, 25, 27, 31, 44-45, 51, 58, 112, 168, 186, 232
Tenth Army (German army during WWI), 164, 170, 174, 176
Tenth Army (Russian army during WWI), 164
Teutonic Order, 19-21, 24-33, 41-42, 166, 250
Thomas of Aquinas (church scholar and saint), 21-22
Thorn, 91
Thracia, 38
Tierra del Fuego, 63
Tiesenhausen (Choiseul-Gouffier), Sophia, 98
Tolstoy, Leo, 81, 126-127, 134-135
Torun, 229
Town Hall, in Vilnius, 84, 108
Trakai (see also Troki), 30-31
Troki (see also Trakai), 99, 113, 213
Turkey, 76, 159
Turkic language, 45
Turkish (Muslim) Quarter, in Vilnius, 185-186
Tuskulėnai, 245, 247
Tyrol, 121
Tyutchev, Fyodor, 154-155

U

Ukraine, 45, 55, 145
Ulubris Sarmaticis, 75

Uniate Church, 45, 56, 61, 83, 128

Uniates, 58, 145

Union of Lublin, 46-47

United States of America, 97, 193

University, in Vilnius, 64, 65-66, 73-76, 77, 84-85, 87, 96, 115, 120, 123, 127-128, 132, 151, 229, 232

Urals, 11

Uxkull, Boris, 113-114, 117-118

V

Vaičiūnaitė, Judita, 231

Vatican, 39

Venclova, Tomas, 227, 238

Venice, 15, 152, 168

Verdery, Katherine, 243

Vienna, 16, 35, 56, 60, 65, 81, 86-87, 90, 101, 120, 123, 125

Vilia River (*see also* Neris) 96, 106, 135, 140, 143, 146-148, 185, 213, 216

Vistula River, 67, 91, 211

Vitebsk, 100

Volhynia, 45, 201

Volozhin, 131

Vossler, Heinrich August, 93, 99-100, 102, 107-108

Vytautas, Grand duke of Lithuania, 29-32

W

Wagner, Richard, 151

War of 1812, 125, 127

Warsaw, 68, 74, 90-91, 96, 100-101, 124, 132, 200, 203-204, 206-208, 210, 216, 218, 225, 232

Warsaw, Grand Duchy of, 90

Washburn, Stanley, 155

Weimar, 67, 73, 131, 193

Western Front, in World War I, 176, 193, 196, 198

Westjuden, 200

Westphalia, 91, 121

Wielka (Didžioji) Street (*see also* Bolshaya and Great Street), 210

Wildnis, 42

Wilhelm II, Emperor of Germany (Kaiser), 170

Wilja River, 185, 213

Wilson, Robert, 115-116

World War I (Great War), 182, 188-189, 196, 198, 214, 232, 244

World War II, 227-228, 245

Wrocław, 229